CC

D1067122

Praise for *Roundtrip from Texas*

"*Roundtrip from Texas* enabled me to experience more lands and peoples than I can ever hope to experience first hand, and it is a great follow-up to *Honk*. Still, I feel the fifty shades of Sonja have not all been revealed … yet."

— Eric Zimmerman, Retired Homicide Detective

"I started reading *Roundtrip from Texas* this morning and ended up being late to my yoga class! I have been jumping around visiting different chapters. The ⋯⋯⋯⋯⋯⋯⋯⋯⋯⋯⋯⋯⋯⋯⋯⋯⋯⋯⋯⋯⋯⋯⋯⋯⋯⋯⋯⋯⋯⋯⋯ ⋯rnia

"So⋯⋯⋯⋯⋯⋯⋯⋯⋯⋯⋯⋯⋯⋯⋯⋯⋯⋯⋯⋯⋯⋯⋯⋯⋯ nny,
fasc⋯⋯⋯⋯⋯⋯⋯⋯⋯⋯⋯⋯⋯⋯⋯⋯⋯⋯⋯⋯⋯⋯⋯⋯⋯⋯⋯ her
own⋯⋯⋯⋯⋯⋯⋯⋯⋯⋯⋯⋯⋯⋯⋯⋯⋯⋯⋯⋯⋯⋯⋯⋯⋯⋯⋯⋯ you
feel **Barbara Bush**⋯⋯⋯⋯⋯⋯⋯⋯**Library Friends** ch a
vari⋯⋯⋯⋯⋯⋯⋯⋯⋯⋯⋯⋯⋯⋯⋯⋯⋯⋯⋯⋯⋯⋯⋯⋯⋯⋯⋯⋯ with
Son *Building a better library*⋯⋯⋯⋯⋯*one book at a time.*

⋯⋯⋯⋯⋯⋯⋯⋯⋯⋯⋯⋯⋯⋯⋯⋯⋯⋯⋯⋯⋯⋯⋯⋯⋯⋯⋯⋯⋯⋯⋯ ator

"You gotta read Sonja's books and essays if you want a view on life and travel from a Texas ranch girl's perspective! But don't be fooled by that description of her, as Ms. Sonja is a woman highly educated by both university and life experiences (read *Honk* if you doubt that). Sonja's writing will take you with her and give you her take on all she sees and experiences, holding nothing back, and never failing to entertain you, to enchant you and to bring you back for more. Dive in now!"

— Bob D'amore, Retired Inspector General,
U.S. Air Force and Planner, HHS/NDMS
Incident Response Coordination Team –
Southwest (Region 6)

"If there was a female Gus in Lonesome Dove, Sonja is it."

— DRK, Executive

"Free spirited Sonja Klein has done it again, serving up a heaping helping of wanderlust for her devoted readers to feast upon! Hop in her back pocket and travel vicariously with this cheeky Texas gal as she explores the world, one adventure at a time. A must read!"

— Linda Koehl, Singer/Songwriter

"Straight from the hip without a quip, Sonja tells it like she sees it, and it is both point blank and insightful. Well worth the time to benefit from her oft too honest observations."

— Tracy Walsh, Retired Honda Executive

"In Roundtrip from Texas Sonja describes her adventures across the planet and at home in Texas in a fun and easy manner. She provides interesting detail, personal insight and witty entertainment. The autobiographical sections have the energy and tone of a conversation between friends sharing a six-pack of Shiner Bock on the tailgate of a pickup truck at the ranch of this native Texan. This makes for an enjoyable read."

— Martin Terry, D.V.M., Ph.D.
Associate Professor, Department of Biology, Sul Ross State University

Praise for
Honk If You Married Sonja

"As we crash through life, we change lives as we change our own. *Honk If You Married Sonja: The Travels and Essays of Sonja Klein* is a memoir from author Sonja Klein who shares her life's journey through Texas and everywhere else, finding her own adventure and experiencing what life has to offer, sharing what she's learned and what she's failed to. *Honk If You Married Sonja* is a strong pick, highly recommended."

— *Midwest Book Review*

"From her ranch, Ambush Hill, in legendary Texas, Sonja produces a stimulating adventure and misadventure book. Readers will be intrigued with her no holds barred essays, worldwide travel adventures and Texas ranch life. The book illuminates the human condition including its joys, heartaches and humor. The book is a literary high quality jewel, not to be missed and a never to be forgotten enjoyable read."

— *The Mindquest Review of Books,* Lightword Publishing

Roundtrip from Texas

More Travels and Essays
from Sonja Klein

Sonja Klein

Ambush Publishing
Barksdale, Texas

Published by Ambush Publishing

PO Box 192
Barksdale, Texas 78828
1-830-234-3156

Library of Congress Control Number: 2013905296
Klein, Sonja 1942 —
Roundtrip from Texas: More Travels and Essays from Sonja Klein
by Sonja Klein

ISBN-13: 978-0-9889863-0-5 (trade paper)

9 8 7 6 5 4 3 2 1

Cover art designed by Chuck Roach, www.roach-art.com
Editing and production by Castle Communications,
www.castlecommunications.com

Printed in the United States of America

About the author

Sonja Rose Klein is a native Texan and graduate of The University of Texas. After retiring, she lives on Ambush Hill Ranch in southwest Texas, where she gardens, writes and raises a few sheep and goats. She is active in the nearby communities of Barksdale and Camp Wood and has won awards for her poetry, essays and short stories. Sonja is an adventure traveler, having visited remote places around the world. She prefers the solitary journeys.

You can contact her by visiting her website, where she blogs quite often: www.sonjaroseklein.com

Acknowledgments

Again, the encouragement of family, friends and readers of my first book has supported me in the publishing of this, my second book. Special thanks to Lee Sweeten, without whose help I wouldn't have the free time and peace of mind to write. For my friend Linda Koehl, a talented singer/songwriter who has accompanied me to book signings, I say you are a Texas princess. And to Eric Zimmerman, I thank you for always answering my phone calls.

For the cover, Chuck Roach captured me after a night of dancing in Terlingua. Chuck, you are an extraordinary artist. Much appreciation goes to Howard and Debbie Simms for their patient research. And to my editor and publishing consultant, Lana Castle, who not only made this book more readable but also created a clearer, stronger, richer map of the journey; you are a wizard who also designed and laid out the inside, produced the cover, advised and encouraged me and calmed my fears.

My heartfelt thanks to you all. I couldn't have done it without you.

For my children, Joseph Klein and Molly Klein,
and my grandson Theiss.
May our branches continue to grow.

Preface

I believe that we are nomads and that traveling helps us find ourselves. Most human contacts have been made through travel by wandering pilgrims who approached the meaning of life through walking. We might be able to think and live better and be closer to our purpose in life if we moved continually across this earth.

I hope that this book will stir the hunger within you to experience the romance of life. My wish for you is to leave the prison of necessity that diverts from the true life of the spirit. Walk through that door, where an untraveled world beckons, for we are all born adventurers. You might as well admit it.

Travel writing is about storytelling and I can only hope that I have told my story well. Most of all, I invite you to join me.

Contents

1 Boots and a Mercedes...1

2 Where are they now?...3

3 Spanish immersion..13

4 South America..16

    Brazil...16

    Uruguay...28

    Argentina...30

5 What's it like?..35

6 Cooking...37

7 The post office..42

8 What's in your trap?...44

9 California...48

10 Comments...55

11 Church..59

12 Sex..61

13 Ex-husbands..63

14 Never give up..66

15 Drought...69

16 Games...71

17 Dancing in Bandera..73

18 What do I do now?...77

19 Itch...80

20 Vietnam and Cambodia..83

    Cambodia..89

    Vietnam..98

21 Cities and Boulevards...101

22 Truth..103

23 The garden...105

24 New Mexico 107

25 Girlie party 110

26 The rodeo 112

27 The concert 114

28 Election Day 116

29 Canada and the East Coast 119

    The East Coast 124

    New England 126

    South Carolina 131

30 My new computer 133

31 Creatures of habit 139

32 Turning seventy, ugh 141

33 Guns 143

34 East Africa and the Indian Ocean 146

    The Seychelles 151

    Kenya 153

    Zanzibar 156

    The Indian Ocean 159

35 Grandmama day care 164

36 The speech 166

37 Bush Library speech 168

38 Two weeks with Theiss 176

39 The scapegoat 178

40 Tennis shoes 182

41 The sorority 184

42 Cuss words 188

43 Cuba 189

44 Used to be 205

45 Trespassers 207

46 Four pages 211

47 Garage sales 214

48 New York City 216

49 Grandmama day care shuts down 223

50 Viva Big Bend 225

51 Pointless..227

52 Tattoo 229

53 China..233

   Beijing..234

   Luoyang and beyond..239

   Xi'an..245

   Cruising the Yangtze 251

   Wuhan...257

   Changsa...259

   Ka'li..264

   Guiyang...268

   Shanghai..271

54 Food as medicine...277

55 Families 280

56 I think I've changed my mind 282

57 Brother John...284

58 India...287

   Delhi...294

   Agra 297

   Jaipur..299

   Cochin 302

59 Thailand, Malaysia, Indonesia and Singapore................306

   Malaysia...312

   Indonesia 314

   Singapore 317

60 The rollercoaster 320

61 I have learned 321

1

Boots and a Mercedes

I purchased my first Mercedes from a high school friend with whom I had stayed in touch. He owned a Mercedes dealership and carried Volvos too. The first car I purchased from him was a Volvo, the sporting model, a P1800. By the time the odometer on the sporty Volvo reached 180,000, I was ready for another Volvo, this time a maroon four-door sedan.

When I took the Volvo for service one day, I couldn't resist the cobalt blue sedan—a Mercedes 280 SE 4.5. sitting in the showroom. The interior was white leather. I traded in the Volvo and purchased the Mercedes.

When I sat in that car to drive it home, I felt like the queen of the road. That euphoria was worth much more than I paid for the car.

I named her Ursula and took her with me when I divorced my first husband. Ursula made me feel much better, even though I had been living in a faithless marriage. She carried me almost 200,000 miles before I bought a Mercedes 6.9, the fastest production car of the times. That one I named the Hell Bitch. I received a few speeding tickets before I discovered the wonders of cruise control.

My second husband became enamored of Mercedes automobiles. To keep him from driving the Hell Bitch, I purchased a used Mercedes 6.3, equally as fast. It was gold, so he called it Goldie. Thank heavens it was a heavy, sturdy sedan. When he hit some cows head on, he wasn't hurt, but Goldie never recovered fully from the accident. She went to live with the insurance company.

The Hell Bitch met a bitter end. After visiting my second husband in prison where he was serving a 10-year sentence for conspiracy to smuggle marijuana, I parked the car in the garage. A strange smell drifted through the air. I ignored it until the next morning when I opened the garage door. The hood was bubbled. Inside the engine compartment was a mass of charcoal, but when I opened the interior door, the car smelled like new leather. I sold the Hell Bitch for $6,000 and quietly experienced a nervous breakdown.

Sonja Klein

For punishment, I bought a little Buick sedan with stick shift, a rolling coffin, and vowed never to rest my happiness in a material possession.

When I divorced my second husband and moved back to Houston, my mother took pity on me and sold me her Lincoln when she purchased a new one. While the Lincoln was a definite step up, it was not a Mercedes.

After I divorced my third husband, I reunited with a long past love and bought a ranch in southwest Texas. I traded the Lincoln for a Ford pickup.

As my fourth husband was dying of cancer, he sent me to town on a fool's errand and ordered a new Mercedes by phone from my high school friend. It was delivered the next week, only a few days before he died. He informed me of the purchase when I returned from town. When I asked him, "Why did you do that?" he replied, "This is my parting gift to you. You have always driven a Mercedes. You were driving one when I met you and you're too tight to buy one for yourself."

"What color is it?"

"I don't remember."

"How am I going to pay for it?"

"Sell the sheep."

"Easy for you to say."

The car was silver. I named it the Hell Bitch too and put over 120,000 miles on it before I gave it to my son, who always loved the car.

Having become computer literate I went online and checked out the inventory of my friend's dealership and decided on a smaller sedan, a Mercedes diesel E320. With only 32,000 miles behind the wheel, the car has yet to identify itself by name. It runs like a silver bullet and I feel bulletproof when I drive it. The great mileage is an added bonus.

I have three pairs of cowboy boots. I don't wear them much because they aren't that comfortable and I can't dance in them. There's always a pair of cowboy boots in the trunk of the Mercedes. I don't know why. The boots just like living in a Mercedes. I like driving one.

2

Where are they now?

The phone rang, "Sonja, this is 'Mary Ann.'" "How are you?"

"Fine."

"I just called to let you know that 'Gary' has been released from jail. Has he gotten in touch with you?"

"No, he hasn't."

"I'm sure he will."

"'Mary Ann,' how is he?"

"Well, he's gained about 100 pounds sitting in jail for a year and a half. He has problems with his heart and swelling feet. They gave him 10 years probation, and he's in Amarillo in a Veterans Domiciliary waiting to be admitted into a drug rehab program. I think they have an angioplasty scheduled for him too. I just wanted to let you know."

"Thanks, 'Mary Ann.' Gee that's terrible. He isn't that old."

"He still smokes a lot, and the years of drug abuse have taken their toll. He's not in good shape."

"Sounds like he'll be in the custody of the Veterans Administration for the rest of his life. At least he's in good hands. What a waste. Another Vietnam vet casualty."

I spent the day in reflection thinking about the men in my life since my husband John died. There had been a few. That first year I grieved; then I decided to live.

'Charlie' was the first one. I met him at the Terlingua Chili Cookoff. My friends knew him and introduced us. We danced. He was a fairly good dancer and sported a full mustache and long hair tied in a ponytail. I was attracted. The relationship lasted less than a year. I visited him; he visited me. He was an oilfield worker from around Midland, 12 years younger. When off his shift he and his friends drank a lot and I mean drank a *lot*, mostly beer.

He took me to the Sand Dunes Park to see the world's thickest oak forest. The trees were about a foot high. Visitors surfed the sand dunes.

With 'Charlie,' I went off-road jeeping in Big Bend. That was quite a day. I could not believe where his jeep and the vehicles of his fellow club members traveled. The modified jeeps climbed boulders, steep cliffs and soft embankments. That night we partied in Terlingua and closed the bar down. As we walked outside in the early hours, a fantastic light display illuminated the skies. 'Charlie' was the first to speak.

"I can't be that drunk. It must be a fire. It looks more like an acid trip."

One of the others agreed, "Wow, what the hell is it? It must be a fire, hell of a fire."

I intruded, "It's the Northern Lights; I've seen movies and pictures of it."

"'It can't be the Northern Lights," 'Charlie' argued, "We're in Texas."

I was adamant, "We'll find out tomorrow. It'll be in the paper or on the news. McDonald Observatory isn't that far away. I know I'm right."

A chorus of yeah, yeahs sounded.

We watched the lights until the drunks sobered and turned sleepy.

At breakfast in Study Butte the following morning, the talk was all about the Northern Lights. It was the first time in recorded history they had been seen so far south. People in Arizona had also witnessed the display.

A few months later 'Charlie' and I visited the Admiral Nimitz Museum in Fredericksburg on the way to Georgetown. We spent hours in the museum. 'Charlie' was fascinated by every display.

As we came to the Japanese mini-submarine captured from the attack on Pearl Harbor, a group of World War II veterans stood close. A life-sized Japanese dummy sat in the sub. Approaching were some Japanese tourists. One of the war veterans commented, "Look, George. They even put a Gook in the sub." I don't think the Japanese tourists comprehended what was said. I did.

'Charlie' and I continued from Fredericksburg to the air show in Georgetown. He and some friends were in a club that set up the pyrotechnics for air shows in Texas. In return for working two days in the hot August sun, the motel rooms were paid and beer and food were furnished after the conclusion of each air show.

We started early. Mostly I followed directions and stayed close to 'Charlie.' Everyone seemed to have a purpose. Lines of wire were laid, and batteries were positioned with controls. After lunch we were instructed to fill garbage bags with airplane fuel. A gasoline truck appeared and we held out the bags while they were filled and tied. Then we positioned them along a line of wires. I tried not to think of the danger.

As workers, we were allowed to watch the show from the inner circle of runways. Radios kept the workers and pilots in touch, and when it was time to go boom, one of the guys pushed the button and moved on to the next controlled area. All of the guys took turns setting off the booms, their highlight of the day. The plastic bags full of airline fuel were part of the strafing display.

The party for the workers was in a hangar. Beer and barbecue were served and no one left until the beer was gone. The following day was a repeat. I was offered the thrill of pushing the button for a boom. I declined. 'Charlie' took my place.

That night the party was even more rowdy. 'Charlie' couldn't perform when we returned to the room. No wonder; he had drunk a shitload of beer, could barely walk. His humiliation was revealed in his words, "I can't fuck with a limp dick." We drove back to the ranch the next day; he dropped me off and never called again. I was relieved.

Every year I see him at the Chili Cookoff with the same group of guys, the jeep crew and the pyrotechnic crew. They are always cordial. Last year 'Charlie' asked me to dance. I accepted. He looked 70 years old. His ponytail was gray. He was smoking a cigar and was so drunk he could only shuffle.

'Daren' was a local. Friends invited me to join them at the Lone Star Saloon in Uvalde for an evening of dancing.

I answered, "I don't think so. It's no fun to go to a dance and just sit. I'm not going unless I have someone to dance with."

One of my friends replied, "We'll ask 'Daren' to go. He's a good dancer. I'll call you back."

I met Vercia Lee and Linton at the Barksdale post office and left my truck there. The 38-mile drive was filled with casual conversation. When we arrived at the Lone Star, 'Daren' was there. Soon other friends from Camp Wood arrived. We danced and drank some beer. Linton was the designated driver, so he drank soft drinks.

'Daren' offered to drive me back to Barksdale, where my truck was parked. I agreed. We talked all the way, getting to know each other. The loud music at the Lone Star had prohibited any serious talking. He owned part of a ranch and lived in an old farmhouse. He was divorced, a few years younger than me, owned property in other parts of Texas, was a graduate of University of Texas and an avid frat boy.

He called the following week and invited me for dinner. I drove to the old farmhouse, following his directions. He grilled fish on an electric grill on the porch and served some frozen mixed vegetables and a baked potato. We talked real estate, children and politics. I was interested.

A pattern developed. About once a week we met for dinner, either his place or mine. He preferred his place. Several times I spent the night, wearing a tee shirt and sharing his bed. Nothing happened. I traveled to Nicaragua for a few weeks. I related the state of affairs in Nicaragua to him. He was interested in the country.

The next thing I knew, he flew to Nicaragua and returned saying he was buying a house there. I was puzzled.

When my brother invited me to his ranch in New Mexico, I asked 'Daren' if would like to go. He said yes.

We traveled in his Lincoln, stopping in Pecos for a crate of cantaloupes. He complained of the smell, but I found it tantalizing. We stopped for dinner at a large truck stop. He piled his plate high from the greasy buffet. Then he took some pills. I asked him, "What are you taking?"

He replied, "Vitamins."

When he stopped at a cheap, shoddy motel, I motioned to the larger one next door and offered, "Since we're in your car, I'll pay for the motel." It wasn't much better.

Our first sexual exercise wasn't that good; he put forth effort that I assumed was pill induced. We arrived at my brother's the next afternoon, stayed a few days, went riding on four-wheelers, took some walks and had a nice visit. My brother David quizzed him on real estate, mentioned a ranch for sale adjoining Big Bend National Park.

From David's ranch near Las Vegas, New Mexico, we drove to my cousin's home for a visit. We had a few drinks; he played bridge poorly. Another sexual attempt failed. I had guessed correctly.

We drove home in a pleasant mood, detouring through Ruidoso, where I bought some cherry cider. I love New Mexico cherry cider.

The phone calls became less frequent. We remained cordial friends. He married an older woman. She died sometime around their divorce.

He's still around. I ran into him in Uvalde at the grocery store. We hugged, exchanged pleasantries and I continued shopping.

My former husband John's friend 'Gary' came for a visit. He would stay a few days, sleep on the sofa and leave. We talked about John, listened to music and I cooked. Sexual tension was present but ignored.

One cold night as he stood before the fireplace, his movements indicated that his back hurt. I went to him and rubbed his back. We ended up in bed. The sex was slow and satisfying. We spent a lot of time under Grandpa Klein's feather comforter. After a few days he left.

Later that month he returned with an unemployed friend, 'Malcom,' who slept in the guest bedroom above the carport. 'Malcom' never left our sight. I finally told him, "We're going for a hike and some ranch sex." He understood.

I received an invitation to a cousin's wedding in Santa Fe. Several weeks before the wedding 'Gary' called. On a moment's whim I asked him if he would like to go to a wedding in Santa Fe with me. He replied, "Sure."

I drove to his house in north Texas. It was mid-afternoon and I assumed we would continue the journey. As I entered his modest house, the smell of incense drifted in the air. The candles were burning and the room was dark. The setting was seductive. I was shocked. He didn't seem the romantic type. We smoked a joint and he gathered his things. Not having any dress clothes, he packed his Indian gear—moccasins, porcupine-quill vest and blue jeans.

As I drove, he held my hand. He was solicitous and charming. The courting felt good. After stopping at a motel, he made love with emotion. I was flattered. I liked the feeling.

With the wedding invitation, my cousin included precise instructions to the motel where the out of town guests were staying. A gift bag full of chocolates and goodies was waiting in the room. The first evening we attended a dinner at her house and the following evening joined the family and friends for the rehearsal dinner. The tables were reserved with place cards. My seat was next to my cousin. 'Gary' sat beside me.

Early in the evening, my cousin looked at 'Gary' and instructed him to go sit at a table of women, "'Gary,' that table needs some testosterone. Go sit over there." He did.

The wedding the next evening was elaborate, held outdoors near the Opera House in Santa Fe. A champagne brunch the following morning ended the festivities. I was partied out.

My brother David attended the wedding and invited us to his ranch for a visit. We went four-wheeling, hiked and enjoyed the slower pace. David left for Houston and we stayed an extra day. As we hiked the beautiful terrain, 'Gary,' stood still, his senses heightened, "Don't move," he said, "They're watching us. Follow me."

He snaked through the trees as if our life depended on it. I silently followed. After what seemed like hours, he stood up, "It's okay now, they're gone." That was my first experience of a Vietnam flashback.

We spent our night alone in the hot tub on the deck, a very sexual night.

We left the next morning. 'Gary' directed me north. The scenery was rugged and beautiful. He said, "I want to show you Mesa Verde."

We spent the night in Cortez and drove around the rim of the canyon. It was mystical and breathtaking. As we returned to Cortez, 'Gary' suggested we stop at an Indian trading post. He looked at vests, moccasins and shirts. I wandered around and spotted a colorful coat. It was big and beautiful. When I looked at the price tag, it was over a thousand dollars. The salesman noticed my interest, "That coat was made by a Navajo woman famous for her coats. This is the last one she made. Try it on."

"It's way too big, a size large."

'Gary' came over and encouraged me to try it on.

When I looked at myself in the mirror in that coat, I knew it was mine.

I offered the salesman $600 for the coat and he said okay.

At that point, 'Gary' pointed out some things he had selected. I said, "Buy them."

"I thought you might buy them for me," he replied.

I don't remember what I said, but it was a polite but definite no. I had paid for the gas, motels, meals and everything. This moment cheapened the trip. He was 12 years younger and just because he was the flavor of the month, I knew there was no future with him. I don't like vanilla but he was too tutti frutti for a long-term relationship. I wanted to go home.

I drove south, dropping him off at his house and headed towards the ranch. The romance and parties were over. I had my colorful Navajo coat. That was enough.

Back at Ambush I returned to my regular routine: reading, writing and a little ranching. The small town of Camp Wood, 20 miles distant, offered the closest shopping opportunity. I carried an account at the feed store, always a good gathering place. On a trip into town, I stopped for some corn and mineral blocks. A new person was behind the counter.

He introduced himself as 'Bart,' the new owner of the feed store. From that moment a mild flirtation began and accelerated when I discovered he was single and had purchased a small but nice ranch outside the town.

I invited him to go dancing with us. He met us at the feed store. He couldn't dance worth a lick. After a while he quit trying, not willing to learn the two-step.

He called and invited me to dinner the following week. His home was nice but far too neutral in colors, typical of a man living alone. We ate grilled steaks, salad and a baked potato after relaxing with a few martinis. As we were cleaning the kitchen he looked at me and said, "I want to kiss you right now."

It was a good line. I replied, "Well, why don't you?"

The kiss was a nice one. We ended up in his waterbed. I drove home the next morning after a friendly breakfast. Pure lust was the dominant factor in the romance. He was younger. The more I learned about him, the less I respected him. His mother owned the ranch and had loaned him the money to buy the feed store. He was always looking for a quick way to make money.

We took one trip together, to Cloudcroft, New Mexico, to look at a small resort for sale. We went in my car. He was not a big spender but did pay for the hotel room. We alternated paying for most of the meals. When he asked if I would be interested in investing with him I replied with a mantra that I had developed after some expensive financial and emotional mistakes, "I don't invest money with anyone I'm fucking, have fucked or want to fuck."

From then on, his interest cooled and soon he was dating a woman that attended my church. Soon she was wearing his grandmother's ring, which I had turned down. They sat directly behind me in church. I quit going to church.

'Gary' called and came for a visit. The romance was rekindled. The memory of the Cortez incident had faded. His commercial coating business had gone under. He explained that a conspiracy had destroyed his livelihood. He was involved in some Indian organization, claimed to be a shaman and wanted me to join the secret organization, at a substantial cost of course. Then he wanted to promote some Indian gathering with my financial assistance. I sent him home.

Life was good until 'Gary' returned for an uninvited visit. A friend dropped him off and left. This time he wanted to get married. I told him, "I will not marry again."

He asked, "Let's try it, live together for six months. I'll help you around the ranch."

Reluctant to commit, I weakened, "Okay, but you have to put the commode seat down, pick up after yourself and let me go away when I want."

He was relieved, "Fair enough."

It didn't take long, "Sonja, I need some running-around money. Why don't you put $500 in my sock drawer on the first of every month? I want you to buy me a truck."

"'Gary,' you can drive my truck anytime."

"Yeah, but I don't want everyone to see me driving your truck all the time. They'll think I'm living off you."

"Well, you are."

Just when I thought things couldn't get worse, they did. He asked me to set him up in business. I delayed as long as possible before saying flatly, "No."

His relationship with his ex-wife and two sons was not affable. His child support payments were erratic at best. He owed back payments. As the summer approached he said he would like to take a trip to Washington State to see his mother, who was in a nursing home after suffering a stroke. His only sibling, a sister, had moved her there and lived nearby.

'Gary' convinced his ex-wife that he was responsible. We met her and the two boys, 18 and 20, in Fredericksburg. They joined us. 'Gary' envisioned a bonding experience. It didn't happen. They smoked pot and listened to music with earphones. I drove the entire trip to Washington

State. 'Gary' spent every evening in the boys' motel room. All of them ate nothing but fast food. Gary' dressed in blue jean shorts and a sleeveless blue jean shirt, both tattered and shredded. His legs looked like stumps.

His sister and her husband received us cordially. Two days passed before 'Gary' and his two sons visited his mother. The rest of the time the three of them laid around, watched TV and ate junk food. We did go to Seattle one day and up to Vancouver another day, but I had to make 'Gary' change clothes. I told him, "I'm not going anywhere with you in those shorts and shirt and work boots."

"Sonja, I don't tell you what to wear."

"I don't care. It's my car and you're not getting in it dressed like that."

He changed clothes.

His sister and I had some frank talks. What I learned I had suspected all along. 'Gary' was not in touch with reality and had an ongoing drug problem.

I drove all the way home, the hostility in the car palpable, and left the three of them at his house late one evening.

'Gary' wasn't happy, "I thought we were going to be together for six months."

"I thought you were going to put the commode seat down."

"Sonja, you expect too much."

"'Gary,' you produce too little. Goodbye."

When I arrived home at the ranch near midnight, I detected a horrible smell. The power transformer had been struck by lightning. The house had been without electricity for days. I called my utility provider. They arrived well after midnight and replaced the transformer. I went to bed, smell and all.

After a few days of nasty work, I cleaned house, decided to make some changes in my life and vowed my days of romance were over.

Some mild flirtations were in play, but none that resulted in bedtime. I continued to write, happy to be alone, until 'Gary' appeared unannounced. He was a mess. The truck he was driving was borrowed. He was drinking whiskey from the bottle and kept returning to his truck. I suspected he was snorting speed.

'Gary' updated me on his life, said he was driving toxic materials cross-country for the government. His house had burned down and he was living with a retired truck driver, a good friend.

He slept on the sofa. The following morning his friend called advising 'Gary' that the state child-support people had called and left a number. After 'Gary' hung up the phone he vented anger like I had never witnessed. He called the state office about the back child-support payments and yelled at the lady who referred him to another office. He yelled at that worker also. When he hung up the phone he informed me that he owed $60,000 in back child support and that they were going to take away his driver's license. He ranted and raved in an alarming manner and then started drinking. I went to bed and slept fitfully and frightened. The following morning, glad to be alive, I firmly told him, "'Gary,' I think you need to go back and straighten this out. Staying here won't solve a thing." He left.

Two weeks later he was in jail, accused of strangling the friend with whom he lived. His defense was that the VA had given him some medicine that caused him to black out for three days. He didn't remember a thing.

When 'Gary' finally called me, he admitted to being in a VA domiciliary in Amarillo but said he was being treated for post-traumatic stress. The only thing that had changed was that he hadn't had any drugs for the 18 months he had been in jail. His reality was still altered.

I told him I was in a serious relationship, was glad to hear he was in the care of the Veterans Administration and wished him the best.

When I told my daughter Molly about the phone call, admitting that the serious relationship was with my grandson, she said, "Mother, you should have told him the truth."

"What is the truth, Molly?"

I cleaned house, no boyfriends in my life. A few men seemed interested, but they were married. I quit doing married, even though I don't believe man or woman is meant to be monogamous. The truth was that I was not attracted to the men who appeared ready to jump in my bed. The magnetic lusty feeling was absent. That didn't mean I wasn't looking.

3

Spanish immersion

In preparation for a scheduled trip to South America, I returned to and consulted my notes from Spanish immersion classes I took in Mexico back when it was safe to travel south of the Texas border. The memories of that experience made me smile.

A moment of splendor convinced me that I could travel to Cuernavaca, enroll in the international college and in two weeks improve my Spanish and become fluent. I was wrong.

I flew to Mexico City, a short flight, and a representative of the university met me and drove me directly to the University Internationale, where I took a test.

Reasoning that the course would be easier if I played dumb, I answered only the questions to which I had the correct answers. After being transported to a lovely hacienda-like motel, I felt comfortable that I could carry out the mission and be chattering Spanish in a few days.

Some fellow students were sitting out by the pool and I joined them for margaritas. Meals were included in my plan, and I dined with a group of various ages from all over the world who had come to learn Spanish. There was a truck driver from Switzerland, a couple from Sweden and two lady Americans The food was tasty. My room was spacious, with a balcony overlooking the courtyard and pool. Lush flowers bloomed throughout the complex. Music echoed from the street. I smiled—one of my last smiles of the week.

A taxi delivered us to the university before 8 A.M. And in the office I received workbooks and a schedule with classes until 4 P.M., including an hour break for lunch. This was serious.

I found the first class of the day. The classroom was small and intimate. There were four of us; I assumed all dummies. This time I was right. Two of the students were middle-aged women, civil service employees from Las Vegas sent to Mexico to learn Spanish to improve their job performance with Hispanics. The other student was a serious young man from Europe.

Sonja Klein

The instructor immediately began with grammar lessons. He hammered us with questions and repetition. I managed quite well.

My scheduled classes consisted of idioms, conversation and vocabulary. Some of the classes were larger than others. Idioms, I couldn't understand at all. Lunch was a welcome break.

Back at the motel, I shared experiences with my fellow students while enjoying a margarita. Some of the students were happy; some complained. I remained quiet.

The second morning of classes, I awoke before dawn and did my homework, studying with a clear mind and carefully writing the sentences. Only two of us were present for grammar. I responded satisfactorily to the questions but was having trouble thinking quickly. My German intruded. I had to translate from the German to the Spanish. The meltdown had begun.

Margaritas were my afternoon pleasure, until I discovered that they weren't priced like the old Mexico I remembered from the 1960's and 1970's. I was being billed $7.50 for each one. I quickly switched to beer. Two weeks of margaritas could become expensive.

On day three I awoke before dawn, studied, and completed my homework, convinced that I could accomplish two weeks of studies. Again there were only two in the class. I lost my voice, could not answer a question. When I tried to explain in English that I was thinking in German, the instructor silenced me and ignored me for the remainder of the class.

After class he allowed me to speak in English. I explained that I had gone blank, that I was thinking in German. He smiled and replied that when a person begins to learn a third language, the second language fights and intrudes. I was so relieved I could have kissed him.

The week dragged. The two women in the class reappeared, saying they had gone to Acapulco to party. The instructor shrugged; I was enraged that they were playing on my tax dollars.

In addition to the classes, we were entertained one evening with a tequila tasting party. Fruit, cheese and crackers were served as we were lectured on the process of making tequila from the agave plant. In front of each of us was a shot glass. We began with tequila in the $20 range and progressed to the $60 range. After drinking five shots, I was worried about arising early and doing my homework.

Before dawn I prepared for class. My mind was clear. I discovered the reason I had no hangover. It was the same about drinking as it was about eating. The ingredients made the difference—fresh food as opposed to prepared with preservatives. I felt a bit stupid. I should have known, especially being a fanatic about what I eat and drink. I don't drink sodas and fruit juices, and I am a cheapskate about beer, wine and liquor. It makes sense to buy the best because it is purer and better prepared. What a double dummy I was—the more expensive the alcohol, the less severe the hangover.

As the weekend approached, I was given the choice of visiting the famous museum in Mexico City or shopping in the town of Taxco. Having visited the museum several times, I chose shopping, lunch and an excursion to the hacienda of Cortez.

My choice was a good one. I purchased silver jewelry for everyone I knew, including myself, and was absolutely enchanted by the ancient walls and buildings of Cortez's hacienda.

My Spanish was improving.

The second week of classes, I again hit the wall, backed off and moved forward. I attended a cocktail party for a recently elected U.S. Senator who was attending classes with his wife. Their lessons were private.

The classes ended. Fortunately, there were no final exams, just a certificate. I completed the course and attended all the classes. I had expected to be immersed in some fountain and come out speaking Spanish. It was not at all like that. The classes were tough, the work was challenging, but I did it.

The experience was revealing, especially the battle with the German. Though I wasn't immersed, I was definitely dipped.

4

South America

I've always wanted to dance the tango in Havana, Cuba, ever since a very older friend told stories from the 1940's of driving a Cadillac to New Orleans, driving the car onto the boat and unloading in Havana to party. The return trip sounded like just as much fun. She and her husband drove the Cadillac onto a boat destined for New York. After partying in New York, they returned home to Olivier, Louisiana.

Since travel to Cuba is restricted to Americans, I didn't deem it worthy of the risk of losing my passport or finding myself on a watch list. My Canadian friends advised, "Fly to Canada and enter Cuba on a Canadian tour. Americans do it all the time, "My outlaw friends have another solution: "Fly to Cozumel; there's daily flights to Cuba. Just don't let the Cubans stamp your passport."

For me, the loss of my passport would be like a prison sentence. I would be confined, and just the thought of being so restricted is scary.

Brazil

After I completed preparations for the printing of my first book, I flew to Rio de Janeiro instead for one last fling, a chance to dance the tango and have some fun before becoming a book peddler.

Since the flight left in the evening, I drove to Houston the day before, had dinner with one of my brothers, his wife and my son Joe and his wife Carla. A good evening of bridge with two of my brothers and sister-in-law completed a long day.

Joe dropped me off at the airport well within the three-hour recommended arrival. The plane was full; my seat on the last row was more comfortable than usual. A movie producer from Chicago and a U.S. Army veteran of Somalia provided interesting conversation during the early hours of the flight before I attempted to sleep. The army veteran and his friend seated elsewhere on the plane were going to Rio for the party of Carnaval. They were staying with friends and planned to immerse themselves in the festivities.

By the time I retrieved my luggage and got on the bus that was to deliver me to the ship, I revived from the long flight. The bustling city of Rio de Janeiro is flanked by Sugarloaf Mountain, shaped like a cone of sugar, and the ever-present statue of Jesus Christ, a landmark always associated with Rio.

My fellow travelers were old and moved slowly. My first impression: What have I gotten myself into this time?

The bus driver as usual was full of conversation and facts. His running dialogue was quite interesting. Rio de Janeiro was settled in the 16th century, having been discovered in January, thus the name. Brazil is pronounced like windowsill, Brazil. Portuguese is spoken in Brazil and is similar to French. My Spanish proficiency helped interpret the signs.

The weather was warm and humid. Rainfall is plentiful, near 80 inches a year, and the rainy season was in full swing.

Leaving the airport I observed the fruit trees along the boulevards laden with bananas, avocados, papaya, jackfruit and guava. The streets were congested with traffic and progress was slow.

The guide continued, saying that the population of Rio was close to 6 million in the city and as much as 12 million in the suburbs and that Sao Paolo was the largest city in Brazil, with 20 million people. The average income is about $350 per month, with surgeons being paid $800 a month.

We drove by the athletic stadium, which has seating for 60,000 spectators. It was the first day of Carnaval and the city was full of tourists. I noticed lots of graffiti on the buildings as the driver pointed to the slums or *favelas* that dotted the hills surrounding the city. The slums are named and the population of each is in the tens of thousands.

A short history of the country followed. Rio de Janeiro was discovered on January 1, 1502, by Portuguese navigators who mistook the entrance of Guanabara Bay for the mouth of a river. Because the French were visiting the area in search of Brazilwood and mineral resources, the Portuguese crown established the city and expelled the French in the 1560's. Portuguese settlers soon cultivated the fertile lands, and the city's importance increased immensely when it became the primary shipping port for gold and diamonds from Minas Gerais, one of the 26 states of Brazil. When Napoleon began the invasion of Portugal in 1808, the Portuguese monarch and his court moved to Rio de Janeiro and remained until 1821, and Brazil was elevated in status from a colony to a Portuguese kingdom. In 1889, Brazil became a republic and now consists of a federation of states. The native population was estimated at 2 million, but today only 200,000 remain, some of them on reservations.

After arriving on the ship and settling in the modest stateroom, I attended a lecture by Dr. Don Klein—no relation. He is an interesting man in his 60's, who has traveled the world, including driving the length of Africa from north to south. He is an accomplished musician, having a Ph.D. in music, specializing in the rhythms of Latin America.

Don explained that where we were docked in Rio was literally a stone's throw from the highlight of the greatest festival on the planet, which was beginning on Saturday. The event is called Carnaval in Portuguese, Mardi Gras in Louisiana. From Saturday evening until the wee hours of Ash Wednesday, the streets of Rio and the world-renown beaches of Copacabana and Ipanema would reverberate with the echo of three million celebrants happily combining merriment with a bit of mayhem.

The over 400 *blocos* (literally blocks or neighborhoods of paraders and musicians) take to the streets in an avalanche of samba-driven exuberance, for samba is the music of Carnaval. The momentum builds for months as the costumes, floats, choreography and inspired new sambas are previewed for and played to eager listeners.

The major venue for all of this excitement is the so-called Sambadrome—a purpose-built, single-street "stadium," with ticketed spectators numbering about 80,000 lining the street's concrete corridor for each of two nights. Along this parade route some of the poorest neighborhoods in Rio compete for bragging rights as Rio's top samba school. Each school has 80 minutes to dance, sing and pound their way along the 800-meter *pasarela* (parade route) in front of the judges and crowds. The samba music has an infectious loud and pulsating rhythm.

Multiple creative criteria are judged during each of the two nights in which 12 different neighborhood schools with names like Beija-Flor, Imperatriz, Tijuca and Mangueira strut their samba choreography in hoped-for harmony together with their 300- to 400-strong percussion sections called *baterias*. All the music is acoustic, with the exception of one amplified, ukulele-like instrument (the *cavaquinho*) that literally drives the entire school of up to 5,000 performers forward.

The cost of producing this event is in the hundreds of millions. Many a *Carioca's* (citizen of Rio de Janeiro) livelihood depends on this event, the ultimate manifestation of a country on the rise economically, politically and culturally. In 2014 the World Cup and in 2016 the Summer Olympics will be held in Brazil.

Following the lecture in the early evening I left the ship to join a party in progress a few blocks from the pier. The music was pulsating, the parade gaudy and the revelers in full swing. Traveling alone, I didn't stay long.

A luscious dinner of sturgeon caviar with buckwheat blinis, a baby spinach salad with pine nuts and steamed Maine lobster tail with risotto primavera put me to bed.

I joined a tour early the next morning driving through the Cosme Velho district, where I boarded the cogwheel train and rode to Corcovado Mountain to view the 120-foot statue of Jesus Christ. The train trip passed through the lush rain forest, where I saw monkeys and sloths. Much of the rain forest in Brazil has been destroyed but efforts are under way to restore and preserve it.

The tour continued along the famous beaches of Rio—Copacabana and Ipanema. People were crowded onto the sand, lying on towels, sitting in chairs under umbrellas or merely strolling hand in hand. Few people were swimming in the water.

Continuing the drive along the beaches, the tour guide dispensed more information. The economy of Brazil is growing at a rate of 11%. Brazil produces 90% of the oil they consume. Taxes are high. Cotton, oranges, sugar, ethanol, iron, gemstones and gold are the main exports.

Frank Sinatra made the beach at Ipanema famous with his song, "The Girl from Ipanema." It was number two when the Beatles had the number one song. There are no private beaches in Brazil and the coastline is crowded with luxurious apartments, some costing as much as $27 million.

That evening I joined a table of interesting passengers. Two were doctors, one from India who flew to disasters and rendered aid, the other, a surgeon from Chicago. Two ladies from Hungary currently living in Canada completed the dinner table. Politics are normally a safe topic of conversation, but the group seemed indifferent to current world affairs. My efforts to engage in meaningful conversation failed. My companions were seemingly just traveling for sheer pleasure, something that is difficult for me. After the light dinner of scallops sashimi, Caesar salad and braised lamb shank on saffron risotto, I skipped the entertainment and retired to my stateroom with a book and my notes.

Through the night, the ship sailed down the coast to the peninsula of Buzios, a fishing village settled by pirates and slave traders. The magnificent beaches and crystal-clear water attract tourists. Brigitte Bardot brought the village to prominence with her visits. The area has grown to international report, likened to Saint Tropez. A life-size bronze of Brigitte Bardot sitting on her suitcase looking out to sea is a favorite spot to people watch and catch the sunset. Since I've ended my bikini and snorkeling days, I ventured into the small town, enjoying the firm land and buying a few trinkets. The shops were filled with bikinis and beachwear. I purchased a tee shirt for my grandson, soon to celebrate his first birthday.

Returning to the ship in time for another lecture by Dr. Klein, I was intrigued by his interpretation of Brazilian Carnaval. According to him, the music comes from west Africa and is not 4/4 timing. The bossa nova, which became popular in the 1960's, is a combination of west coast cool jazz plus the samba.

Carnaval is about social inversion—formal versus informal, masculine versus feminine, authoritarian versus egalitarian, black versus white, home versus street, rich versus poor, elite versus the masses. The roles are reversed. The women take to the street, the poor dress rich, the rich dress poor, the men dress as women and so forth.

The African influence in Brazil is prominent. Though most Brazilians are Catholic, over 30 million of them believe in and worship African deities.

The wearing of masks is not popular as it is in New Orleans. In Brazil the theme is to be recognized. New stars are discovered at Carnaval. Standing on top of the float is called *destaque*. Everyone wants to be on top of the float to be discovered and become famous. Huge feather farms are maintained just for costuming during Carnaval.

Most of all, samba is the music of Carnaval. Drums or *pandeiros* are played or spun. This drives the parade. Musicians strike the tambourine with a flexible plastic stick. The floats are powered by as many as 100 people underneath.

Following the lecture I retreated to the bar for the afternoon game of Trivial Pursuit. As I approached a group that included one of the doctors I had met previously, I asked if I might join them. Politely, they said they had their team of eight. The next group was also full so I sat by myself and waited. An attorney from Iowa of all places approached and asked if she and her husband might join me.

I replied, "Are you smart?"

"No."

"Please join me." We laughed. Her name was Linda and her husband's name was Rich. They were brilliant. Our team of eight soon filled. There was a doctor from New Jersey, a couple from Florida and a retired teacher. We regularly placed in the top three. Every evening before cocktails we competed for points to buy bookmarks, caps and tee shirts at the end of the voyage.

The teams were serious and a fierce competition soon developed. All was forgiven after the game and we adjourned to the bar. Often I joined some of them for dinner.

The evening of our stop in Buzios I dined with the couple from Florida, having crab cakes, vegetable salad with feta cheese and steak with cognac sauce. I skipped the evening's entertainment by a British comedian. Their humor is difficult to comprehend.

Moving south along the coastline of Brazil we stopped at Ilha Grande, meaning Big Island. The island is largely undeveloped and is one of the most pristine remnants of Brazil's Atlantic rainforest, one of the richest ecosystems in the world and a hotspot for biodiversity and conservation. The pristine condition of the island is due to its unusual history. First it was a pirates' lair, then a leper colony and finally a prison for the most violent and deranged criminals. Cars are not allowed in town except for emergency vehicles, but during high season, the beaches become crowded.

Ilha Grande holds some of the largest remaining populations of many endangered species, including the red-ruffed fruit crow, the brown howler monkey, the maned sloth, the red-browed Amazon parrot and the broad-snouted cayman.

Here it is also possible to see corals and tropical fish, along with Magellanic penguins and Southern right whales. The entire island of 193 square kilometers is a protected area.

I walked along the beach and strolled through the small village, absorbing the smells of outdoor cooking before I returned to the ship for another lecture by Dr. Klein, more on Brazil.

Sonja Klein

I found it quite interesting that Dr. Klein referred to the countries of South America as Latin America, including Central America and Mexico. Educators tend to refer to the American continent as North America, Central America and South America.

From Dr. Klein I learned that Brazil contains one third of the world's rain forests. Congo is second. Between the coast and the rain forest, cattle and soybeans are raised. There are 4,500 miles of coastline in Brazil.

Among the first exports after the discovery of Brazil in the 1500's was red dye from the native trees. The word *brasa* means coals in a brazier. The country was named after the red dye that was a popular export.

Brazil is approximately the same size as the mainland United States minus Alaska. There are 195 million Brazilians and 310 million Americans. The literacy rate is 87% and life expectancy is 71.5 years. Per capita income in Brazil is $7,600, whereas it is $40,000 in the United States. An earlier guide stated that the per capita income was $350 per month. Perhaps that was just in Rio. Information is at best vague, not absolute truth.

Brazil exports textiles, iron ore, shoes, chemicals, steel, aircraft, small arms, automobiles, ammunition, cement, lumber, cattle, cocoa and jet fighters. Brazil is the number one exporter of rice, coffee, soybeans and cane sugar. Metals such as platinum, nickel, tin, gold and manganese are also exported. Brazil ranks number one in beef and chicken exports. Brazil is so big that all of Europe except Russia fits inside the country. Brazil is number five in the world's population as well as in area and number eight in the world's economy. The United States is third in both categories.

The ethnicity of Brazil is 50 to 55% European, 9% African and 35 to 40% mixed. Sao Paolo, the largest city in Brazil, is second or third in the world's population, thus making two of the five world's largest cities being in Latin America, the other being Mexico City.

Learning is one of the adventures of travel, and in this lecture I learned something new. After the American Civil War thousands of Confederates moved to Brazil, choosing not to live in an oppressive society that had lost to the Union. The immigrants believed in states' rights and slavery, which existed in Brazil until 1888. The climate was such that two cotton crops a year could be raised. Many of the immigrants were from Texas, Alabama and South Carolina. Dr. Klein recommended the book by E. C. Hartner called *The Last Colony of the Confederacy.*

The predominant religion is a combination of Catholicism and animism, with spiritualism capturing 15% of the population.

Another interesting fact is that if you don't vote you cannot have a driver's license or bank account, not a bad idea.

The ship bypassed the port of Santos, from which the products of Sao Paolo are shipped, mainly industrial goods and sugar. The town was swamped with tourists and Carnaval celebrations. The harbor was crowded with cruise ships.

The capital of Brazil is Brasilia, designed by the Swiss architect Oscar Niemeyer and by Lucio Costa, a socialist. The capital was located there to encourage settlement from the poor north. The city is arranged in blocks and is utopian in design but has grown so dynamically that it has outgrown its design. The per capita income in Brasilia is the highest in the country—$28,000 per year.

As if that were not sufficient information for the day, I moved on to the Trivial Pursuit game. The competition was tough as ever. Our team tied for third. The tiebreaker question was, "What is the speed of light?"

Rich said 186,000; our opponents said 186,640. They were closer. We received no precious points. Happy hour drinks dulled my muddled brain and I dined with new friends on zucchini with cherry tomatoes and arugula salad, Indian pachadi, carrot salad marinated with yogurt and curry leaves, grilled lamb chops and a summer vegetable casserole with parmesan.

Refreshed with food and happy hour I again skipped the evening festivities to read a book by one of my favorite travel writers Paul Theroux. I had purchased the book at the Houston airport. The book was a fairly recent account of his repeat trip covered in *The Great Railway Bazaar.* Theroux in this book travels from London to Japan and back, journeying through some of my favorite countries in central Asia. Theroux is now older and I sensed his tiredness in the book. I was hoping to share his enthusiasm for central Asia and the Trans-Siberian railroad. Instead he skipped over the wonderful cities of Bukhara, Khiva and Samarkand, almost not mentioning them, hardly offering a detail. The Far East he relives in his past experiences. As for Siberia, he offers little or no detail. I realized at that point that the Far East is his favorite and that he is not a fancier of dry, arid plains. I am. So much for me being another Paul Theroux. We are all partial and ruled by perception. I will finish his book.

I awoke to bright sun and dazzling white beaches. The ship docked in the harbor of Parati with its history of piracy, gold, slaves and sugar. Founded around 1600, the town was at one time the second most important port in Brazil. The main export was gold brought down from the mines along the infamous Caminho do Ouro, or Gold Trail. The primary import was slaves transported in shiploads to work the mines.

I visited three churches from the 1700's that separated the races—one for the slaves, one for the freed mulattos and one for the colonial elite.

The slaves worked in the production of sugar and its potent liquor, *cachaca*. When slavery was abolished in the 1880's, the residents fled; the population dropped drastically and the town was forgotten.

Tourism rediscovered the town in the 1950's and Parati now supports a thriving tourist industry. I strolled the streets and art galleries; there were no bargains.

I noticed that every port we visited along the Brazilian coast was filled with schooners and sleek modern yachts, so many I could not count them. The wealth of Brazil was obvious from their toys.

Trivial Pursuit was disappointing that afternoon. Our team was fifth. With eight people volunteering an answer, it is difficult to select the correct one. We usually managed to discard a few correct answers.

I dined on marinated salmon tartar with cucumber and green asparagus tips, salad with creamy goat cheese, miso and anchovy dressing and lobster Thermidor over jasmine rice. As always I skipped dessert.

Since the cruise ship had avoided the port of Santos, we stopped for a day at Ilhabela, Portuguese for beautiful island. The archipelago, island and town are all named Ilhabela. The city is situated four miles off the coast. The largest island is Ilhabela. Together, the islands cover a total of 130 square miles of pristine beaches, rain forest and waterfalls. Earlier in the decade the population of the island was 26,000, but during the holiday months up to 100,000 people may be on the island. The island is accessible by ferry from Sao Paolo.

Before the Portuguese colonized Brazil an indigenous tribe called the Tupinambas inhabited the island, giving it a name that meant tranquil place. They were displaced, like most of the indigenous tribes.

I went ashore and visited the church and some of the shops. The drizzling rain dampened my shopping instincts and I returned to the warmth of the ship. Second place in Trivial Pursuit livened up the team's spirits. That evening we relaxed over a delightful meal. I selected pink roasted veal loin with creamy tuna sauce, yogurt-marinated cucumber salad and pink sautéed ostrich filet with Jerusalem artichokes on pasta. The menu descriptions read like a culinary novel. I always keep them for a reminder of the combinations now called fusion as well as the memory of elegant evening dining.

Our next port of call was Porto Belo, located south of Rio de Janeiro in the Brazilian state of Santa Catarina. It is located on the most beautiful part of the Catarinense coast, an area famous for the beaches, emerald green waters and diving opportunities. The temperature averages about 80 degrees year round, with cool ocean breezes.

Porto Belo is named for its beautiful harbor and gives access to the city of Florianapolis and nearby Blumenau, named after Dr. Hermann Bruno Otto Blumenau. Blumenau is a small piece of Germany in the middle of Brazil and it was my destination for the day. I wanted to travel the countryside and since Blumenau was over an hour's drive from the coast I welcomed the opportunity to go inland. You can view only so many pretty beaches before they all look the same.

We passed through the city of Florianapolis with its white, high-rise apartment buildings looking out to sea. Construction was in evidence and the town appeared to be flourishing. The yachts in the harbor were larger and sleeker than in the smaller ports. I could have been on the Mediterranean or in Florida.

The double decker bright green Volvo bus was unlike any I had ever seen, modern with a bathroom, cappuccino machine, snack bar and observation deck. I never saw the driver. Hopefully he was somewhere down below.

As the tour guide spoke I kept busy with my notebook. The Portuguese and Azores Islanders settled Porto Belo in the early 1700's. The population of the port area is 35,000. The president of Brazil is elected directly by the voters and can serve two terms.

Gas is about $8 per gallon.

Porto Belo is a large container port. The region ships pork and is a big textile center. As the bus passed through the countryside and small villages, I saw underwear shops on both sides of the road. This valley is very European and bills itself as the underwear capital. The guide said that since 1950, Italians, Germans, Poles, Austrians and Belgians have populated the area.

Arriving in Blumenau, I was surprised to find myself in a city of 350,000 with two universities and European architecture. The area was settled by Dr. Blumenau in the 1850's. The first stop was the Colonial Family Museum, where I toured several homes from the early period. I visited the Oktoberfest Pavilion and enjoyed a German buffet lunch before wandering through the downtown area of the city.

The lecture continued during the return trip. The smallest bikini is called dental floss and topless bathing is frowned upon. Topless beaches are located in remote areas and toplessness at the city beaches results in arrest. Since there are thousands of miles of coastline in Brazil, the beach culture is part of everyday life and is integrated with dance and music.

I learned that 55% of the sugar cane grown is used for ethanol and that 25% of the cars in Brazil use only ethanol.

The current president is a woman whose father was a Bulgarian immigrant. Brazil has strong ties with the United States. Hillary Clinton attended the Brazilian president's inauguration.

While on the trip, an earthquake in Japan devastated the country. We were assured that Brazil is considered geologically inactive or "mature."

The large consumer economy and huge economic potential of Brazil are important to the United States. Brazil and the United States exchange $45 billion in trade per year and Brazil is twelfth on our list of trade partners.

I was told that there was unity in Brazil—unity of church, language, celebrations, sports and rituals. Words installed in our language that were given to us by Brazilian natives include hammock, barbecue, canoe, tapioca, hurricane, manioc and cashew.

Contrasting Brazil and the United States, the guide noted that Brazil was settled by southern European Catholic men with hopes of returning home rich; whereas, the United States was settled by English Protestant families who wished to make a new life, with no intentions of returning to their homeland.

Roundtrip from Texas

The guide admitted that the settlers decimated the native population, that there was disparity between the rich and the poor and that Brazil is best described as a rich country with mostly poor people.

Having missed Trivial Pursuit I dined on the top deck, enjoying sushi and a light meal and turned in early with my books and notes.

On a low sandy peninsula at the entrance of a large fresh water lagoon lies Rio Grande, the ship's last stop in Brazil. The town was founded in 1737 at the southern fringe of the Portuguese Empire. With the growth of the frozen beef industry, Rio Grande became an important distribution center for the southern part of the state of Rio Grande do Sul, which borders Argentina and Uruguay. The inhabitants are strongly independent people—pioneer farmers descended from European immigrants.

The first German immigrants arrived in 1824, and in the following century an estimated 250,000 Germans settled in this part of Brazil.

Beaches stretch for more that 125 miles around the city, including one of the longest uninterrupted beaches in the world.

Rain was falling as the ship docked and the planned welcoming by a group of young dancers was dampened. Their enthusiasm was contagious as I joined them in some circle dances. When the music stopped I wandered around the harbor area and entered a small shop that invited tourists. Inside were a few tables with leather goods, some jewelry and ceramics. Being the only customer, I had their attention. A young man fluent in English spoke with me as I asked the purpose of some of the leather goods. On the table were also the gourds, filters and straws for drinking the famous South American drink, *yerba maté*. He explained the ritual of drinking the tea, saying it was not full of caffeine but rather relaxing, that he drank it in the morning and before going to bed in the evening. He went to a back room and brought out his own cup, a thermos of hot water and a bag of the green powdered tea. I tried some. It tasted like chamomile. I purchased two of the gourds, straws and filters after being assured I could buy the tea anywhere. After taking more pictures of luxurious private yachts I returned to the ship for an introductory lecture on Uruguay.

Sonja Klein

Uruguay

The small country of Uruguay became independent in 1828. José Artigas and 33 rebel soldiers founded the country, which became a buffer between the Portuguese in Brazil and the Spanish in Argentina.

In size, Uruguay is similar to the state of Washington. Pasture comprises four fifths of the country and grass-fed beef is the main export, along with timber for paper pulp in addition to hides and wool.

According to Dr. Klein, the name Uruguay means river of birds He said that Uruguay eradicated the native population, explaining that there were no hills or trees for the natives to hide from the invading settlers. There is no evidence of a native population and there are no reservations, as there are in Brazil. Dr. Klein recommended watching the movie, "The Mission," starring Robert de Niro, citing it as an honest representation of the Jesuit's treatment of the native Indians.

The population is around three million and nowhere in the world is the disparity between rich and poor so close as it is in Uruguay. Uruguay is one of the most developed countries in the world and ranks 41st in the quality of life.

The country has no oil and imports all it uses from Africa and Venezuela. Education and medical care are free

The famous German ship that preyed on the Allies during World War II was sunk off the coast of Uruguay in 1939, scuttled by Captain Langsdorf, who then committed suicide.

Dr. Klein then changed the subject to *yerba maté*. He said it was highly addictive, full of caffeine and tasted like dirt. I disagreed from my earlier experience but kept quiet.

After a disappointing afternoon of Trivial Pursuit, I consoled myself with dinner—Norwegian salmon, Caesar salad and a sirloin steak.

The ship docked in Punta del Este the following morning and I availed myself of a long day's tour. The tour began with a scenic drive through the residential district. The homes along the waterfront were of every style and design, mansions visited by the Bush family, the Clintons and even the Roosevelts.

Uruguay was different from Brazil, very European and resort ritzy. Punta del Este's population is said to be 150,000, with more during the high season. Apartments along the waterfront range from $150,000 to millions.

Hibiscus and oleanders were in bloom and I was surprised to see pine trees.

Few resorts in South America rival Punta del Este for glamour. It might be in Uruguay, but it's where the glitterati and elite of Buenos Aires make their homes. The main town of Punta del Este is on a small peninsula where the Rio de la Plata meets the Atlantic Ocean. Hotels and casinos dominate the riverbanks on the widest estuary in the world, over 150 miles across. An estuary is the wide lower course of a river where it flows into the sea. Estuaries experience tidal flows and their water is a changing mixture of fresh and salt.

The coastal highway is filled with high-rise hotels and condominiums, reminiscent of developments in southern Florida. After driving through the coastal residential area, we stopped for a visit at the private Ralli Museum containing famous artwork owned and displayed by the wealthy collector.

We visited the icon of Punta del Este, Casa Puebla, an architectural masterpiece built on a peninsula overlooking the waters by the famous Uruguayan painter and sculptor Carlos Páez Vilaró The spontaneous construction took 36 years to complete. There are no square lines. Rather, it is a domed white structure where he lives and displays his sculptures, paintings and ceramics. After being treated to a glass of champagne I strolled through the many rooms and met the artist, now in his 80's. His son was one of the rugby players who survived the plane crash in the Andes. He and some of the survivors lived for over 70 days before being rescued by the efforts of his father who never gave up hope. I purchased the book he had written about the search and rescue effort. He signed the book and several small prints I purchased. His work is colorful and vibrant. One of his originals on the wall had a price tag of $35,000. He was quite charming, an international figure who knew many famous people.

Some of us on the bus were given the option of being dropped in the center of town after being assured that it was a short walk to the dock and the ship. I joined a couple for some famous grass-fed beef. The man grilling the meat was in a corner of the dining room and I walked over to see what he was cooking. After selecting a beef tenderloin I posed for a picture with him and returned to my table. The meat was close to the best, tasting much like we used to raise on the farm north of Houston.

The couple with whom I dined went shopping and I decided to return to the ship, walking in the direction the guide had pointed. After many blocks I could not see the ship or the harbor, only the open ocean. I almost panicked before I spotted a small pizza place and asked directions. The port was two blocks away. I barely made it back in time for the afternoon brain game.

We won first place and celebrated in the main dining room. I enjoyed vegetable caponata, daikon, carrot and broccoli stem slaw and roasted rack of lamb with vegetable ratatouille.

Montevideo, the capital of Uruguay, greeted me the following morning. The weather was in the middle 70's and the sun was shining. Montevideo is a cosmopolitan city located on the river Platte and the countryside inland is home to many working ranches. The city is the commercial center of Uruguay and much of the South Atlantic fishing fleet is based here.

Uruguay exports frozen and canned meats, fish, wool and grains as well as textiles, dairy items and wines.

Montevideo's origins lie in the colonial rivalry of the Spanish and Portuguese. The Portuguese constructed a fort in 1717; the Spanish captured it in 1724. Montevideo became the capital in 1828.

The city is attractive, with tree-lined avenues and beautiful parks. After a short overview tour of the city, the magnificent Legislative Palace and a visit to the main square, I wandered the market and food courts along the docks, this time with the ship in view. I purchased a blouse and ran into some fellow passengers and joined them for some more of the famous grilled beef.

I skipped dinner after enjoying happy hour and some finger food. Argentina and the tango were waiting.

Argentina

The ship docked in Buenos Aires in the morning. I scribbled notes in the taxi on the way to my private tango lesson. The driver became a tour guide. Dubbed the Queen of the Platte River, Buenos Aires is the capital of Argentina and the country's center of manufacturing, banking, culture and intellectualism but shows very little of its Spanish heritage. It is often referred to as the "Paris of South America." The city was laid out around a central plaza, bordered by a fort and armory, city hall and cathedral.

Parisian architects were hired to design parks and villas for the landed gentry.

Most of Argentina is grassland, and the Europeans found that cattle, horses and pigs thrived. The gauchos were the South American cowboys who became the expert horsemen of the pampas. They threw the bolo to trap the emu and rhea.

According to the tour guide there has always been a conflict in Argentina between the city and country people.

Spanish taxation led to independence, but the British then occupied Buenos Aires in 1806 and 1807 before being repelled by the Argentines. In 1810 the upperclass Creoles formed their own government and under General Jose de San Martin defeated the Spanish. On July 9, 1816, Argentina became independent.

Between 1840 and 1940, 6.2 million immigrants, mostly Italian and Spanish, immigrated to Argentina. In 1929, Argentina boasted the 10th largest economy in the world. Sadly, it is not so now.

It was mid-morning when the driver left me at La Ventana, the tango school. I had dressed for the occasion—a red, white and black polka-dotted short skirt, cut on the bias with insets so it flared, a top to match and black heels. As I entered the school I noticed other tourists attending for lessons. They were dressed in sweat pants, jeans, tennis shoes and flip-flops. I was the only student wearing a skirt.

My instructor was young, early 30's and very serious, quite slim with a thin mustache. He showed me the basic eight-count step. I practiced a few times and then did it with him. It was easy. He asked, "Are you a dance instructor?"

"No."

"Are you a professional?"

"No."

"You're good."

Of course, I beamed, but it was that easy and natural. He added some twists and I danced the tango. I thought of my artist friend Chuck, who is a great dancer. One time he said, "I can learn any dance in 30 seconds." He was right.

I had my tango moment and left to explore the town, going to the square where the "disappeared ones" were memorialized. Over 30,000 people disappeared between 1976 and 1983 under government oppression. Today, so many years later, the mothers still walk the circle on Thursdays and leave flowers. I reverently made the walk and said a silent prayer.

On one side of the square was the Casa Rosada, the presidential palace where Eva Perón appeared on the balcony shortly before she died. The cathedral was at the other end.

I returned to the ship for a last lecture by Dr. Klein. He spoke of Juan Perón, a military man who became the leader of Argentina, married Eva Perón, his second wife, and ruled Argentina. He was on the side of the workers and, with his wife, was either dearly loved or dearly hated. He was elected president in 1946.

Eva Perón died in 1952. She was one of three influential women in 20th century Latin America. The other two were Frieda Kahlo and Carmen Miranda. All three of them died young within two years of one another. Eva died of uterine cancer.

Argentina today is suffering economically; there is high inflation. Argentina defaulted on its loans in 2002 and unemployment is 15%.

And then Dr. Klein talked about Butch Cassidy and the Sundance Kid. At the end of the 1800's the Pinkerton detectives were getting better at their job. The Wild Bunch was a real group of outlaws that included Butch and Sundance. Fearing apprehension in the American West, Butch, Etta and Sundance fled to New York. Sundance and Etta Place went to Buenos Aires; Butch went to Europe and had plastic surgery. They reunited in Buenos Aires and took a train to near Cholila, where they purchased a ranch of about 12,000 acres. Their neighbors liked them. They stayed out of trouble.

In 1905 Harvey Logan, one of the Wild Bunch, came to visit. They reverted to their old ways. The ranch was sold in 1907. Sundance was killed, Etta disappeared and Butch died years later in the United States. Dr. Klein's source of information was the book, *In Search of Butch Cassidy*, by Larry Pointer.

My last evening of the trip was spent at a tango show at La Ventana. I was not surprised to see my instructor as the featured dancer with his partner. It was spectacular, with singing and dancing and a closing with the song, "Don't Cry for Me Argentina,"—very emotional.

The next morning I disembarked the ship for a day tour before catching my plane that evening for Houston. I kept my pen and notebook busy most of the day. I learned more information about Argentina as the bus traveled through the city parks, where the blue plumbago and hibiscus were in bloom.

The population of Argentina is 14 million, with four million living in Buenos Aires. The city was founded in 1580. Che Guevara and Fanzio the race car driver were from Argentina. The main boulevard in Buenos Aires, named Ninth of July, is wider than the Champs Elyssees and is the widest in the world. The average salary is less than $1,000 per month.

We stopped at the Recoleta Cemetery to visit the grave of Eva Perón. The cemetery was full of miniature chapels that held the remains of prominent citizens. It was peaceful and clean, except for all the stray cats roaming among the mausoleums. The guide said, "Eva's gravesite is the only one in the cemetery that has fresh flowers every day."

When we arrived at the site, I felt the flowers. Not one of them was fresh. So much for the veracity of the guides.

As the day progressed I learned from this guide that tango is the fusion of Cuban, African and polka dances and that Carlos Gardel is the tango musician supreme. The guide said that tango had originated among the gauchos, men dancing with men. The lower classes began to tango and when the French discovered the tango, the wealthy people of Latin America adopted the tango as their dance.

Argentina exports crude oil, steel, beef, leather goods and soccer players. The guide was an avid soccer fan.

She commented that Buenos Aires has a large Italian population and that the citizens are very Italian in their behavior and culture—noisy, opinionated, passionate, insulting and shouting.

When I asked her about *yerba maté*, the tea, she said it was a cultural thing, that there was no caffeine in it and that it was about sharing the straw and passing it around. Only friends drank out of the same straw; it was a ritualistic custom.

The trip home was full of reflection. The east coast of South America was more African than the west coast. The South Americans think of themselves as Latin Americans, including Central America in that term. Brazil is an impressive country, but I could not bring myself to admire a country that is proud of their slums.

Uruguay is a country I could live in and return to visit, but it's still not Texas.

Argentina is struggling with economic problems. Eastern South America is much more Latin than western South America. Beaches are beautiful but my beach days are over. The view of the beach is nice, but congested cities, traffic and lots of bodies on the beach don't thrill me. Jungles and rainforest are not my passion, rather wide-open spaces and open vistas and skies excite me. But most of all I'm still looking forward to a trip where I don't take a pen and notebook and feel compelled to learn everything and write it down. I do enjoy the tango, the *yerba maté* tea that I purchased in Puentes Arenas and my new Che Gueverra tee shirt and Che magnet for the refrigerator.

Old people on cruises are more interested in the food, Trivial Pursuit, bridge, the spa and holding hands than learning about the history and facts of the countries they visit. The lectures are not well attended. They don't carry notebooks.

Waiting at home were boxes of my first book. The marketing would begin.

5

What's it like?

After I finished *Honk If You Married Sonja,* I was asked, "What's it like having your first book published?"

"I'll let you know when I hold it in my hot little hands."

The galley copy arrived first. It was covered in glossy white paper. I inspected the book to see if the pages were correctly aligned, that there were no smudges on the pages and that they were all right side up. I signed the paper accepting the book and went to South America to dance the tango and mailed the check for the balance due for the printing and shipping.

When I returned home two advance copies were waiting. My daughter Molly handed them to me. There it was, my first book. It looked just as I had designed it. It was more substantial than I had originally imagined. I held it my hands.

I felt a sense of accomplishment. Then I realized, "Oh shit, now I have to market and sell this book." The best part was over, the writing. Now the publicity and peddling had to begin.

For a week I didn't do a thing. My mind went off in a million directions. It was overwhelming. Sanity took over reluctantly. I finished the press release; my friend Linda fine-tuned the words with me.

Then I drove to Houston to catch a plane with son Joe and his wife Carla. We were flying to California to attend my niece's wedding and spend a week driving up the California coast from Los Angeles to San Francisco.

But before I drove to their house I stopped by the family farm where my brother David officed in Mother and Daddy's home. Having earlier called his secretary from my cell phone to be assured he was there, I surprised him. I walked in his office and handed him the second of the advance copies, "David, this is yours, the second copy. You gave me the courage to do this and the second copy is yours."

He was delighted and I inscribed it for him. After a short visit I drove to the cemetery where my family is buried. I walked to Mother and Daddy's grave and showed them the book. I was crying, "Here it is; this is for you. I love you."

I drove to my son's home, blinded by the wetness in my eyes. I remember the traffic was bad. I carried advance copy number one in my arms like a baby.

I didn't care whether the plane crashed. I had done what I set out to do. The trip was enjoyable. I returned home to develop my marketing plan. My daughter had set up the website. The work had not begun but the feeling was one of accomplishment. I had done due diligence, attended seminars, spent days at writers' conferences, read books on publishing, spoken with agents and publishers, hired an editor, solicited bids from printers, purchased an ISBN number, obtained a Library of Congress number, bought the bar code and commissioned the artwork.

No longer was I a writer, I was an author. And now it seemed like I was a publicist.

What is it like? It's like work. I'll have to make it fun. That's my job.

6

Cooking

I can't remember the specifics of my first intoxication with cooking. My earliest memories include my grandmother's farm kitchen north of Houston. I remember her frying chicken and serving it with mashed potatoes and cream gravy.

Weekend visits to her farm always ended with her sending our family home with butter-and-jelly sandwiches. They weren't really jelly but homemade fig or pear preserves. My three brothers and I munched them during the hour-long drive back to Houston. I suppose it kept us quiet while we listened to "The Lone Ranger" on the radio.

My mother was a great cook; her yeast confections were our favorite, especially the cinnamon rolls. I remember setting the table but not really helping with the cooking.

When I was a young teenager I spent summers with my Aunt Ella in Spring, Texas. She was always cooking, preserving or canning. She put me to work, whether it was shredding cabbage for sauerkraut or peeling fruit or vegetables. While we cooked in the heat of the kitchen, either music or preaching on the radio kept us company. God was always there.

I didn't realize that men could cook until I met my first husband. His father and uncles were Louisiana men. They cooked. The German men in my life did not. I'll never forget an incident with my father after he retired from Humble Oil. One of my brothers, I think it was David, challenged him to open a can with a manual can opener. He couldn't. We laughed until we cried. Daddy did too.

When I first married, I often consulted a cookbook but found many recipes that used canned soups and prepared ingredients. I couldn't cook that way and so I developed my cooking skills, consulting a book only for desserts.

Even though my first husband was from Louisiana, he didn't cook. I suppose it was because he was an only child. I don't know another reason.

Sonja Klein

Cooking for two was not easy for me, but I managed to scale down my efforts. I paid attention to the Louisiana cooking, preparing dishes I learned from his parents. They were both good cooks.

Over the years of my first marriage, I cooked as my family had done, enjoying it but always alone in the kitchen. My pleasure came from serving a pretty table and watching my company eat. As Germans, we were not allowed outward displays of affection. The women hugged but not the men. Our way of conveying love was by feeding. If the food was eaten, we were loved—silly, but true.

Raleigh, my second husband, was a great cook. So was his father George. From them I leaned to make a roux, cook chicken stew, gumbos and boiled seafood, etouffée, catfish sauce piquant and moc choux. From my mother-in-law I learned to make alligator balls. From Raleigh's aunt I discovered garfish roast.

Descending from a farming family, I have always enjoyed fresh vegetables and always complimented my meals with sautéed, baked or steamed combinations.

I taught my children to cook at an early age, setting them on the kitchen counter and letting them stir whatever concoction I promoted. I bought Molly a children's bake oven that worked. She loved it.

I recall coaxing them to crack their first raw egg. They had courage, just like when I convinced them to pop their first balloon. It was fun to see the wonder in their eyes.

Growing up in a farm atmosphere, we raised cattle and butchered them for the deepfreeze. Uncle Pete would shoot a young grass-fed calf, then Daddy and my brothers would string the animal up with a block and tackle attached to one of the pecan trees in the orchard by the barn. The animal was skinned, gutted and quartered. I was usually given the job of dragging the guts to the end of the orchard for the buzzards.

Sheets were laid in the trunk of the car, Mother and I drove the quartered animal to the Klein Store in Tomball and it hung for a week or so before Mother and I returned to wrap and label the packages of meat that the butcher cut, chopped or ground.

Butchering day was always a treat because Mother cooked the brains, tongue, heart and liver. She scrambled the brains with eggs; I didn't eat that. She boiled the tongue with spices, and chicken-fried the liver and heart. Those were my favorite. Of course, cream gravy makes anything taste good.

Roundtrip from Texas

Summers with Aunt Ella, I learned to make blood sausage, a pretty messy procedure. I ate anything Aunt Ella cooked.

Recently I became acquainted with sweet breads and mountain oysters (calf balls), more good food.

Living on a ranch, we eat mostly what we raise—sheep, goats, rabbits, wild hog, domestic deer as well as exotic hoof stock, doves, turkey and fish from the creek. I don't eat chicken because of the hormones and overall nastiness of the bird. My daughter and her family, however, do eat quite a bit of chicken and order fresh seafood shipped from south Louisiana. We buy bacon because every German recipe starts with, "Melt a pound of butter and fry two pounds of bacon."

When it comes to seafood, I enjoy raw oysters and cold-water fish but not bottom feeders or farm-raised anything, except for crawfish and crabs, which I love. I believe that farm-raised seafood is full of antibiotics and hormones. One has to make a few exceptions.

Having Molly and her partner at the ranch provides the opportunity for me to cook. Usually I will go down to their house and snatch the baby and bring him up to my house to keep me company while I cook. I give him a pot and spoon and bites of what I'm cooking. He's good company and never complains about what I feed him.

Some of my fondest memories are of cooking to music, country and western mostly, and drinking some wine while visiting with whoever I can draft to sit at the bar and keep me company.

House of Praise, the nondenominational church I attend in Barksdale, follows a wonderful custom every Sunday. Everyone brings a dish and we enjoy lunch together. The variety is always a surprise and the goal for my contribution is to have it eaten entirely. Deviled eggs or a tossed green salad are my staples.

Desserts are not my forte, except for my famous pecan pie. My crust always rolls out easily and there is no corn syrup in my recipe. The yearly festival in Camp Wood, aptly named Old Settlers, hosts a pecan pie contest. The first year I entered, I won first place. The following year Molly and I entered the same recipe. Her pie won second; mine did not place. In subsequent years, I was awarded firsts, seconds and sometimes nothing. I always bake the exact same pie but the judges are different.

My duck gumbo is rumored to be the best, even by those from Louisiana. My brothers Allan and John are avid hunters, especially of birds, and they furnish the ducks. Their wives don't cook duck. I'm thrilled they don't.

Every year at the Terlingua Chili Cookoff, the men do all the cooking. Their elaborate kitchen setup is complete with spices and condiments. For breakfast, they cook eggs and sausage or bacon in a giant propane-heated wok. Snacks are fried pickles or pork tenders. The women in camp enjoy sitting in the shade and watching the men prepare food.

For some unknown reason, Mexican food is my favorite. I am always on a quest for the best enchiladas. So far, the best I have eaten were in Terlingua at the motel restaurant near the site of the Chili Cookoff. The meat and seasoning is hot enough to satisfy my palate.

I am also a pepper *aficionado*. I eat hot chopped raw peppers with everything. I even have books on the medicinal benefits of capsicum. I add cayenne pepper to my coffee in the morning and the garden always has a variety of peppers—serrano, jalapeño, poblano, tabasco and cayenne. In addition, chili pequins grow wild in my yard. They are the hottest. I don't care for habañeros because they have a rank flavor similar to the smell of a billy goat.

Highly seasoned curries are among my favorites. I don't make my own curry powders but instead have a variety of green and red curry powders. My daughter Molly cooks the best curry I've eaten.

Next to peppers, I love raw onions, serving them chopped with most of my meals. Garlic is right up there with onions and peppers. I once read that during World War I, wounds were treated with raw garlic, that garlic is nature's antibiotic. I peel and chop fresh garlic for most everything I cook. It would be much easier to use the dried, flaked or chopped garlic in jars, but I prefer the fresh for the purity and flavor.

One of the many benefits of travel is the discovery of new foods. From a trip to Mexico, I concocted a dish called *chili enojado*, meaning angry chili. I stuff a poblano pepper with a mixture of most anything and then cover it with a pecan béarnaise sauce and sprinkle that with pomegranate, thus making it look like an angry chili. I have stuffed the pepper with anything from squash to lamb or goat with rice. The presentation is dramatic.

Food served on nice linens and colorful dishes with a lovely centerpiece always tastes better. Plastic or paper is not used in my kitchen, and I am a sucker for pretty dishes and glassware.

Visiting my cousin in Santa Fe, I admired her cabinet full of hand-blown glasses. The following day she drove me to the pueblo where the glasses were made. When I discovered the price per glass was $35, I felt relieved that the artist had only four in stock. I protect those glasses carefully.

Cooking always leads to cleaning the kitchen. Being German, I always begin with an empty dishwasher and clean as I go—filling, running and emptying the dishwasher prior to arrival of my guests. There are no microwaves on the ranch. Cooking is a pleasure, not a chore.

Before I go to bed, I return the kitchen to a spotless state so the next morning I'm ready to enjoy the pleasure of giving love through food. My pantry is full.

7

The post office

Barksdale, Texas, is a small rural town located in the middle of nowhere. To the inhabitants the town is significant. The population is about 80; the town is not incorporated.

The local consolidated junior high and high school are located in the middle of the broken and pot-holed streets. Students number less than 200. Septic tanks serve the individual, mostly neglected and dilapidated homes. Some are abandoned.

Two businesses exist: the United States Post Office and Taylor [sic] Made Saddle Shop. Three churches reign supreme—the Methodist Church, Barksdale Baptist and House of Praise.

A small yellow frame building that was once a schoolhouse in Vance sits on the edge of the school grounds. Once the general Barksdale library, the locals are converting it into a genealogical research library. It has been a long process.

But the post office is the center of the town's activity. Effie is the genial postmaster. Candy sits on the counter facing the lace-trimmed windows, seasonal decorations are always present and the bulletin board by the post office boxes reads like a local newspaper.

If I am looking for a particular person, I will invariably find them at the post office, where I believe the best deal in America exists. Whether I need to overnight a check to Michigan or mail books to my brothers, Effie finds the best way. At the prices the post office charges, it is a bargain.

Eric drives the rural mail route. About a mile from my ranch are located a bank of bent and rusty mailboxes. There, he delivers the mail to the few families that neighbor the ranch.

Every day except Sunday Eric sorts and drives the miles on the winding roads, dodging deer, hogs, turkeys, buzzards and an occasional exotic animal that has managed to escape the deer-proof fences that line the road.

If I have a package or my post office box is full, Eric calls and brings it out; sometimes I meet him at the boxes if the package is too large.

When the school bus collided with the bank of mailboxes, Eric fixed them, restored the stand and returned the seasoned boxes to use.

For me, it is more than comforting to know that my correspondence is in the hands of Effie, Eric and the new assistant Crystal. If the post office closes due to government cutbacks, I will have to drive an additional four miles to Camp Wood, where the post office serves the town of 600.

For now, I rest in confidence that the Barksdale post office is well run and operating efficiently.

8

What's in your trap?

The first time my husband John and I set a trap, we caught three javelinas. I had seen pictures of them but never experienced a close encounter. They were in the hog trap we borrowed from a friend. It was a heavy steel-and-wire cage about five by seven feet. On the end was a trap door that was activated to close when the animal stepped on a back panel in the rear of the cage to eat the bait.

For bait, John poured some corn in a five-gallon bucket, added water, covered the top and let it sour for a few hot days. The result was a smelly mash, really stinky. Our purpose was to trap feral hogs. We failed.

As we drove the pickup to the site and saw the javelinas, John remarked, "Oh no, we've got javelinas."

I replied, "What's wrong with that? At least we caught something."

"Javelinas are native and not invasive. They're mostly vegetarians and don't do any harm. We're trying to get rid of the invasive species that damage the land and inhibit and interfere with the native species."

"Okay, John, now what do we do?"

"We very carefully let them go."

As we approached the cage, I saw that we had trapped a female and two young half-grown ones. When they saw us, they clacked their tusks and charged the wire, bloodying their snouts. The stiff hair on their backs bristled. It was quite scary. Even though they were in a cage, I felt threatened.

Being from a west Texas ranching family, John knew what to do. He carefully backed up the truck, tied a rope to the trap door, crawled in the bed of the pickup and released the door. I was beside him. The animals fled into the brush, bloody noses dripping.

Our next experience was with coons. They invaded feed sacks, garbage cans and sacks of dog food. We purchased a live trap, a smaller wire cage, and baited it with dog food. In a few weeks we trapped over a dozen coons. John shot them and we baited the hog trap with their carcasses. Nothing ate them so we again resorted to baiting the hog trap with sour corn. We managed to catch a deer and some turkeys, carefully releasing them, but never a hog.

After John died of cancer, our friend came and picked up his hog trap and I forgot about trapping until a neighbor stopped me on the road, "Sonja, you've got a lot of hogs on your place. Are you doing anything to get rid of them?"

"No," I told him.

"Well, you need to control them or at least try."

I drove to Rocksprings and purchased a hog trap. It was loaded in the back of my pickup and when I returned to the ranch, I hooked a chain to the trap and the other end to a tree and drove it out of the bed of the pickup. Once again, I started baiting the hog trap. I caught nothing.

When my son Joe came for a visit with some of his firefighter friends, I had them move the trap to what I thought would be a better location, a site where I noticed the hogs had been rooting.

With persistence, I started catching hogs. The problem was what to do with them. I dislike killing anything, so I relied on my neighbor to come and shoot them. The small ones he took home and butchered, sharing a front or hindquarter with me.

Over the years, I caught wild turkeys, deer and feral hogs as well as Russian boars. A caged wild animal is ferocious and will injure itself for freedom. The noises they make are frightening, desperate screams and growls.

One singular experience stands in memory. A friend had come to visit and as we checked the trap, we discovered that a red-tailed hawk was caught. He had been lured by the deer guts in the trap. As we approached, he flapped his enormous wings, squawked and flopped over on his back as if dead. His piercing eyes were frozen. With his wings in the way, we could not open the door, so we attempted to turn him over or move him with sticks. He remained still. Deer entrails hung from his hooked beak.

I said, "He's dead."

"No, he's not. Watch his eyes, they follow our movements. I think he's in shock. Maybe had a stroke."

"I don't think hawks have strokes."

We waited a while and still he did not move. My friend bravely pushed him back and opened the door. The hawk just lay there. Finally, we pulled him by the wings out of the cage and onto the creek bank. He was heavier than I imagined and remained on his back, wings outstretched.

I ventured, "Maybe he broke his wings, flapping around."

"I don't think so."

We left him there. Several hours later, when we returned to check on him, he was gone. I remarked, "I thought for sure a hawk would be more aggressive and would have attacked us. That was weird. He played dead like a possum."

My friend from Dallas spoke, "What an experience to be so close to a wild hawk. I didn't realize they were so big. They don't look that big when you see them flying. His wings must have been at least five feet. That was really neat."

I continued to catch hogs occasionally.

And then the coons began to invade my utility room. Normally, I leave the door open so the ranch cat can eat and seek shelter. Since my dog moved down to my daughter's house in the creek bottom, the coons felt safe trespassing in my yard and eating the cat food in the utility room. When I began to shut the door at night, the coons jammed the metal storm door when trying to enter and eat the cat food.

In retaliation, I resurrected the old coon trap from the barn and baited it with the cat food they seemed to love. In a month's time, I trapped over 20 coons—big ones, smaller ones and twice even trapped two at once. Coons in pictures look like cute little masked bandits. They are not cute when approached. They snarl and hiss and bare their teeth. At first, my daughter's partner shot them and hung their tails from the fence. Now he just shoots them.

When a few days passed without trapping a coon, I figured I had thinned them sufficiently but soon discovered that the cat food still disappeared. Setting the trap within close sight soon revealed that cardinals in the dead of winter eat cat food. So I had to wait till dark to bait the trap.

When my daughter moved back to Alpine, Texas, to complete her master's degree, I resurrected a second coon trap from the barn and set it by her house, now vacant, thinking the coons would invade the garden with an absence of humans.

I was correct, except it was even worse. Not only did the coons invade but the rabbits ate the tomato plants and okra plants, the porcupines chewed the bark on the fruit trees and unknown predators killed three lambs within a few weeks of their birth. The predators can range from mountain lion, bobcat, hog, hawk, owl or coyote to *chupacabra*, the legendary "goat sucking" monster.

I tried deer repellant to deter the rabbits. We put wire cages around the trees to keep the porcupines away and I moved the sheep to a larger area where they might perhaps have more room to run.

The hog trap has again been moved from the back of the ranch to a more convenient spot for baiting, checking and killing hogs in the trap. The bucket of corn is fermenting. In a few days I'll bait the trap. I hope I find hogs in my trap.

9

California

For months I complained about going to California for my niece's wedding, wondering why anyone would want to leave Texas to get married. Nevertheless, I made plane and hotel reservations for my son and daughter-in-law and myself at the plush resort on the California coastline, the setting for the destination wedding.

Choosing an outfit for the occasion was difficult, but I settled on an over 30-year-old Giorgio original my mother had purchased in California when she flew out there to pick up a black Stutz Bearcat car. She purchased the dress to match the car. It was a black chiffon off the shoulder with red roses and a bias flared skirt with matching sash. My thoughts were that if Mother couldn't be there, at least her dress would be present for the celebration.

When I checked the weather and discovered it would be chilly, I added a red fringed shawl with lots of holes, knowing it would do little to keep me warm. For the evening before the wedding festivities, I packed white slacks with a long flowing silk tunic complete with feathers—frivolous, but in character.

The anxiety of flying disappeared the minute I strapped myself into my assigned seat on the plane. I was no longer in control. Most of the flight I worried about the rental car and directions from the Los Angeles airport to the resort—irrational, but worthy.

Fortunately, my son Joe is technically adept. Once in the Chevrolet Malibu, he plugged a small GPS device into something and without effort drove to the resort. Comfortable in the back seat, I smiled all the way, admiring the flowers and beautiful homes set on the hillsides. It was unusual for me to not be in charge, and I determined to not take notes and to relax for sheer pleasure—difficult, but definitely attainable.

As we approached the resort, the view became breathtaking. Joe parked in front, we entered an elegant lobby and were given a glass of champagne before I checked in and Joe unloaded the luggage. After parking the car, we found our adjoining rooms overlooking the terraced landscape leading to the Pacific Ocean. The weather was chilly and I yearned for my colorful Navajo coat.

As I was unpacking, Joe knocked on my door. When he entered, I could tell he was uncomfortable about something, "Mom, I know you're paying for the rooms, but isn't this a bit extravagant?"

"Oh Joe, we're on vacation. Don't worry about the price."

"But, Mother, really, we could all go to Europe for this."

"What do you mean?"

"Did you see the price of the room?"

"No, where is it?"

"Look inside your closet."

I opened the closet door. The posted room rate was $2,100 per night.

"Joe, we're not paying that."

He sighed in relief.

Since airlines no longer even provide peanuts, we were hungry. A chauffeured golf cart took us to a casual restaurant on the grounds. I enjoyed fish tacos while Joe and Carla split an order of fish and chips, the chips being French-fried sweet potatoes. Fortunately, the price of the meal was nowhere near the posted rate of the rooms.

The agenda for the evening included cocktails and snacks in a private suite to be followed by dinner at Hermosa Beach, transportation provided. Brother Allan and wife Alma as well as other family members joined us for music, drinks, delicious finger food and the view. My niece Katie and the groom were so obviously happy I could not help but tell her, "Thank you, Katie, for drawing us out of Texas and our comfortable shells to such a beautiful place."

At the prescribed time, we were ushered to waiting busses and driven to Hermosa Beach and an upstairs dining area reserved for the wedding guests. Brother John sat with me on the bus and entertained us during the 30-minute drive to the restaurant. The food was bountiful and tasty, barbecued ribs and trimmings. The outdoor deck was warmed with tall heaters, and I enjoyed visiting with the friends and family who were in attendance. The toasts and speeches later in the evening were funny and lively, quite entertaining. Before we were driven back to the resort, warm and satisfied, Joe remarked, "It's really nice to be with family and not be as intimidated as I was as a kid. Your brothers are really fun to be with."

Sonja Klein

Since the wedding was in the evening, we had a free day to relax and explore. But first, we went down to the dining area for breakfast and were soon joined by Allan and Alma, Allan's son and daughter-in-law and then brother John, the father of the bride. The breakfast was extended; we shared French toast and bacon, wired by the $5 a cup coffee.

Allan, Alma, his son Cameron and wife Mary drove into Los Angeles for sightseeing and shopping. John went to the spa for a massage. Joe and Carla and I drove along the coastline, stopping at the lighthouse and museum and then enjoyed a nice walk along the footpaths. After a light lunch, I retired to my room to read and nap for the coming evening.

The setting for the wedding was a gazebo overlooking the ocean. Roses were everywhere, decorating the white chairs and the gazebo. The music befitted the scene. John and Maria together walked Katie down the aisle. Her dress was elegant and the ceremony short and touching, and we adjourned to one of the resort's terraces, where we were served drinks and trays of snacks and warmed up once again by the tall heaters. I never left the one I commandeered until we were escorted to the grand ballroom and found our assigned tables. The dance floor separated me from Joe and Carla, and I sat with my niece and nephew, as well as one of the law partners for whom Katie, an attorney, worked. We did our best to behave.

Dinner was served at stations. Rack of lamb and trimmings was my first choice. Cedar-planked salmon was next. The pasta station was delectable, and breads and cheeses complimented the meal.

Then the dancing began; the band was lively, playing songs for the young attendees. We joined in the dancing. I danced with friends and then just went out there and danced. John and Maria were on the dance floor as well as Allan and Alma and the rest of the family. Even son Joe and his wife Carla shared space with us on the crowded floor. I was proud of him, knowing full well his reluctance to dance, and told him so. Earlier I had whispered, "Joe, if you can wear Spandex and ride a bicycle, you can get out on the dance floor."

We all ate wedding cake, both groom's and bride's, and received mementos of the wedding, small living succulent plants, touchingly packaged. Instead of rice, everyone had a wooden wand with a tangerine silk streamer to wave at the end of the reception. Midnight found me in my luxurious bed.

Roundtrip from Texas

Joe and Carla and I left the hotel early the next morning, skipping breakfast. Stopping for coffee and donuts in Hermosa Beach, Joe drove north along the famous coastal highway, consulting his technical devices to direct us to San Simeon.

The scenery occupied our vision as we commented on the beauty of California. A moment of revelation occurred to me. I had been traveling all over the world for 10 years and had not appreciated the beauty of my own country—the roads, scenery, homes, clean environment and efficiency. Perhaps I was a fool.

I had set my taster on eating some abalone, a fond memory from my first marriage, one of the few fond memories. We had flown to California to visit my aunt and uncle and had spent a weekend in Santa Barbara at the Biltmore Hotel, dining one evening at a famous restaurant. I had eaten abalone for the first time and loved it. Never since had the opportunity arisen to eat it again.

Internet research had revealed that there was an abalone farm on the way to San Simeon and that several restaurants in the area served the local abalone. We stopped in Cayucos and dined on abalone for a late lunch. It was as good as I remembered but expensive, actually very expensive. Abalone sells for $70 a pound. The meal was worth it.

From Cayucos, the drive was short to the Best Western Hotel in San Simeon. Again, we had a delightful surprise, a gorgeous setting overlooking the ocean. The rooms were large, complete with fireplace and balcony overlooking the Pacific. Outdoor fire pits lined the walkways along the cliff.

Visiting Hearst Castle was our plan for the next entire day. Joe had booked us for three separate tours, allowing a break for lunch and time to watch the movie at the guest center.

The temperature was chillier than I liked. Our first tour began at 9 A.M. The bus trip up the winding road to the castle lasted 15 minutes. The views were fantastic.

When we reached the castle, the guide related its short history. William Randolph Hearst was an only child. His father purchased the ranch of nearly 100,000 acres in 1865 with money realized from mining discoveries. William was born in 1863.

The family added acreage over the years until the total land owned was close to 250,000 acres. As a child, William Randolph Hearst enjoyed camping on the mountaintop on which he was to build his castle.

Sonja Klein

When his mother died in 1919, he inherited the ranch and began construction on the site. Taking advantage of the chaos and economic conditions in Europe following World War I, Hearst purchased remains of bombed monasteries and architectural remnants, instructing his architect, Julia Morgan, to build rooms around the pieces, fabricating matching relics when needed to complete the room.

Being an only child, he could have lived well on the family fortune but instead built a publishing empire that still leads the worldwide industry today. Hearst died in 1948, not having finished the castle, which contains 160 rooms.

In 1957 the family donated 150 acres, including the castle, to the state of California. They still own the surrounding ranch and raise beef cattle.

The setting, grounds, castle and swimming pools are magnificent. I was proud to see a castle of such proportion and style in California. Hearst Castle rivals most that I have seen throughout the world.

For the first tour, we walked the grounds and visited the larger of the two guesthouses. The outdoor pool with statues and columns has been enlarged three times to conform to the surroundings. It was by far the most beautiful pool I have seen.

After watching the movie at the visitor center, we returned back up the hill to tour some of the main rooms, the reception or living room, some guest bedrooms and the library. The tour guide advised us to remain on the carpet runners installed to protect the marble and wooden floors. As our small group entered the library, a beeper barked at intervals. I was so awestruck by the volumes of books, the size of the room and the elaborate carpets that I did not realize I had left the zone of tourists and was standing in the middle of the room.

Son Joe gently took me by the arm and said, "Mom, you set off the Persian rug alarm."

Profuse apologies to the tour guide salvaged my pride and the tour continued to the tennis courts and indoor pool, decorated with over a million golden mosaic tiles.

Following a light lunch at the visitor center, we journeyed up the hill for the final tour of the day: a tour of the kitchens, master bedroom and multiple marble bathrooms. We climbed up and down staircases being informed that there were 16 staircases in the castle.

The kitchen was fascinating and an open drawer displayed silver bone marrow spoons, dozens of them. I had first seen a bone marrow spoon at the Hermitage in St. Petersburg, Russia. Returning from Russia as a lover of bone marrow, I ordered one from the Internet. I use it often.

The tour guides were excellent, telling snippets of Hearst's life and the famous people that were entertained at the castle. The trip was well worthwhile and made me proud to be an American, confident that Americans can replicate the splendor of Europe.

Since lunch had been light, we dined early at the Mexican restaurant near the motel. We ordered their advertised agave wine margaritas. I was unfamiliar with agave wine. The drinks were so good that we each consumed two, being only a block from our lodgings.

The beef enchiladas were made with Hearst beef, very tasty, and we returned to our rooms to recap the day around the warmth of my fireplace and view the sun setting over the Pacific.

San Francisco was our next destination. The drive along vineyards, fields of produce, scenery and freeway traffic consumed half the day. Since we could not check into the boutique hotel in the heart of the city, Joe drove across the Golden Gate Bridge to the John Muir Natural Park Reserve. He and Carla wanted to see the redwoods. This time there were no Persian carpet sensors, and we took the two-mile path through the forest, laughing at the warning signs to watch for banana slugs. At least we laughed until we saw a six-inch slug , creepy, slimy and smashed in the path.

Joe's expert navigating led us back into the heart of the city, and we found ourselves going down Lombard Street, the most crooked street in the country. It was scary but fun when it was all over. The other steep streets were disconcerting until we reached the tops.

A friend of Joe's was in San Francisco on a business project, so after checking in the hotel we walked a cold few blocks to his hotel and enjoyed complimentary wine before going to a French restaurant in the area. The food was outstanding. We dined and drank long into the evening.

Since it was drizzling the next morning, we took a taxi to Fisherman's Wharf and walked through the Maritime Museum and outdoor portion, which displayed an array of ships from an old ferry to a schooner.

As we shopped the many stores along the wharf, Carla purchased a miniature boat and I purchased a tee shirt that read, THE BEATINGS WILL CONTINUE UNTIL MORALE IMPROVES. The pirate flag was on the front of the shirt. I thought it would be funny to show the crew at the ranch.

We lunched on fresh crab and continued shopping, entering a chocolate shop that had every sort of chocolate confection imaginable. Fortunately, we had just eaten and purchased only some truffles.

Joe guided us to a trolley stop and we boarded the trolley for a ride back to the hotel. The trolley really went clang clang clang.

Early that last evening, we walked to China Town and did some fun shopping. I purchased an outfit for my grandson that was black-and-white striped and said, "Alcatraz reject. Too cute." Carla purchased a red silk dress.

Though I couldn't find any abalone on the menu in China Town, the food was delicious. The following morning we returned our rental car at the airport and flew back to Houston. I drove home to the ranch reflecting that destination weddings were a lot of fun, a step outside the traditional wedding box.

10

Comments

After publishing my first book, I thought I was prepared for comments and reviews. I wasn't.

The first came from my brother David who complimented me on baring my soul and added that I was the female "Gus" in *Lonesome Dove*. I was amazed. He even said he couldn't put the book down. Since he was my brother, I was flattered but assumed he was prejudiced.

I then received an email from his wife Mary who wrote, "I stole David's copy of the book and couldn't stop reading it."

Israel, the father of my grandson remarked, "I started reading it in the bathroom and carried it into the bathtub. Had no idea you were so raunchy." Lee, a friend in Barksdale, said, "I'm almost two thirds through. It's very revealing; I didn't know those things about you. You really tell it like it is. I especially liked the chapter about pets not being free. I suppose the sequel won't be quite as bold."

I replied that the sequel will be even more so and that I hoped the book's language won't offend some of the local people.

Lee admitted that the language was a bit rank, but that knowing me, the book was truthful.

I confessed that I could not be who I was not. The book is me.

The next offer was from Chuck, the artist who designed the cover. In an email, he said he had received the book in the mail, put it on the kitchen table and went for his daily run. When he returned, his wife had already read the first chapter. Chuck wrote, "She doesn't read much for pleasure. That's a real compliment coming from her."

One of the praise contributors emailed me that he couldn't put the book down and that he felt I had a winner. I was not prepared to receive compliments from men; I had assumed that the book would be a chick read since the majority of readers are women and a woman wrote the book.

A friend from church agreed with Lee, "I especially liked the chapter about pets not being free. It made me laugh."

Sonja Klein

In my mind, the translation of her comment was that she did not approve of some of the more graphic chapters. Of course, that is merely my perception.

My son called. I asked him, "Joe, have you read the book?"

"No, Mom, Carla has been reading it for two days. She wouldn't even talk to me. Then she put the book on the table on my side of the bed. I haven't had time to start it."

"Joe, what did she say about it?"

"She said it was a great book for people with ADHD, short stuff and long stuff."

"Joe, that's the symphony of the book, a natural rhythm."

Brother Allan called on family business. I couldn't restrain myself, "Allan, have you read the book?"

"I started it but my son Erich was here for the weekend and he took it downstairs and I haven't seen it since. Send me 10 copies and be sure you sign them."

Brother John called, "I received your book, couldn't put it down. Very nice. Send me five copies and be sure you sign them."

A lady friend remarked, "The most interesting thing I find is that you read and research the countries before you go." She hadn't yet read the book.

And then the shit hit the fan. My cousin called and said she found a mistake in the chapter about rafting. For some weird reason I used her mother's name instead of hers. That was her only comment.

I spoke with my attorney; I've known him since college. His comments, "It made me laugh a lot. I didn't know you gave blow jobs. I don't remember reading that, but my secretary did."

My cousin Ida emailed me, "I like your style of writing."

My CPA emailed, "I'm almost through reading every word. I didn't know you were such a hottie, though I always suspected."

And then a lady friend who is featured in the article about the hat replied to an email I sent. Three weeks had passed since I mailed her a copy of the book. Since she remained silent, I emailed her and asked her how she liked the book. She emailed in bold black large letters followed by many exclamation points, "I'm stunned."

Not to be denied the truth, I asked in a reply, "What do you mean?"

I never heard from her again until she called, "Sonja, I am so disappointed in you. I introduced you to my friends and you betrayed us."

I was speechless for a moment before I replied, "I'm sorry you feel betrayed; I wrote the truth as I perceived it."

She was brutal, "I introduced you to my friends and you wrote about us without asking permission."

"I only used first names and didn't say where they live."

"Yes, but anyone who reads the book will know who they are. You could have at least changed the names and the events. The book won't be a best seller anyway. No one's going to read it."

"No, I couldn't do that. I have to keep the integrity of nonfiction."

"You are not welcome in our camp at the Terlingua Chili Cookoff. Don't set foot inside the camp."

I fixed a drink of vodka and water, even though it was before noon and resolved to spend more dollars on promoting the book to prove her wrong.

Kathy from Utopia asked, "Do you think you'll ever marry again?"

My answer was a definite no. Then I saw the look on her and her new husband's face.

"Well, if the right guy came along, I probably would."

Her husband smiled, "Yeah, you'll follow him around like a little puppy dog."

A young vet who had done tours in Iraq and Afghanistan commented, "It's so intimate and so real."

I replied, "It's real, for sure."

A friend from California called, "I started your book last night. I stayed up until 2 A.M. Can't wait to finish it. It's the most honest book I've ever read. I laughed and I cried."

A lady friend called, "I especially like the story of your mother building a church. Your book is extremely candid."

"Yes, it's all true."

"I remember when your second husband was arrested. We were living in Louisiana when that happened. I remember it. Do you remember who the first Scarface was?"

"Not really."

"It was Al Capone."

"You were married to him a long time."

"Fifteen years."

A friend with whom I play bridge commented, "I read a chapter to my son at breakfast. I'm going to finish the book today. I really like the part about Russia. I was there in the 1970's. From your writing, it is a lot different now, except for the fact that no one smiles. It was like that in the 70's too. About Mongolia, is it really that modern?"

"Very much so. Since the 1990's, the population has moved to the cities. Ulan Bator is quite cosmopolitan. Asians from the south travel there to purchase designer items."

A lady friend who had purchased a book called, "I would like for you to mail a copy of the book to my friend. She travels a lot and I think she would enjoy the book."

That's the best review I could ever expect.

11

Church

Attending church is a great part of my life. As a child, my father was at times president of the Missouri Synod Lutheran Church, Trinity, on Houston Avenue in Houston, Texas. At times, my mother was president of the Women's League.

My three brothers and I attended the Lutheran parochial schools either St. Matthews on South Main Street or Trinity. Every Sunday we were in church, sitting in the second pew on the right in the front of the church. If we misbehaved, we received a spanking when we returned home. We did our best to behave. Sometimes it worked, sometimes it didn't.

Only Lutheran teachers taught at the Lutheran schools. God forbid a Baptist or Methodist teacher instructing in the schools.

Since the schools were small, often the grades were combined into one room. In the early years, I remember having one grade per classroom. But from the third grade up, there were at least two grades in the same room. One year at St. Matthews, the fifth through the eighth grades were in one room. I loved being with the older students.

We played volleyball and basketball, competing with the other Lutheran schools in Houston. Over the years, all of us Missouri Synod Lutheran kids became acquainted.

I remember the old German teacher in the eighth grade. We learned to write long hand using the old script method and every time I would pick up my pencil with my left hand, he would hit it with a ruler. There were only two lefties in the class and Judy and I were persecuted and given C's in handwriting. It's a wonder I wasn't emotionally scarred from the experience, or maybe I was and just don't know it.

Every Sunday found our family in church and Sunday school. When we spent the weekends at the farm, we attended the Lutheran church in the country, as we called it.

In the spring of the eighth grade, we were all confirmed and the church held a family dinner with all the relatives invited. It was a big deal and we wore special outfits and were given gifts.

Sonja Klein

The Sunday school even presented me with a Bible for 10 years of perfect attendance, though I don't understand how that was possible. I must have been sick or missed at least one Sunday.

When I went to college, my father questioned me every time I spoke with him, "Are you going to church?"

Of course, I wasn't going to church. I was free and away at college. When I went home I went to church. I didn't go to church when I finished college either. I was churched out. My early married years didn't find me in church, but when I became a mother, I went back to church, sending my children to the Episcopal school in New Iberia, Louisiana. The closest Missouri Synod Lutheran Church was in Lafayette.

Until I divorced my second husband and moved back to the area north of Houston where my family originated, my children attended parochial school, going to chapel every day and being confirmed around Easter. We sat on the second row from the front on the right. I couldn't sit anywhere else.

My children's high school years were a bit chaotic; I occasionally attended church with my mother, sitting front right as always.

Another failed marriage and a new one found me in west Texas on the ranch I purchased. We didn't attend church. After John died, I went back to church, attending a local charismatic church in Barksdale, population around 80. It was comforting. The second row front right was open.

Having been Episcopalian for my children's years, I once attended the Episcopal church in Montel. The liturgy and rituals did not sing to my soul as the music at House of Praise in Barksdale had. Perhaps my spiritual journey had led me elsewhere.

Now that my daughter and partner are living at the ranch, we attend church. Her son is a year old and his children are 14 and 16. The second row front right is just long enough to hold us all.

Within a year, the teenagers returned to live with their mother. My daughter and family moved to Alpine. Now I rarely attend church.

The God to whom I pray does not live in a church. He lives in me. I talk to him every day. We walk together.

12

Sex

Sitting around the campfire in Terlingua at the Chili Cookoff, the conversation lulled in the late night. After listening to the mainly male company for hours, I posed a question, "Have any of you ever had enough good sex?"

After a slight pause, a chorus answered, "No."

I pursued, "I thought any sex was good for the man."

Again, they answered, "No."

To the few women present I asked, "What about you? Have you ever had enough good sex?"

The answer was the same.

As I grow older, erections seem to become an issue with men. I have known men to experience the limp dick syndrome from the 40's and up. You might expect this with older men, but not with younger.

The ads all tout Viagra as the answer, but to women, the idea of a man taking a pill to have sex is abhorrent, contrived and humiliating. After all, we want to be pursued naturally, courted and petted to stir the hormones.

Having sex with an old man doesn't appeal to me; I like young men but suppose that classifies me as a cougar, a new term for an older woman with a younger man. The double standard isn't fair.

Old men with young pretty women prompt remarks like, "Good for him." Old women with young men inspire the comment, "Isn't that disgusting?"

Comedians make jokes saying that blacks don't lick the honey pot. If you're too old to cut the mustard, you can at least lick the jar. Oral sex isn't my favorite. I have to be drunk to enjoy it. Anal sex is out of the question. I will die a virgin. Bondage is fun, but not whips and chains.

Never have I wished to be a man. I have no desire to be governed by something hanging between my legs. I love being a woman and I love sex.

Friends in west Texas invited me to a sex toy party. When I inquired what that was, I was told, "It's against the law in some parts of Texas to sell sex toys, so you have these home parties like Tupperware and buy all sorts of paraphernalia."

"No, thanks."

"But it's fun."

"My sex habits are private."

Between boyfriends, my brother David advised me, "Sonja, you need some recreational sex."

I asked him, "What the hell is recreational sex?"

"Simply put, it's sex for fun. Sex produces all sorts of hormonal changes, all good, just like laughing."

"But, David, what about all the sexually transmitted diseases?"

"Just use condoms."

"That's no fun."

David's answer was frank, "Then take your chances."

"No thanks."

As my brothers and I were approaching puberty, the question was posed, "Do you think Mother and Daddy have sex? Sonja, your bedroom is next to theirs; do you ever hear anything?"

I replied, "That's disgusting. What we do know is that they had sex four times because there are four of us."

After my father died, my mother had a boyfriend. My brothers were appalled to think of their mother with another man other than our father. I was happy for her and told my brothers, "Look, Daddy was sick with cancer for quite a while. She probably hasn't had any for a long time. I say good for her."

They didn't like it.

I didn't like it when I discovered that my children had become sexually active. I worried about pregnancy and disease, but somehow the children and I survived those scary years.

I have always believed that what one does in privacy is their business, never being critical of sexual preference. By the same token, what I do in privacy is my choice.

13

Ex-husbands

Ex-husband number one, 'Montgomery,' is still alive, living in my house with his wife of over 30 years. He married her within months of our divorce. She moved in with him the week after I left. I suppose she is still enjoying some of the furniture and decorator items I left behind, probably still sleeping in my bed too.

She had never been married, and according to my brother David, who was a groomsman, the wedding was quite an affair. Years passed before I forgave David for being in his wedding.

Fifteen years after the divorce I attended a real estate auction with David and 'Montgomery' was there with his wife. I didn't recognize him. David pointed him out. He had a potbelly and was holding a drink. I don't remember what his wife looked like, except that she had dark hair and wasn't fat.

When he saw David and recognized me, he walked over and said, "Well, well. Look who's here."

I turned and walked away, bitter memories returning. Ten years passed before I quit hating him. Seeing him brought it all back. I didn't want to go back to bitterness.

David has a bad habit of bringing up exes when we are all together. Allan has two and David invariably asks, "How is _____?" We've told him over and over again that divorce is just that and we don't wish to be quizzed about people no longer in our life. Yet he persists. Over the years, he told me that 'Montgomery's' father died, that his mother had moved to Conroe, that she died, that 'Montgomery' has a pacemaker. He doesn't understand that I don't care.

As for Raleigh, we remained friends. He called me often and called Joe and Molly on a regular basis. One year, Joe and Carla and I drove to New Iberia for the Sugar Cane Festival. We stayed in a bed and breakfast on Main Street. Raleigh came and spent time with us, tried to tempt me with some cocaine and asked me to go home with him for the night. I declined.

Sonja Klein

Several years later, he called and asked if he could come for a visit since Molly was staying at the ranch. He said he wanted to see her. I agreed. He was recovering from a hernia operation. He chose to stay with me in my one-bedroom house. I told him he would be sleeping on the futon on the sun porch. He asked to sleep with me. I told him that was not an option.

He stayed a week, asking me for money. I returned a pearl and diamond ring he had given me. He wanted more. I asked him to leave. He did, but he still continued to call.

A phone call from Raleigh's sister informed me that he had been killed in a car accident. A teenager under the influence of drugs and alcohol and driving a borrowed Mercedes hit him head on, driving at a high speed. He was killed instantly. That was about five years ago. The children and I drove to the funeral. The coffin was closed.

A young woman claiming to be his daughter made the arrangements for the funeral. Raleigh's uncle paid the bill. A young man came to the funeral claiming to be his son. Doing the math, I realized he would have been conceived during my marriage. The daughter of another acknowledged illegitimate son was also there. The son had died. I knew about those two but not about the young punk who appeared. I was furious. My children were stunned. He was the only father they ever knew. None of these other pretenders had ever lived with him.

The pretenders preempted the front chairs and sat staring at the coffin. I wanted to go kick the coffin and scream. The older alleged daughter took the ashes after the cremation.

I contacted an attorney friend in New Iberia. She filed a wrongful death suit against the owner of the Mercedes. The owner's daughter had loaned the vehicle to the young driver, who incidentally had outstanding warrants. He was jailed.

The story did not have a happy ending. One of Raleigh's friends vouched to the insurance company that the older girl was his daughter and she received the nominal proceeds from his auto insurance policy. Since my children were legally adopted, they were his heirs, not any of the others. Louisiana is a different world and abides by Napoleonic law.

The wrongful death suit proved that none of the others were his biological children and after a year and a half, my children received about $50,000 each, after attorney fees. My children did not go to court but settled. There were no winners. The driver of the car went to jail, the young alleged son also got in trouble and went to jail for a while. The alleged daughter went back to Mississippi with the insurance money and the granddaughter never said a word.

The story didn't end there. The young girl who loaned her father's Mercedes to the killing driver committed suicide a year later on the day of her sister's wedding. Drugs and alcohol created a catastrophic set of events.

Raleigh's friends erected a wooden cross at the site of the accident in Broussard, Louisiana.

As for husband number three, 'Rodney,' he lives between Lafayette and New Iberia. Mother's boyfriend, Eloy, now dead, told Mother that he saw 'Rodney' out in the yard down the street from where he lived. Eloy stopped to visit with 'Rodney' and relayed to Mother that 'Rodney' was managing a sugar mill in the area, that his mother in South Africa had died and that his house was quite nice.

Months later, I was cleaning out my TV cabinet and discovered a videotape of his daughter as a child. With a clear conscience, I couldn't throw it away, so I tried to find him in the phone book. No such luck. Eloy had died.

Raleigh was still alive and I called him and asked him to go find 'Rodney' and obtain his address. The following day Raleigh called with the address. I smiled when he told me that 'Rodney' had acted scared. Raleigh's reputation was not a good one. I mailed him the tape.

The next news I heard about 'Rodney' was from Raleigh's cousin. He heard that 'Rodney' had married a chubby Cajun woman and had purchased a home on the prestigious golf course between Lafayette and New Iberia.

Several years later, I attended a social event. One of my brother David's partners was there. He asked, "Guess who I ran into in Santa Fe?"

I declined to speak. He continued, "'Rodney's' daughter. Look, I have her number on my cell phone. She's quite attractive."

"That's nice," I answered, but I thought, *Who the hell cares?*

As far as I know, they are both still alive, which lends truth to the saying that only the good die young. The sorry-assed sons of bitches live forever.

Did I say I had gotten over those husbands? Maybe I haven't. Easy to forgive but not to forget.

14

Never give up

I am reluctant to write about bad things, but an incident occurred on my trip to South America that took months to resolve. On the last day of the cruise that took me from Rio de Janeiro to Buenos Aires, south along the east coast of South America, I was robbed.

As usual, the ship kicked the travelers off the luxurious ship early in the morning. Since my flight home did not leave until late that evening, I signed up for a full day tour of the city and boarded a bus at 8 A.M. My luggage had been sent to an airport holding area, and I carried only my purse and a carry-on with some modest jewelry and overflow purchases. The bus first stopped at Recoleta Cemetery, where Evita Perón is buried.

I always notice the driver and guide and pay close attention to their demeanor. I noticed that the driver was smoking and seemed nervous. The guide was young, anxious and quite pretty.

Most of us on the bus were in the same situation, trying to kill time before boarding a late evening plane for home.

The bus stopped at the main gate of the cemetery. The guide loudly admonished us to leave all valuables on the bus, to remove our jewelry because there were thieves in the cemetery. Everyone dutifully removed their jewelry and left it on the bus in their tote bags. I was wearing no jewelry but left my carryon in the bus, carefully arranging it so that I would be able to tell if it had been disturbed. My purse with my passport and money remained with me.

An elderly lady spoke, "I'm staying on the bus. I visited this cemetery yesterday."

Before we entered the gate, she joined us.

"I thought you were staying on the bus," I remarked.

"The driver made me get off."

Never in my travels had a driver insisted that an elderly person could not remain on the bus. I almost returned to the bus to retrieve my bag, but since it was early in the morning, I ignored my instincts. Big mistake.

Roundtrip from Texas

The young guide talked too much, took too long in the cemetery and even admitted that she was perhaps spending too much time there. We returned to the bus. I checked my bag. It had been disturbed, but a perfunctory check revealed nothing missing. We toured, shopped, had lunch and toured some more.

By 8 P.M., we were left at the airport, reclaimed our baggage and departed for the various gates assigned to our flights. By chance, I was in line with some of my fellow travelers. One of them remarked that her wedding rings were missing, that she had left them on the bus during the cemetery tour. Some of us began to examine our bags. One lady was missing a gold necklace, another was missing some money and I was missing the amethyst and gold ring my mother had given me. Comparing notes, we all determined that the theft had occurred while at the cemetery.

I was sent to call the cruise line's emergency number and report the theft. We recalled the bus number, the driver's name and the guide's name. The cruise line recorded my report of the theft. I urged the cruise line to contact everyone on that bus to check their belongings. I received a number to call when I returned home.

When I called the cruise line upon my return, they replied that they were investigating to determine if an incident had occurred. I was adamant, "An incident occurred. Our belongings were stolen."

I was assured that they would contact me. Days went by. I checked with my insurance agent, was told that I was covered and delivered pictures of the ring as well as an estimate of its value. The adjustor contacted me and said that the ring was worth $200 less than my deductible. He had depreciated the ring. I asked him, "How can you depreciate 18 carat gold?"

He replied, "It's our policy." '

I replied, "You are wrong."

I called my agent. He agreed to investigate. Actually, he did nothing but agree with the adjustor. I took another estimate and a blown up picture of the ring to his office. Still I received no satisfaction.

In the meantime, I was communicating with the cruise line, which said they had no liability in the issue. I disagreed, telling them, "You arranged the bus tour and paid for it, collecting the money from me for the tour. You are liable. If you think I'm going away, you are wrong. I'm from Texas and I will not go away or give up."

Sonja Klein

As time passed, I blamed myself. I thought it was my fault, not paying attention to my instincts, being stupid and vulnerable. I had traveled all over the world and never had anything similar occurred. I was never careless or flashy. Surely it was my fault. Then reason prevailed. I was the victim and I demanded recompense.

Months later and many phone calls billed, I received a letter from the cruise line, offering me the amount of the appraisal for the ring. I accepted.

I mailed the letter of acceptance and a copy of the check to my insurance agent, admonishing him to correct the adjustor.

Since then, I replaced the ring and have traveled to Vietnam, Cambodia and quite a few countries in east Africa. I will continue to travel the world and pay closer attention to my instincts. But most of all, I will never give up.

15

Drought

The animals are starving. I have lived in these canyon lands for 17 years and log the amount of rainfall. Before the year 2011, the least amount of rainfall had been 18 inches; the most was 46. The annual average according to the *Texas Almanac* is 22 to 24 inches. By July of 2011, the heavens only dropped 2 inches.

Where my ranch was grassy in the creek bottom, there is now only dirt. I culled the goats down to six and the sheep to seven and still fed them. The oak trees are dying. The cedar, elm, pecan and mesquite are stressed. Even the prickly pear cacti are shriveling with some sort of fungus.

I can't keep sufficient birdseed in the feeders around the house. Ten pounds might last a day or two. The hummingbirds hover around the three feeders I attempt to keep full. I have noticed all sorts of birds that normally do not frequent the feeders—orioles, buntings, Mexican jays and woodpeckers. They compete for seeds in the feeder and those that fall to the ground. Even the cautious rock squirrels are bold,

In several months, I trapped over 40 coons within a few feet of my home. Twice I have trapped two at the same time. Rabbits have eaten all my petunias. I replanted periwinkle and found that rabbits don't eat that particular flower. The native deer and exotic deer stand beside the roads, ribs showing.

A high-pressure ridge dominates the central area of Texas, blocking any moisture from the Gulf of Mexico that might try to drift in.

By the end of October, we'd received nearly 10 inches. The grass tried to grow but the warm weather is nearly finished.

My brother David in Houston called to say the pine trees at the farm are dying and that he is forced to harvest the dying and dead ones. Even his live oak trees are dying. According to David, Houston has only received three inches this year.

At church, we pray for rain. Towns are hosting rain prayers. Camp Wood, Leakey, Junction, all small towns in the area, are rationing water and low on water reserves. The Nueces River at Vance has stopped running. I received an email that the Llano at Junction is no longer flowing.

If ever we needed a hurricane, this is the time. While we are suffering from a shortage of rain, the Midwest is flooding. As the summer has progressed with no rain, people are going crazy. A local lady drove off the mountain. She survived with cuts and abrasions, but they had to cut her out of her truck. A young man, no stranger to guns, shot off his foot while cleaning his shotgun. Machinery is failing, computers are crashing and people are acting irrationally.

Forest fires are burning all over Texas. The winds have blown them out of control. Thankfully, the creek still has water. The springs are flowing but perhaps not for long. The newspapers say that this weather pattern will last for the next five to ten years. If that is true, we will be living in the desert.

No matter, I'm staying. This is home.

16

Games

How much of life is a game? I grew up playing games, dominoes, cards, board games and yard games. I don't remember when I first began to play games. Winning was always important. I was never told, "It's just a game; have fun playing."

The object was to become number one, to win victorious. Even in neighborhood games like kick the can, my three brothers and I were fiercely competitive. At the Lutheran schools we attended, we participated in football, baseball and volleyball. We played to win.

As we grew older, the games became less physical and more mental. Bridge and 42 dominoes were family favorites. My brother David often called them war games. We competed fiercely.

My father was not the best bridge player, but when he was winning, he whistled. When the card gods did not deal him good hands, he would often rise from the table and say goodnight. The games were over.

My brother John is known to throw the cards in the fireplace and burn them. He changes decks, hoping to change his luck.

My mother was a good bridge player. She competed at tournaments and often won. Even into her upper 80's she still played a good game of bridge. Every morning she read the bridge column. When the brothers and I played with her, she corrected our every mistake.

One evening, brother John was playing. He was a good bridge player but this particular evening and year, his bridge was sloppy. When Mother commented, "John, you are playing poor bridge," John replied, "Who gives a damn? I have better things to think about."

That's when the siblings at the table realized that no longer do we have to win. All in our 60's, we have nothing left to prove. We have all made our mistakes and achieved successes, not that we can't continue to fail and succeed, but it doesn't really matter anymore.

In fact, it's time to have fun, what time there is left. However, being German, it is very difficult to have fun. Only once have I splurged for business class airfare and used frequent flyer miles to upgrade.

Sonja Klein

I still enjoy a game of bridge. Since my mother died, we still play bridge, but it's just not the same. It is as if she is still with us at the table, watching over our shoulders.

Even in sparsely populated Real County, games are popular. Just within 20 miles of the ranch are three bridge clubs and several domino clubs and, in Rocksprings, about 45 miles north, duplicate bridge is available once a week.

In my travels, I often have occasion to play bridge. I have played with Jordanians, Australians, New Zealanders (also known as Kiwis), Canadians, Brits and Americans. Some have been good; others awful, but it has always been a game. To some of them, it was not a game but a matter of life and death.

I'll never forget an experience in Houston at the Shamrock Hotel. I was in my mid-twenties. My mother had signed up for a bridge tournament. Her partner canceled at the last moment. She convinced me to be her partner and as always encouraged me, saying, "You can do it."

I was so intimidated by the vast ballroom with tables of players. I played awful, or at least I think I did. My mother smiled and gave me confidence. I think we scored horribly, but in my mother's eyes, we had a great time. She made me feel comfortable. My mother never made me feel that she was disappointed, even when I made some of my worst mistakes and was at my lowest.

Today I play bridge, substituting for the clubs in the canyon. Most of the players are retired and very forgiving. We have all come to realize that it's just a game and we merely enjoy the company and companionship as well as the snacks and desserts. How we play is no longer important. What is important that we show up to play.

17

Dancing in Bandera

Memorial Day weekend arrived. My artist friend Chuck was coming for his yearly visit following graduation ceremonies in Merkel. Chuck was the high school teacher for the gifted and talented students, and this year was special. He was retiring; this was his last graduation.

When my friend Linda from Uvalde called and invited Chuck and me to join her and friends in Bandera for a night of dancing, I was elated to accept. Any time spent with Linda and her husband Milton is enjoyable. Her other friend Linda, from Dallas, was coming as well as some other friends from Utopia.

Chuck always arrived well after midnight and stayed in the hunter's cabin in the creek bottom. Saturday morning he walked up the hill for a visit and breakfast. We shared observations about books and travel and caught up on our artistic lives. Chuck is one hell of an artist and designed my first book cover. His dancing skills match his artistic skills.

I drove the long way, out the back of the ranch. The route was scenic through the terrain often termed the Little Switzerland of Texas.

Chuck and I shared thoughts. Chuck observed, "The first time I came to see you, I couldn't believe I was in Texas."

I added, "Yeah, not many people are familiar with this area. They think the Hill Country is just rolling. I love these badlands. How does it feel to be retired?"

"I think I'm going to like it. Now I'm a full-time artist. I'll be working every day."

Chuck and I share our love for the creative life. His insights often give me courage to overcome the fear of being read, of expecting approval. Both of us are dedicated solitary travelers, and we communicate about geographic highlights.

"What was the advice you gave your last class?"

"I try to keep it short because it's more easily remembered. This year it was, 'Travel light.'"

Sonja Klein

"What a great message. It can be taken literally or philosophically. Anger, jealousy, resentment are a heavy load as well as a big suitcase. Negative emotions are like bricks in a backpack."

"I taught a unit on art, focusing on a Belgian artist who painted things like a derby hat. His critics said it wasn't art. He said it wasn't a hat; the painting was oil colors on canvas, not a hat. I thought my students got the idea. I really knew they had the concept when they gave me a tee shirt with a bong on it that read, THIS IS NOT A BONG. My Taiwanese exchange student told me that he put it on to wear to church. His host mother told him it was not appropriate for church, and he replied that it wasn't a bong. The student said his host mother didn't think it was very funny."

Chuck dozed as I drove portions of the Twisted Sisters, Highways 335, 336 and 337. Garven's Store, at the intersection of Highway 41 and 83, sells tee shirts that brag, "I rode the Twisted Sisters." Every weekend hundreds of motorcyclists and bicyclists ride the winding roads. This year I noticed the new highway signs warning about the hazards and enumerating how many deaths had occurred. One sign cautioned that 10 people had been killed in the next 12 miles.

The party was in full swing when we arrived at the guest ranch on the outskirts of Bandera, where Linda had rented a cabin that slept eight. The temperature was three digits. A couple from Utopia was there. The girls and Milton were damp from a swim in the pool. Linda poured me a glass of wine and we caught up on the weekend's events. The girls had spent the previous day and evening in Kerrville at the Kerrville Folk Music Festival and had partied late.

When Milton said Bandera was a zoo, we decided to avoid the crowds and instead purchased a barbecue plate dinner at the guest ranch. As the girls dressed for the dance, they made elaborate preparations, debating jewelry and outfits. I had dressed in jeans, a short sleeve long shirt and jeweled moccasins. I had come to dance not to attract. I couldn't compete with the pretty girls in camp or at the dance.

By the time we arrived at the dance hall/saloon on a side street in downtown Bandera, the sun had dropped but not the temperature. Since Chuck doesn't drink, he was the designated driver. We lucked into a parking place at the front door. The music resonated out to the street, pure country. I smiled. We paid our $20 per person cover charge, then Chuck and I walked straight to the dance floor and danced three songs:

a two-step, a waltz and a polka, as good as it gets. I told Chuck, "I had forgotten how much I love to dance. It's been a while."

By the time we were finished, I was wringing wet and half sick, having just eaten a heavy barbecue brisket dinner. Hundreds of partygoers were crammed into the open courtyard. There was no air conditioning. A few fans were blowing. There were no available seats or stools. We all stood in the middle of the crowd, trying to stay alive. I could barely breathe. Chuck was wringing wet; so were the others who had danced. No relief was expected.

I thought, 'I can't do this. I think I would rather lie down and die or at least throw up first before I die.'

I tried distraction. There were so many people crowded in the courtyard, drinking, laughing and talking. Chuck brought me a bottle of water. I inhaled it. Then I really felt sick and convinced Linda from Dallas to walk outside. We sat by the car on a big rock and attempted to recover before returning to the oven of sweating bodies and pulsating country music. I found an empty stool close to where our group was standing and asked permission to join two pretty girls drinking tequila. They said sure and invited me for a drink, which I'm sure would have killed me stone dead with one sip. Instead I sucked on water.

The women in the crowd were diverse, from the very young in short tight-fitting Western glitz to the older polyester and tee shirt matrons. Big jewelry was common. Linda from Uvalde wore a short black knit dress with red designs that matched her black cowboy boots, initialed to match her big silver necklace. Linda from Dallas wore tight jeans and a halter top. All of their makeup and preparations meant nothing at this point. We were all dying of the heat. No one gave a fuck what they looked like.

Those were the only dances I danced. As the evening progressed, I drank more water and yearned for a cool room and a bed. The two girls I had joined asked me to take my stool and move back to my friends. One of them said, "You're in our way."

I knew better than to argue with people drinking. I moved. Linda from Uvalde and I walked out to the car. We sat in the front seat of her gold Lexus with the air conditioning on high blast until the windows frosted.

I told Linda, "Great, Linda, now we're going to get pneumonia for going from boiling to freezing"

We returned to the misery of the heat, which had increased as more people entered the open-air dance hall. I told Chuck, "I hate to admit it, but I'm a fair weather dancer."

"No, you're not. I've seen you dance at the Chili Cookoff in the rain and in the cold wearing gloves, hat and thermal underwear." We returned to the guest ranch and went for a swim. The air-conditioned cabin and hard bunk bed felt like heaven.

Being an early riser, I was up and dressed at 7 A.M., searching for a cup of coffee. I found one in the office and sat outside in the cool of the morning admiring the view, feeling pretty rotten for not having been able or inclined to dance. I got over it. Chuck joined me, and we reflected on music, life and love. Linda joined us, and we three artists—a painter, a writer and a singer/songwriter—hatched plans to promote each other and our careers. As we became energized, we went over to the dining hall for breakfast tacos, continued our dialogue and went back for seconds. Linda from Dallas and Milton joined us. The company had been great, the temperature oppressive. On that, we all agreed.

Chuck and I said our goodbyes. The two Lindas went to Kerrville for another day at the festival. The rest of them returned home.

Chuck dozed as I navigated the Twisted Sisters. As I dropped him off at the hunter's cabin he mentioned, "I'll be coming more often now that I'm retired. My wife will be proud of me. My first day of retirement, and I have two commissions. Kathy and Butch want me to do their portraits."

"That's great. Come back anytime, Chuck; we'll go dancing in air conditioning."

18

What do I do now?

A friend called, "Sonja, why don't you write about growing old, approaching 70?"

"That's not a subject I wish to address. But it is a good idea. I am working on a sequel to my first book."

"I think you would do a good job of it."

"I'll think about it."

Aging is not fun and definitely not for the faint-hearted. When I look in the mirror, I am appalled. Inside I feel about 35; outside I see the wrinkles. I can't wear the cute flashy clothes I favor or chase the young men I desire. Instead, the only men to whom I appeal are older with saggy butts and wrinkled throats. They walk slowly or shuffle and are in need of knee and hip replacements, thus they cannot dance well. In addition, most of them are looking for a nurse or a purse.

I have come to the conclusion that the only way to combat aging is to fight tooth and nail, never giving in to being old, resisting every way possible.

I have seen friends succumb without resistance to the monthly round of doctors, separate doctors for the skin, kidneys, heart, thyroid, eyes, ears, bones, nerves, plumbing and so forth. There's a specialist for every ache and pain. Their lives are planned in advance with scheduled appointments.

I prefer appointments for a pedicure and a manicure, a planned trip to Cambodia or an evening of dancing. If it's no fun, why bother?

Volunteer work is satisfying but often turns into disillusionment once the truth surfaces. Negativity is bad. If it doesn't make you feel good, don't do it. Sounds simple, but often it is not easy to extricate yourself from someone else's drama.

Learning and dreaming are the keys to staying young. Without dreams, there is no life and without learning, there is no challenge.

I love books, the feel of a substantial bundle of pages, the sensory satisfaction of turning the paper. An afternoon with a good book is almost as good as sex. And speaking of sex, I don't relish the thought of going to bed with some old man who relies on Viagra. I would have to be drunk and the room midnight dark to engage in a romp in the hay, not that it would be much of a romp.

But then, if I were an old man, I suppose I would feel the same about going to bed with an old woman. Old women have saggy butts and cottage cheese skin too. So far, I haven't reached that stage, but I do work at it.

What do I do now? There is not a day that passes that I don't have a question for my mother. Whether it's advice or some question about the family, the answer is the same. There's no one to ask. My brother John is older but he doesn't know. My Aunt Stella is in her '90's, quick and sharp-witted, but not a wealth of information. It's awful to think that I have to be the source of information. My life has been full of mistakes and bad choices. I'm left without guidance that I can absolutely trust. My mother knew me best of all. Her love was absolute and her advice was always in my best interest, whether I followed it or not.

Most of the time, I have to rely on my own judgment. I usually revert to her admonition, "You can do it. Just go for it." So far, she hasn't been wrong. The best advice came years ago. Mother said there are two lessons in life. Once you get them, you will survive, "Time takes care of everything" and "Accept what you cannot change."

I was recently with friends and ventured the subject of aging with a male friend who is near my age. I asked him how he was dealing with old age. He replied, "I don't like it one bit. It sucks."

I revealed my thoughts, "I try not to think about it either. It would be easy to sit at the ranch, drink and eat myself fat. Just plain give up. I think about why I have been so thrifty all my life. I think about the money I have accumulated by saving and traveling coach, using coupons. And then I realize that the government will take a big chunk out of my estate and my children will spend it with glee. The solution might be to just start spending it and cheat the government out of their share. But that is difficult to do if you are German. And then I recall the months I spent with my father when he was losing his battle against lymphatic cancer. He was nearing 80. He had married a beautiful woman of 19 at the age of 46. She was a faithful wife and good mother to the four children they had together. He had worked hard and saved all his life, and when he died his estate was substantial."

"Daddy's advice as he was dying was to enjoy life. He admitted that he had worked so hard his entire life that he never took the time to learn how to enjoy the fruits of his labor. He advised me to enjoy life. After he died, my mother, then 54, enjoyed her life. She lived to be 89."

I told my friend, "But that is so hard for me to do. Perhaps I should work harder to spend money and live in fun. I think that's the best answer to growing old. Enjoy life, learn and continue with dreams and accomplishments. Publish a book, take a luxury trip, love your family and friends, laugh a lot, play cards, eat well, dance and accept what you cannot change, but most of all, plan to die while you are living."

19

Itch

I was living on Lake Livingston, out in the middle of nowhere, feeding my anger over the breakup of my first marriage and the bitter divorce that left me somewhat broke. I spent most days clearing, grubbing a hardscrabble garden and attacking brush with a venom that had to be exorcised.

One hot summer day as I was mowing along the bulkhead that protected me from the waves of the lake, I managed to stall my riding mower, as well as clog the blades with the stubborn Johnson grass that thrived on the yellow clay.

Since I was 30, fine and slim, I was mowing in shorts and a halter top to encourage a tan on my pale skin. In the 1970's skin cancer was not yet an issue. As I crawled under the mower in an attempt to free the blades and inspect the extent of the ground center, I took no thought of the flora in which I was lying. It was a mistake.

After freeing the mower, I finished the job, finally exhausting myself and returned to the house to shower and have a cold beer. The next morning I was miserable, covered with red welts and itching beyond comprehension. As the day progressed, the itching became unbearable. My personality changed. I drove 12 miles to town and the small hospital emergency room where I was diagnosed with poison oak and given a shot of Benadryl. I barely made it home, desperately trying to stay awake before I fell into the comfort of my double bed in the loft. The pills the doctor gave me helped, but I spent a miserable week fighting the urge to scratch off my skin.

Not long after, I drove to Laredo with a girlfriend. She had never been to Mexico. We took a taxi across the border, shopped and had an enchilada dinner, enhanced by a few margaritas. I used the restroom. Back in Livingston, on the lake, my crotch began to itch. I knew it wasn't the poison oak and discovered tiny red things making their home in my pubic hair. I first thought it was red bugs/chiggers or tiny seed ticks. When I examined the critters closely, they resembled tiny crabs.

Roundtrip from Texas

My first instinct as a woman living alone was that I could solve the problem. I tried just about everything I had in the house before I resorted to the Clorox. God forbid I drive into town and tell the pharmacist I had crabs. After all, it was the 70's.

Soaking in a strong bath of Clorox is not pleasant. It burned but I conquered the nasty critters and my crotch returned to normal. I never told anyone about it, too embarrassed.

Many years later, I moved to west Texas. There, I encountered big ticks, scorpions, spiders, centipedes, hornets and killer bees. Having my husband John with me helped. He picked the ticks off my back, and then I realized that many itches were in places that were unseen and hard to find and scratch.

Six months after a supposedly simple cataract surgery, I managed to detach my retina while tilling the garden. After working myself tired, I returned to the house to discover that I was blind in the left eye. Thinking I'd ruptured a blood vessel, I went to the computer and researched. That was when I knew I had detached the retina. The information was alarming. Time was of the essence, like several days, if I wanted to save the eye.

Early the next morning, I drove to Uvalde for an emergency eye appointment with the ophthalmologist. He confirmed my diagnosis and made an appointment with a retina specialist in San Antonio. I continued on to San Antonio, where again the detached retina was diagnosed. Surgery was scheduled for the next day. The surgery was successful; a bubble was inserted into my eye, along with a silicon belt to keep the retina together. The retina is like layers of wallpaper and the belt is intended to secure the layers. The gas bubble is intended to push the retina back in place and cause it to reattach to the part of the eye where it belongs.

After the surgery, they sent me home to lie flat on my stomach for 22 hours a day to allow the bubble to press the retina in place. Fourteen days of this torture were required before the bubble dissolved. Since I could only be up for two hours per day, I divided the days and nights into segments. The first few days weren't too bad, but after the fourth day, I was unsure. As soon as I could detect movement in my eye, I knew I would recover, but the mental anguish of lying flat on my stomach became unbearable. I tried to sleep as much as possible. In order to sleep, I moved a barstool to the side of the bed, slept crossways and put my head on a pillow on the barstool and rested my eyes in the gap between the bed and barstool. I wished for a knockout pill that would last the days remaining. I didn't have one.

In retrospect, I think I had a mental breakdown, fought insanity and sanity in waves. I couldn't read, shunned TV and finally resorted to every audiobook the small library in Camp Wood had on the shelves. Then came the itch. The eye itched so badly that I wanted to scratch it out. I tried Benadryl. Nothing helped. I scratched all around the eye until the skin was raw.

By the twelfth day, I knew I would make it. And on the last day, I put on my tape of "Lonesome Dove" and spent eight hours crying and listening to my favorite movie, except for "The Searchers" with John Wayne. The bubble became a dot and then was gone. My vision returned, somewhat blurred, but I had vision.

Since there are few fire ants on the ranch, the red bugs/chiggers/no see 'ums are numerous. I warn visitors who hike to protect their skin from the pesky critters. Few listen. I keep remedies. Over the years, I have gone from nail polish to sulfur to diatomaceous earth to Absorbine Jr. The sulfur and earth are preventatives and Absorbine Jr. works after the fact. I've had guests who've scratch their legs raw before they'd admit there is a problem.

I still manage to claw the skin on my ankles before the remedy works. It usually takes a few days.

When I stepped on a centipede for the first time I thought my foot would fall off. The pain was worse than a scorpion's sting. I made a paste of toothpaste and baking soda. When that didn't alleviate the pain, I resorted to an ice pack. That helped. I kept the paste on too. Once the worst was over, a severe itch occurred. It was so bad I wanted to scratch off the skin on the bottom of my foot. I prefer a scorpion or hornet sting.

The most recent itch occurred after a tetanus shot. The itch was top of the scale. The welts were huge red lumps all over my arm. The rash spread to my stomach area. I resorted to Benadryl and went to bed to sleep it off and allow my immune system to take over. Eventually, the rash disappeared.

I hope it's quite a while before I have another itch. In fact just thinking about it makes me itch.

20

Vietnam and Cambodia

As I stepped off the plane in Hanoi, Vietnam, shortly after midnight, that old familiar feeling intruded. What had I done to myself? I'd never see my children, grandchild, family and Texas again. I always seem to resist the first few days of a trip before I immerse.

The flight had been long but comfortable for a change. I had flown coach to Los Angeles and then flew business class to Seoul, Korea, and then on to Hanoi. Korean Airways was quite comfortable. My chair folded down into a bed and the service was exceptional, the flight attendants young, beautiful and smiling, in contrast to my fellow passengers, mostly Koreans who never smiled or spoke except with each other.

Nevertheless, the flight time had been over 20 hours. I was ready to stretch out on a soft bed. The airport in Hanoi was modern but quiet, absent of the bustling activity in most countries' main airports. I later understood the reason. The citizens of a Communist country cannot travel freely and Vietnam is one of five Communist countries in the world. The other four are Cuba, North Vietnam, Laos and China.

The hotel was luxurious, with lovely tropical landscaping and a central courtyard. After a short night of sleep, I emerged at the bank of elevators and pushed the first button I saw. Unfortunately, I realized too late that I had pushed the fire alarm button. At first, I hoped that it didn't work and then I worried that it would. I casually pushed the correct button and descended in the elevator and entered the lobby. Expecting the alarm bells momentarily, I strolled out to the courtyard and admired the landscaping.

Reassured that the hotel would not be evacuated, I entered the dining room for breakfast. The display was lavish and plentiful, the food exactly what I had been prepared for. There were all sorts of fish dishes cooked every way possible. Pho, the Vietnamese soup with noodles, rice dishes, cheeses, grilled tomatoes, beans, lovely fresh fruit and assorted vegetables occupied the buffet tables. French pastries, sushi, omelets cooked to order, pancakes, French toast and interesting breads completed the spread. I ate lightly, dining on pho, fruit and fish.

I met my guide, Mr. Thinh, in the lobby and embarked on a city tour. His English was better than any I had encountered so far, but I had to listen closely to understand. He was a man in his 40's and very kind and gentle.

During a short lecture, I learned that Vietnam is a little larger in area than Italy and almost the size of Germany. Vietnam has a population of more than 84 million and is the world's 13th most populous country.

North Vietnam enjoys the weather of the four seasons, whereas South Vietnam is predominantly sub-equatorial with two main seasons, the wet, rainy season and the dry season.

The Vietnam currency is the dong. One United States dollar buys about 20,000 dong. Dollars were accepted everywhere.

The traffic was intimidating. The population of Hanoi is 6 million. There are 3 million motor scooters in Hanoi, each carrying one to four persons. They clog the lanes. Horns honk and the traffic moves slowly. Helmets are required.

I spent the morning visiting the Temple of Literature, the Ho Chi Minh Mausoleum, the One Pillar Pagoda and Ba Dinh Square. The Ho Chi Minh Mausoleum is a massive structure that houses the embalmed body of Ho Chi Minh. Upon entering the mausoleum, talking is not allowed, shoes must be removed and head and shoulders must be covered. Being dead, he didn't look that good.

Following the walk through the mausoleum, we entered the surrounding park, which contains the modest house on stilts in which he lived, as well as the presidential palace where state ceremonies take place.

I toured the oldest university in Vietnam, dating from 1,000 A.D. It has been restored with foreign donations. President Clinton attended the opening of the now tourist destination. The flowers and landscaping were quite delicate and lavish. The park was full of Vietnamese tourists. Few Americans or Europeans were visible.

Vendors waited outside the gates, selling tee shirts for $3, fans two for $1 and embroidered tote bags for $2. I purchased a tote bag and two fans.

I learned from my guide that citizens pay 10% income tax over $500 and that most Vietnamese convert their money to gold and keep it in their homes. Robbery is not a problem because families live together in the same house, each generation occupying a floor. There is always someone at home. The homes are less than 30 feet wide but are multi-storied, some four and five stories high. The youngest generation always lives on the top floor because they can climb the stairs easier. Land is sold by the square meter and is very expensive.

Walking in the morning August heat and humidity was miserable. I was soaking wet. Having left the heat of Texas, I thought I could certainly survive the heat of Vietnam. My 50-cent fan most likely saved my life.

As I was suffering the heat of Hanoi, I thought of our young men and women during the Vietnam War walking through the jungles in uniforms with pounds of equipment on their backs, and I felt bad for the waste and oppression of war. Better for the opposing leaders to have a duel than destroy so many lives.

Following a light soup lunch, I embarked on a rickshaw ride. My bicycle navigator was old and wiry, with muscled legs. We set off from the hotel for the French Quarter. I had not realized the peril of riding behind a bicycle in the frantic Hanoi traffic. There I was with no protection in the midst of motor scooters, cars and trucks on the streets of Hanoi with no red lights or no stop signs. I tried not to pay attention but rather enjoyed the sensory delights of the city. I left the rickshaw in the French Quarter and walked among the many stalls that lined the narrow streets, observing live eels in buckets, frogs with their legs tied with twine, fresh crabs, fish of all kinds, shrimp, fresh meat, fruits and vegetables. Laundry stalls advertised one kilo of laundry, 2.2 pounds, could be washed for $1. I continued through the French Quarter and visited the Jade Emperor Temple and observed the Huc Bridge.

At the end of my walk, I attended a water puppet show in a theater. The puppets performed on water, the stage being a large pool. The puppets were controlled by cables behind a curtain. There were horses, dragons and elaborately costumed people dancing on top of the water. The puppets and the show and synchronicity of the performance was amazing. At the end of the show, the puppeteers came from behind the water stage, wading in the waist deep water to take a bow, displaying the cables with which they controlled the characters. I have never witnessed anything like it. It was a highlight of the trip. That evening, I dined on vegetable spring rolls with garlic, light but very tasty.

For breakfast I feasted on noodles with herbs, a rice pancake rolled over beef and herbs, fresh mango, papaya and watermelon chased by a shot of fruit smoothie. Most of the fellow diners were British. I found a copy of the international paper and read about judicial reform and improved maritime facilities featured in the Vietnamese headlines. Following breakfast, I joined a group of 13 on a coach ride to Ha Long Bay in the Gulf of Tonkin, traveling north from Hanoi. There were Americans, a couple from Ireland and a lady from Venezuela

The guide lectured during the ride, informing us that 75% of the population are farmers, that Vietnam inflicts a 10% value-added tax on all goods purchased and that ladies cover their hands to keep them white and use whitening cream. Corn, rice, tapioca and sweet potatoes are grown.

In the past, the Communist government allowed only three suits of clothes. The material was given to the citizen. The citizen then hired a tailor or sewed their clothing.

Books are censored. The guide told us of a book he wanted to read. It could not be sent into the country. Instead, a tourist brought the book to him.

His life story was interesting. Part of his family was South Vietnamese and part from the north. They fought on both sides of the war. His uncle spent 10 years in a re-education center and his father spent three years being re-educated. His mother fled with him to the Thailand border but could not cross because of the land mines. He spent 13 years in a refugee camp on the Vietnamese/Thailand border and attributed his success in life to the United States and the United Nations, who educated him, taught him English and kept him fed. When he returned to Saigon, now Ho Chi Minh City, he was drafted into the army. Being of South Vietnamese origin, he was given the dirtiest work, clearing land mines in Cambodia for 18 months. He witnessed many of his friends being killed and observed that the bad memories caused the soldiers to become mentally ill.

The Vietnamese pay for education and health care. Many of them use herbal medicines, lemon grass and eucalyptus. Family culture is strong.

Snakes are very much a part of the culture. Wine is mixed with the blood of the snake and drunk for male vigor. The beating heart of a snake is also eaten. If a poisonous snake bites them, they cut off the finger that was bitten.

As we observed the rice fields being tended with equipment pulled by water buffalo, the guide said that water buffalo have no upper teeth. He then told a mythological story about why the water buffalo has no upper teeth. I could not quite follow his English.

Coal and hydroelectricity furnish power. The Vietnamese do not trust the Chinese to the north. They purchase power from China, and it's in short supply. China is currently building dams along the Mekong River, north of Vietnam, adversely affecting the water levels and migration of silt.

Along the route, we stopped for a bathroom break. Our guide called the bathroom the happy house because after you come out you feel happy.

The guide spoke of the effects of Agent Orange. Three generations later, the birth defects are still in evidence.

I was quite surprised to hear that Vietnam is second in world production of coffee beans, first in the production of pepper and second in the production of rice. Rubber is also produced in Vietnam.

The narrow road was congested with people, animals and vehicles. Progress was slow. The mountains were to the west. The morning was consumed by the 100-mile trip that lasted three hours. Traffic moved slowly on the narrow, uneven roads. Upon arrival at Ha Long Bay, I was surprised by the luxurious resorts and casinos. The guide informed us that the Chinese and Koreans vacationed on the bay in great numbers and that the Vietnamese are not allowed in the casinos. Rather, they bet on football and soccer games and travel to Cambodia to gamble.

When I asked the guide, "Have you ever been to America?" he replied that he cannot go to America. The government will not allow him to travel except to neighboring Cambodia, Laos, Thailand and China.

A tender took us to a teak Chinese junk festooned with mustard-colored sails. The boat was clean and luxurious. My stateroom was spacious and cool, a welcome relief from the oppressive heat.

Ha Long Bay is a designated UNESCO World Heritage Site and deserves the recognition. It is a bay of over 300 islands, dark green waters surrounded by cliffs and peaks. The sandy beaches were inviting. I half expected to see a hobbit or elf frolicking on the verdant islands.

Lunch was served on the boat: beef, shrimp, chicken and fish, delicately flavored with herbs. As the ship cruised the bay, a rain shower fell upon the boat and was followed by a rainbow, a beautiful visual serenade. I rode a small tender to an isolated beach. Some of the passengers swam; I waded into the green water and returned to sit on the beach and savor the beauty of the early evening.

A return to the ship and a wine tasting party previewed a dinner of elephant clams, caramel tarragon pork, garlic beef, chicken, shrimp and vegetables with rice and fruit. As we enjoyed dinner, the boat cruised among the islands.

The following morning we visited a floating village. We left the boat on tenders and were then rowed among the 100 floating homes occupied by over 600 residents. The school was also afloat. Solar power was in evidence. For work, the men and women fish. Many of the boats have no motors.

After a short stop to visit a cave, the boat returned to dock and the little group of 14 boarded a coach for the return trip to the Hanoi airport and a short flight to Siem Reap, Cambodia. The coach stopped midway for lunch at the Chi Linh Star Golf Resort, partly financed by the Arabs. As the coach arrived, a group of lovely young Vietnamese ladies stood outside, smiling and welcoming the bus. They were the caddies and quite disappointed that we were not a busload of golfers.

The lunch consisted of pho soup, pizza bread and French fries, not very Vietnamese but adequate. At the golf course, we lost one of our travelers to an ambulance that transported a lady to the hospital in Hanoi. She had awoken with a loss of long-term memory, very disoriented. Fortunately, one of the passengers on the boat was a Spanish doctor honeymooning with his new wife. He examined her and recommended that she be sent to the hospital for tests. Her companion accompanied her.

As we arrived at the not busy Hanoi airport, another of the ladies became ill, very ill with diarrhea and vomiting. The situation was messy. The airline declined to let her on the plane, so she was sent to the hospital in Hanoi. We later learned that both ladies were hospitalized for a few days and sent home for further testing.

Cambodia

The flight to Siem Reap was an hour and a half. A lavish meal for such a short flight was served. Our number had shrunk to eleven. On the flight down into Siem Reap, we flew through cloud cover as the sun was setting. Every window was covered in pink or orange. It was a surreal introduction to the famous site of Angkor Wat.

The Sofitel Resort in Siem Reap was an absolutely beautiful tropical lush resort. Everywhere there were attractive young people in native costumes bowing with hands clasped, greeting us in French. The resort surrounded flowering ponds, bridges and walkways lined with greenery.

The evening meal was served in a private dining room crested with three layers of decorative wooden molding, with native dancers and singers performing throughout the dinner. We were served fruit, fish, chicken, beef and pork and finished the meal with French pastries.

Due to the expansiveness of the elaborate resort, each of us was personally escorted to our rooms. Mine had a private balcony overlooking one of the ponds. On my bed was a silk scarf and chocolate truffles. On the table by the patio was a bowl of fresh fruit. I slept in heaven.

Breakfast was served early. Everything imaginable was available. I began with pho, roasted pork and garlic and fresh fruit. The chef cooked omelets. Beans, curry, cheeses, bread and rice were served. The buffet was fully 60 feet of feasts. I traversed over the bridges, through the gazebos and between the blooming lotus to my room to prepare for a day in the temple ruins.

We began with a visit to the ticket center, where we were given a badge that admitted us to all the temple grounds. The cost was $40. We moved on in our small coach to the south gate of Angkor Thom, where we began our walk through Angkor Thom. Monkeys pestered us from all sides.

Cambodia was the richest and biggest country in the world from the 9th century to the 13th century. In 1863, Cambodia became a French protectorate. In 1953, the French returned Cambodia to its citizens.

We spent the entire morning walking the steamy jungle ruins of Angkor Thom. It was magnificent, with stone carvings of everyday life in contrast to the carvings at Angkor Wat, which display images from the Hindu religion.

Angkor Thom thrived in the 12th to 13th century and is a vast temple and palace complex, which also includes Bayon, Baphoun, the Terrace of the Leper King and the Elephant Terrace, all of which we visited.

Returning to the hotel, I dined on pho, the soup I found so tasty, and took a short nap before rejoining the group for a trip to Bantey Srei. The road was narrow and bumpy as we journeyed through rice fields, observing thatched huts on stilts with no electricity. Car batteries are charged for TV viewing. The road was lined with cashew trees and sugar palms. Few cars were on the road, mostly just bicycles and motor scooters.

Along the route, I observed open-air furniture stores featuring carved furniture of ironwood and rosewood.

The Cambodian guide lectured during the trip. Forty-seven percent of Cambodians attend primary school. Education is not compulsory and the country is not literate. The Cambodian language has 73 characters in its alphabet.

Bantey Srei is a pink carved stone temple palace dedicated to women. The ruins were in excellent shape and the cloud cover prevented the extreme heat we endured during the morning tour.

Since the noon meal is the main meal in southeast Asia, we dined lightly that evening. The meal began with raw fish. The main course was sea bass wrapped in a banana leaf and baked with sticks of ginger. Dragon fruit served with cheese completed the meal. Dragon fruit is white with black specks or red with black specks and tastes similar to kiwi.

The evening gift in my room was a woven basked with rose petals, chocolate truffles and more fresh fruit.

Following the breakfast buffet fit for kings and queens, we visited Angkor Wat. Angkor Wat is the largest temple complex in the world. A 60-foot-wide man-made moat filled with water surrounds the complex. The entrance is a bridge across the moat to a massive carved stone gate and walls. After a long walk across the open space, we approached the Hindu Temple complex, with its many rooms, towering spires and courtyards. We spent hours wandering through the ruins and admiring them before returning to the coach for a ride to Ta Phrom, a temple complex located in the area and built by a king for his mother. The movie "Tomb Raiders," with Angelina Jolie, was filmed in this complex. A walk through the jungle took me to the complex overgrown with roots and trees from the encroaching tropical forest. While many of the stones lie disassembled, much of the complex is still standing. The roots of the towering trees were features to be admired.

We returned to the hotel for a scheduled free afternoon. Skipping lunch, I rented a tuk tuk for the remainder of the day with an adventurous lady from Florida. A tuk tuk is a motor scooter that propels a four-seater canopy-covered vehicle. His price for the remainder of the day was $10. We first returned to the ruins for an elephant ride through the jungle. We found the elephant by the ruins of Angkor Thom. With dread, I anticipated climbing on an elephant, but it was surprisingly easy. The elephant stood by the tree. We climbed a wooden staircase and crawled from the platform built around the tree to the wide seat on his back.

Of course, we wanted pictures, so we engaged a young man through a series of laughable hand gestures to follow us through the jungle on his bicycle and take pictures with my camera. The ride lasted nearly an hour. There were ancient ruins at every turn through the jungle. The affable elephant browsed on trees. At the end of the ride, my friend purchased a kilo of bananas, which we fed into his mucus-filled trunk. Laughter filled the scene.

We then traveled to the main market of Siem Reap and shopped for jewelry, spices and silk shirts. Fresh fruit sold for 50 cents a kilo. The purchases were quite inexpensive. Our tuk tuk driver then took us to a restaurant, where we ate a full evening meal accompanied by beer and wine. The bill for both of us was $12. I chose fish and green curry. The choice was a good one. On the way back to the hotel, we stopped at another jewelry store, where my companion purchased some Cambodian rubies, beautiful gemstones. The day spent with the tuk tuk driver was so much fun that we tipped him $5. The annual per capita income of Cambodia is less than $900 per year. The people are Buddhist and very sweet and pleasant.

While in Siem Reap, I learned that 2.4 million tourists visit Angkor Wat per year and that not many of them visit Phnom Penh, the capital of Cambodia. Most of the visitors are from Vietnam, with Korea and Japan ranking next. America is fourth and Australia is fifth.

I also discovered that the words wat, temple, pagoda and monastery are interchangeable.

Sonja Klein

The following morning after the usual breakfast feast, we boarded a coach that delivered the 11 of us to the river barge that was to be home for the next seven days, the La Marguerite. There, we joined 55 other passengers for a cruise through Tonle Sap Lake onto the Tonle Sap River and then down the Mekong River to Saigon, now known as Ho Chi Minh City.

As we cruised the lake, I noticed an unbroken stream of houses on stilts along the river. Fish were drying on the roofs. The children threw kisses. Commercial fishing is not allowed from June to September. I learned from the guide that millions of people live along the lakes and rivers and that Cambodia is a farming culture. Only 10% of the population works for the government. Cambodia exports many tons of rice per year.

Our Cambodian guide tendered a lecture in the lounge of the comfortable riverboat. The Cambodian flag stands for universal compassion, the middle path, blessings, purity, liberation and wisdom. Cambodia was formerly the Kingdom of Kampuchea and is about the size of Oklahoma. Laos, Thailand and Vietnam border the country. The waters of the South China Sea and the Gulf of Thailand touch Cambodia. The capital, Phnom Penh, has a population of about 2 million.

The Mekong River flows through the country, beginning in Tibet and flowing through China, Burma, Thailand, Laos, Cambodia and Vietnam. It is 4,200 kilometers long. The Mekong River is home to near 60 million people in the countries through which it meanders. Over half a million tons of fish are harvested per year.

A national event is held every November in Cambodia, the Festival of the Water and the Moon. The festival is famous for its dragon boat races. Over 400 dragon boats manned by 60 to 70 men and women compete.

Before 1863, the only education available was for boys, who were taught in the Buddhist temples. Their curriculum consisted of religious education, didactic poems, folktales and the Sanskrit epic, *Ramayana*. When the French colonized Cambodia in the mid-nineteenth century, they built schools. Though the children can begin school at the age of three, education is not compulsory. There is a shortage of schools, but the students can move up by passing exams. College tuition is $450 per year.

In the past, marriages were arranged but not now. Wedding dresses are colored and the day of the wedding is chosen by first consulting a fortune teller. Funerals are held in the homes and white is the color of mourning. The bodies are cremated and the ashes are kept at home. Ceremonies of mourning occur seven days after the death, 100 days after death and then on a yearly schedule.

The French occupied Cambodia from 1863 to 1953. Why? The Angkor civilization collapsed in the 1400's. Cambodia's neighbors began to invade the country. The Khmer king petitioned the French government for protection, and the country became a French protectorate. In 1887 the French forced Cambodia to sign over Indochina—Vietnam, Laos and Cambodia. And in 1941 the French chose King Sihanouk. The people respected the king.

After the French left Cambodia, the king was overthrown by General Lon Nol who ruled from 1970 to 1975. During that time, North Vietnamese troops were traveling across Cambodia to fight in South Vietnam. As a result, the United States dropped 20 million bombs on Cambodia, killing 600,000 Cambodians.

In 1975 the Khmer came to power. Most Cambodians are Khmer, the natives. Pol Pot was a guerrilla fighter, educated in France and a Communist. He absorbed Maoist teachings from China and persuaded students to see the difference between the poor and the rich.

The American bombings made the Cambodians angry. They wanted equality. China and Pol Pot supported King Sihanouk. The king supported the Khmer army. Pol Pot ordered the evacuation of Phnom Penh, citing that the Americans were going to bomb the city. The city was evacuated in three days. No bombs fell. Pol Pot then massacred half the population, estimated to be over 2 million people, in an effort to return the country to an agrarian society. Frankly stated, he killed everyone who could read or write.

Four years later, in 1979, the Vietnamese army liberated Cambodia from the Pol Pot regime. Cambodia is forever grateful, and the two countries are very friendly.

In the aftermath of the Pol Pot regime, 389 killing fields, 200 prisons and over 20,000 mass graves have been discovered, some not excavated.

A new king was crowned in 2004, and Cambodia exists as a constitutional monarchy. Peace reigns.

Sonja Klein

When the lecture ended, my notebook was full. Some of the fellow passengers, most of them Australians, remarked that it was too much information. A few Americans agreed. I was shocked. I had traveled with Australians, been to their country. Never had I received too much information. From my fellow Americans, I was not surprised.

During the night, we cruised the lake and entered the Tonle Sap River. By dawn, we'd anchored midstream at Chong Koh village, a busy rural port town. Following a buffet breakfast equal to that at the hotel in Siem Reap, we took a motorboat past floating villages to the town and walked through the local market. For the first time in Cambodia, I saw the betel leaf, beans and lime. Vats of resin were offered for sale to be used for cooking. It was a visual and sensory heaven. The people were smiling and friendly. We returned to the boat and continued down the river to Kampong Tralach where we were met by oxcarts and after donning a polka dot rain poncho, I crawled onto the back of a wooden oxcart and held on for dear life as I traveled down a muddy path in a thunderstorm trusting my life to two Brahma cows. Every bump was a delight, and there were many.

At the end of the dirt path, a small bus drove us through the rice fields to Oudong, an elaborate and beautiful Buddhist monastery, funded primarily by Buddhists not currently living in Cambodia. After climbing the many marble steps in the rain, we removed our shoes and entered the monastery for a water blessing by three Buddhist monks. Sitting cross-legged on the carpet, I closed my eyes and went into a meditative state. I was startled by the drop of light pellets. Determined to stay meditative, I continued with my eyes closed until the chants ceased. When I opened my eyes, I was covered with jasmine blossoms. The fragrance was overwhelming.

The serenity dissolved when two of the group put on their closed-toe shoes and were stung by scorpions. So much for blessings. Wisely, I'd worn sandals.

We walked through a muddy field and were met at the ship by a crew of foot washers. Our shoes were removed and put aside to be cleaned, our feet were washed and we were shod with clean flip-flops. Later that evening, after an outstanding meal of pork with coconut milk and sea bass with tarragon, I found my sandals outside my stateroom door. It was days before they were dry. Luckily, I had another pair.

Later that evening, we were entertained by a movie depicting the life of Pol Pot. He wasn't a nice man. I fell asleep.

I awoke moored midstream near a small handicraft village, Chong Koh, located south of Phnom Penh. After the usual breakfast, we took a leisurely stroll through the silk-weaving village. The looms were set under the thatched houses and were worked by hand. The children followed us. I purchased silk scarves for $5, made onsite. They were very nice.

After we returned to the boat, we set sail for Phnom Penh. I spent an afternoon of leisure in the capital and largest city in Cambodia. Once known as the Pearl of Asia, Phnom Penh is considered one of the loveliest of French-built cities in Indochina. Founded in 1434, the city is noted for its beautiful architecture as seen in the Royal Palace and other French-style buildings. Situated on the Tonle Sap, Mekong and Bassac Rivers, Phnom Penh is home to more than two million of the 14 million inhabitants of Cambodia.

I took advantage of the leisurely afternoon and joined newly made friends for a tuk tuk ride to the central market. The shopping was fantastic. Anything imaginable was available, from knock-off Prada, Coach and Gucci handbags and wallets to silk dresses made in hours. The jewelry was intriguing and quite cheap. We returned to the ship with full bags.

The evening's entertainment was provided by local school children, who danced and sang Cambodian style.

The following day was emotional. I had decided to visit one of the killing fields and visit a prison used during the regime of Pol Pot. I had come to Vietnam and Cambodia to feel the effects of the war. A morning excursion took me to the Royal Palace built in 1866 as the home of the Cambodian king. Located on the grounds is Prasat Park, which means Silver Pagoda because over 5,000 pieces of its floor tiles are made from silver. Inside the pagoda is a masterpiece of a Buddha statue along with hundreds of antique gifts, works of art and sculpture. The Buddha is made from pure gold, has 2,086 diamonds attached to it and weighs over 90 kilograms, close to 200 pounds of pure gold. It was magnificent.

After the Royal Palace, I visited the Cambodia National Museum, which features art, statues and sculptures dating from the pre-Angkor era through the 20th century as well as antique traditional dancing clothes, weapons and the king's bed.

Sonja Klein

Following another fabulous Cambodian lunch, I joined a coach tour for a ride to the killing fields of Choeung Ek, located about 10 miles from the city. The ride lasted about 30 minutes while our guide lectured.

I learned that life expectancy in Cambodia is 59 years for men and 61 for women, that unemployment for people between the ages of 15 and 24 is 61% and factory workers earn $3 per day. We drove through the factories on the outskirts of town. As we left the city, the rice fields and banana trees dominated the landscape.

The Killing Fields were a number of sites in Cambodia where large numbers of people were killed and buried during the Khmer Rouge regime. The Cambodian Genocide Program was one of the worst human tragedies of the last century. Pol Pot is sometimes described as the Hitler of Cambodia and a genocidal tyrant.

As we pulled into the parking lot, a quiet hush descended upon the bus. As I stepped out of the bus, the most horrible smell pervaded the air. I will never forget that smell. It was the smell of death. Ahead was a four-story glassed enclosure about 10 feet square stacked with human skulls. I put my camera away. The path through the partially excavated area was well defined. Bits of bone and teeth as well as clothing leached out of the earth. There were glass boxes stationed along the path to deposit what one might pick up. I felt death and fear.

When I commented on the smell, the guide replied that a village dump was located in the vicinity and that the smell was from the dump. It didn't matter. I returned to the bus as quickly as possible.

On the return trip to the city, our guide told his personal story. His parents were teachers. They were taken away when he was seven and killed. He never saw them again. He was blindfolded and thrown into the back of a truck and driven 10 hours to a re-education center, where he remained for two years. At the age of nine, he was sent back to his village, where he no longer knew anyone, and given a rifle and taught to shoot at live running targets. Then he was sent to the prison to clean the buckets of feces and urine from the cells and to witness the tortures. He admitted that he still has nightmares.

He told us that he remembers being so hungry as a soldier that he picked up a kernel of corn from the ground and put it in his mouth. Another soldier told him to spit it out, but it was too late. He was hit on the head with a rifle butt and lay unconscious for days. A Cambodian woman saved his life.

Returning to the city, we visited the S21 Detention Center, home of the Tuol Sleng Genocide Museum, located in the former Tuol Svay Prey High School, only a kilometer or so from the city center. It was used as the notorious Security Prison 21 by the Khmer Rouge regime from 1975 to 1979. Many of the schoolrooms were divided into cells. At any one time, the prison held up to 1,500 people. They were repeatedly tortured and coerced into naming family members, who were in turn arrested, tortured and killed.

Again, I put my camera away and left as soon as possible. It was a sad place. The pictures were gruesome beyond description.

To dispel the somber mood, the ship hosted a DJ dance. Some of the tunes played were "The Twist," "YMCA" and "La Bamba."

After a hearty morning breakfast, the ship sailed for the border crossing into Vietnam. The day was spent cruising the main Mekong channel, an international shipping route.

My morning treat was a Cambodian massage. The young girl crawled on my back and rubbed the kinks out of my worn body with strong hands. She was working to send money home to her family. The massage was among the best I ever received.

The afternoon lecture began with "Welcome to Vietnam." The history of Vietnam began around 2,700 years ago. Successive dynasties based in China ruled Vietnam directly for most of the period from 111 B.C. until 938 A.D., when Vietnam regained its independence. Vietnam remained a tributary state to its larger neighbor, China, for much of its history but repelled invasions by the Chinese as well as three invasions by the Mongols between 1255 and 1285. The independent period temporarily ended in the mid- to late 19th century. During World War II, Imperial Japan expelled the French to occupy Vietnam.

Rather than peaceful reunification, partition led to the Vietnam War. During this time, the People's Republic of China and the Soviet Union supported the North, while the United States supported the South. After millions of deaths, the war ended with the fall of Saigon to the North in April 1975. The reunified Vietnam suffered further internal repression and was isolated internationally due to the continuing Cold War and the Vietnamese invasion of Cambodia. In 1986, the Communist Party of Vietnam changed its economic policy and began reforms of the private sector similar to those in China. Since the mid-1980's, Vietnam has enjoyed substantial economic growth and some reduction in political repression, though reports of corruption have risen.

Indochina is the former French colonial empire in southeast Asia. Having gained early influence in establishing the Vietnamese empire in the early 19th century, the French colonized the area between late 1850 and 1890, using the term "Indochina" to designate the final union of their colonies and dependencies within Annam, Cambodia, Cochin-China, Laos and Tonkin. Nationalist movements sprang up between the world wars, and the collaboration of the Vichy colonial administration with the Japanese fatally undermined the French influence in the area in the early 1940's. French rule ended in 1954.

Vietnam

Having entered Vietnam, the ship stopped at Tan Chau, a small town untouched by tourism. The day began with a rickshaw tour as we visited factories making rattan mats and slippers. The factories were primitive, but the products were charming. We then went by motorboat, navigating narrow channels, to an evergreen island. There we walked the dirt path through the jungle to a small village. The people live in thatched huts on stilts. Again, no electricity was in evidence. The children appeared healthy and happy. We then traveled to a floating fish farm, where fish are caged under a floating platform. The family purchases fingerlings and feeds them five times a day. After several months, when their weight has reached about two pounds, they are sold and processed for the European market for about $1.20 per kilo.

The evening performance of Mekong folklore was better than dessert. The day had been quite full.

The ship left the town of Tan Chau as we cruised the river to Sa Dec. In Sa Dec, we disembarked for a walking tour and visited the old house of Huynh Thuy Le, now known as the Lovers' Museum. The story of the love of a Chinese man and a young Vietnamese girl was portrayed in a movie called, "The Lovers."

From the museum, we walked to the local market, where vendors sell live grub worms, live eel, frogs, rats and what I call minnows. Ladies sit on the ground and, with a tiny pair of scissors, behead and gut the tiny minnows. Tarantulas were also available, deep-fried.

Leaving the market we drove an hour inland to Xeo Quy, a site located in the villages of My Hiep and My Long in Cao Lanh district, where I spent an hour walking the narrow dirt path over twig bridges, the jungle growth uncomfortably close. It is an area of 50 hectares, including more than 20 hectares of cajuput forest. From 1960 to 1975, the Province Party Committee of Kien Phong chose this locality as a base to lead the province's people to contribute their strength to the anti-French and U.S. resistance. Formerly, this place was a wasteland covered by wild grass. The cajuput forests have been restored and expanded.

After returning to the boat and a wonderful lunch, we sailed to Cai Be, a town of 275,000, best known for its floating market. Although the wares on sale were not that unusual, the manner of shopping was, as every part of the transaction was conducted on the water. The stallholders sold from larger boats, hanging out tasting samples from poles while shoppers milled about on smaller craft.

The entire scene took place against the photogenic backdrop of Cai Be's 19th century French Gothic Cathedral. We left our tender to visit a rice-paper mill and a coconut candy factory in Cai Be, walking the narrow streets. We observed rice being popped over an open fire and made into candy, similar to the familiar rice-crispy candy we enjoy. We were shown the process of making rice paper used to construct spring and vegetable rolls. The samples were quite good.

The following morning, we docked in Ho Chi Minh City, formerly know as Saigon. Because of being South Vietnamese, our guide called it Saigon in private. In public, he referred to it as Ho Chi Minh City for political reasons. The city is home to 8 million people and 4 million motor scooters. The traffic was extremely congested at all hours of the day, with few traffic lights or stop signs. Those that do exist are widely ignored. Riding in a taxi was a nightmare. Rainfall is 72 inches a year and the climate is tropical with 75% humidity.

We visited the Notre Dame Cathedral, the city post office, the Thien Hau Pagoda, the presidential palace and the Bin Tay Market and enjoyed a seven-course meal before checking into the hotel.

Since the afternoon was free, I joined three others in hiring a taxi to take us to the Cu Chi Battlefield and underground tunnel system, north of Saigon. We had been assured that the ride would last 20 minutes. Twenty had become a humorous number. Anytime we asked

99

how long, the answer was always 20 minutes. Never was it actually 20 minutes. This trip lasted an hour and a half. The Ben Duoc underground tunnel complex is over 250 kilometers long. The entrances were well disguised as we followed the guide through the jungle. The torturous, killing devices rigged with spikes were on display. A battlefield tank was hidden under camouflage. I found it difficult listening to the guide from my American standpoint. Other tourists were mostly European and Oriental. The documentary movie at the end of the tour was very anti-American. To the Vietnamese, their people were heroes.

The return trip in the evening traffic was arduous, as we passed through the suburbs observing the factory workers going home. A light dinner put me to bed.

I spent the last day in Saigon shopping with friends. Silk shirts, spices, puppets, inexpensive jewelry, leather goods and carvings filled my suitcase to capacity. To occupy a long afternoon, I spent time in a Saigon beauty parlor. For $49, I was treated to a pedicure, foot massage, manicure, hand massage and a shampoo and blow dry. The pampering was delicious. My plane left Saigon near midnight, the first leg of a long journey home.

As I reflected during the long flights and layovers, the food of Cambodia and Vietnam was the best I had ever eaten. Great attention is paid to spices and presentation. The food is always fresh, most likely fresher than we obtain at our local grocery stores. The people eat healthfully and their appearance tells the story. There are no fat people in southeast Asia.

The trip had been one of learning and silent humility. While we complain of a hangnail, these people have endured hardships beyond description. Never have I been so happy to be an American.

21

Cities and Boulevards

I don't know why I always write about the wide boulevards, parks and flowers of every foreign city I visit. Somehow, I am always surprised to see that the flowers I grow in my yard are the same across the world.

Having traveled extensively, I would begin to think that I would tire of the big cities. Each and every one of them has wide streets, parks and monuments to soldiers, leaders and other notables. All cities are proud of their edifices of worship, whether it be the temples of Angkor Wat, the Buddhist monasteries of Bhutan, the cathedrals of the Christian world or the mosques of Morocco.

Every large city has a historical museum and an art museum, as well as nature displays full of stuffed animals and birds native to the country. Most have specialty museums too, like the carpet museum in Turkmenistan, the ceramic museum in Morocco, the music museum in I forgot where and replicated villages depicting how the inhabitants lived in the old days.

I'm more concerned about the political, economic and social situations of the countries I visit. I have usually read and studied the history before I leave my ranch.

I want to learn who they are now, what they're doing and where they might go in the future. I travel for the now, as well as the past.

Of course, it's always breathtaking to view the wonders: the ancient temples, grand palaces and magnificent ruins of which I've read.

The works of nature can only satisfy so much. I don't care if I ever see another waterfall, a big lake, a glacier, a giant tree or a big rock that looks like something other than a big rock.

And then there is always the native dance troupe. God spare me if I ever have to see another native dance troupe. The production is always the same. They dance in native costumes, with artificially painted faces and frolic about; and near the end, they pull members out of the audience to join them, where everyone makes fools of themselves smiling and laughing.

Sonja Klein

My favorite destinations to visit in cities are the food stalls, flower shops and open markets. There I can mingle with the people, see what they eat and drink, how they dress, what they have to sell and who is doing the buying and selling. In addition, I always ask for samples. Some of my favorite memories involve sampling varieties of honey in Tajikistan and Tasmania, eating roasted acorns in Morocco, sampling slivovitz in Serbia, olives in Turkey, marinated eggplant in Egypt and golden dates in Syria.

Why do I travel? I don't know. Maybe I'm trying to escape, or maybe I crave to be free. I do know that I travel to meet people from other cultures who are different than me, but what I always discover is that inside we are all the same. We care about our families, we eat and drink, we worship a higher power, we know we should be good and we dress for comfort according to the climate. That is the now and that is where I hope to stay.

22

Truth

I was innocently and calmly watching the local evening news. The featured story was about a woman who had killed her toddling child. The broadcaster reported with serious words, "Three to five children nationwide are killed every week by parents or step-parents."

I sat erect and spoke out loud, "What? Three to five?" That's a big percentage difference and a wide range. Where do those figures come from? It's very simple math; take the total number and divide by 52. The answer cannot be three to five. What a fucking lie. And we all sit like sheep and believe the bullshit figures the media, politicians and informed authorities spout off with confidence.

I have arrived at the point of not believing anything I see on TV, read in the paper or hear on the streets. In the last 10 years, I have seen the death of truth. Everyone lies on a daily basis.

Being a numbers person, I find the falsehoods with numbers most awful. Budget projections, statistics, body counts and raw data can all be manipulated. We have a tendency to believe specific numbers when, in fact, they lie.

We all lie on a daily basis. I call my daughter and ask, "What are you doing?"

She answers, "Working on the computer." I hear water running. She's probably in the bathroom. How hard is it to say, "I'm in the bathroom, Mother."

She in turn asks, "What are you up to?"

Playing the game of untruths, I reply, "Working on my latest book." The truth is I have been playing dominoes on the computer. Why can't I say it? Because we all answer with words that make us look good or we answer with what we think the questioner wants us to say. How stupid.

We lie about why we are late, why we weren't in church, why we can't attend a wedding shower, why we don't pay our bills on time or why we didn't accomplish a task on time.

How easy it is to tell the truth. How about answers like, "I couldn't decide what to wear. I had a hangover. I dislike wedding showers and think they are stupid. I spent the money on clothes. I didn't want to do it."

Instead, we lie and think nothing of it, don't even consider it a lie. We think a lie is more like, "I didn't have sex with him. I don't have a sexually transmitted disease. My blood pressure is always normal. I don't have a problem with my weight. I always eat healthy. I don't smoke pot. I haven't had a speeding ticket in years."

If lies made our noses grow, we'd all be deformed. We expect people to lie, confirming silently, 'I know he's lying.' And then we think that it's okay, that everyone does it. It is not okay. Truth should reign supreme.

23

The garden

I've always had a garden, no matter where I lived. In my first apartment, fresh out of college and teaching school, I found some hard bare earth out behind the apartment complex. I hoed and scratched to loosen the dirt and planted some peppers and tomatoes. I spent hours and hard-earned dollars for a few puny tomatoes and peppers. It was satisfying.

I've had vegetables growing in pots. I've purchased tillers and worked until my body ached, spent hundreds of dollars for $10 worth of produce, but I have to grow food. I am descended from many generations of farmers. It's that simple. In fact, it is so simple that all three of my brothers have to grow food too. We also plant fruit trees. Often we neglect our gardens, but by God, we have to plant a garden whether it produces lavishly or scantily.

I once grew a full head of cauliflower. That was exciting. I've never had much luck with eggplant, no matter where I lived. One year I grew a bumper crop of carrots, almost 10 pounds. They were sweet. Every few years I forget and plant green beans. They are very tiresome to pick and don't have that much flavor. Squash, I do well, tomatoes, not so well. The bugs usually eat them before they mature. I have the best luck with the cherry tomatoes and Roma tomatoes. Peppers and okra perform great, both of which are among my favorites.

My daughter is a much better gardener. She faithfully weeds the garden and pulls off diseased leaves and treats the plants with fish oil and rapid-bloom formulas. She installs an underground drip system and lays down black cloth to combat the weeds. She fertilizes organically. She chooses the placement to avoid cross-pollinating. Her gardens are planned and well tended; however, she rarely picks the garden.

I'm quite the opposite. I plant the garden and leave it alone, picking it faithfully, tenderly lifting the leaf to see what Mother Nature has provided. The two of us make a good team.

Since Molly's come to live at the ranch, we've done round gardens, maze gardens and just plain straight row gardens. Every year after preparing the ground and planting the seeds, we stand in agreement, "This is the best garden ever."

This year we've gone a step further. Molly invested in a beehive, carefully building the box and ordering a variety of bees that are resistant to diseases. She has assured me, "If all the bees in the country die, we'll have our own to pollinate the garden and provide us with honey."

Every year, I realize that after purchasing the organic seeds, black cloth, supplies and new hoses and connections and paying for the tiller to be repaired that each squash costs about $10, tomatoes maybe $15 and so forth.

But by June, satisfaction reigns supreme. I cook a dinner of smothered goat or lamb chops, the meat raised on the ranch. The side dishes are baked butternut squash, smothered scalloped squash, cucumber salad with dill, roasted beets and butternut lettuce and tomatoes, all ingredients fresh from the garden. I raise herbs up at my house on the hill. There's not enough dirt for a full garden.

Our rabbit enterprise didn't go so well. We built a hutch and started breeding rabbits for food. We love eating rabbit. After eating the first of them, the remaining breeder killed her first litter and then ate the second. We gave her away and abandoned the project.

Ducks, guineas, quail and chickens have replaced the rabbits. Somehow, a varmint entered the hutch and killed all the guineas, quail and ducks but three. A few of the chickens died.

A rooster and three hens grew to adulthood. My daughter moved away to complete her education. The rooster crowed every morning at 5:45 A.M. I found it comforting. I arise early. The chicken shit on the patio and outdoor furniture at the guest lodge was not. I gave the chickens away and turned the surviving ducks and quail loose.

From the garden, I pick several varieties of peppers, cherry tomatoes, okra and parsley. The squash succumbed to the heat. There were four cantaloupes. The coons ate two and left me two, an even split.

The fruit trees were doing well until a porcupine feasted on the young succulent bark. Wire cages around the base of the trees saved them. Rabbits discovered the okra plants and stripped the leaves from the lower stalks. I pick the upper okra; the rabbits eat the lower leaves. Sharing is good. Everyone gets a bite.

24

New Mexico

The cool mountain breeze of northern New Mexico had not yet reached the deck at my brother David's ranch, but the heat did not deter us from our first glass of wine and ceremonial toast for our July "land cruise." His wife Mary brought out the ceremonial cheese, crackers and cholesterol-saturated nuts.

I was the first to toast, having barely recovered from the 640-mile drive from my ranch in Texas. I insisted on driving because I habitually stopped in Pecos and purchased the famous flavorful Pecos cantaloupes and whatever fresh vegetables and fruit were on display. Once I reached northern New Mexico, I halted at a convenience store on a crossroads and purchased New Mexico raspberry cider and cherry cider.

On this, our fourth year, we were the only three. Brother John was coming later in the month for the opera season in Santa Fe and brother Allan and his wife Alma instead planned to travel to Costa Rica with her sons.

I made a toast, "Here's to family. Without you, there would have been no book. Just think, last year at this time, you gave me the courage to publish and before a year passed, I had a book. Thank you. Maybe next year I will have the second one finished."

The mountain air cooled, but the yearly afternoon shower was far away. Tecalote Creek, which never runs dry, was indeed dry in most places. The drought that covered Texas extended to New Mexico. There was no green grass.

Without Allan and Alma to regiment our evening meal, we instead performed like the children we all are. We snacked our way through dinner, relishing the rebellion.

But the following morning's guilt propelled us on a two-mile hike before the guests arrived. David and Mary had invited a couple, friends from Austin. They fit in quite well. The men grilled the meat and the women provided the side dishes. Wine flowed freely and the deck was our meeting point.

David, the interrogator, caught up on Sean and Kimberly's four children and family life. The proud parents spoke of their teenage twins, both at camp. Once the preliminaries were over, we surrendered to a few days of fun, four-wheeling, hiking and a trip into Las Vegas for Mexican food and a stroll around the central plaza. I mostly read and loafed and planned the meals.

Over the next few days, David met with his new foreman and drove around the ranch with Sean, and we entertained the foreman and his wife with grilled steaks and an evening of guitar music and storytelling. The best stories involved how the couples met, honeymoon adventures and anecdotes of children in high school and college, the scary stuff.

Most of the fun involved eating and cooking and drinking and sitting on the deck. One evening, we watched three coyotes yipping, yelling and playing below in the valley. We listened to the crows calling back and forth and witnessed the big blue jays cackling in the pinyon trees around the house. Hermitage Peak stood watchful in the distance.

After Sean and Kimberly left, Steve, a long time friend of David's, and his nine-year-old daughter arrived. We played silly card games: spoons, hearts, 99 and "Yea me, screw you." But we changed the name to "Yea me, bad for you" to accommodate the young girl. David and I played some straight dominoes. I won the majority of the domino games. It felt good. I wasn't very successful on the silly games, too German to enjoy them.

The evening deck talks and stories were frank and cathartic. We spoke of multiple marriages, painful divorces, travels, raising children and trying to fill holes in our souls. We solved the political and economic problems in the world and commiserated on the aging process. I gained new perspective, ideas for stories.

And then the land cruise was over. Facing the return 10-hour drive, I arose at daybreak and drove off, splashed through the creek, over the rocks and drove up the hill. The tire pressure light lit up the dashboard and then a giant red light saying stop the car and check the tires and then another yellow flashing icon illuminated the instrument panel. I panicked, turned around and drove back to the house, killed the engine and listened for a hissing sound. There was none. David and Mary were awake. It was 6:30 A.M.

Even with David's assurance that the cool morning and cold creek water were to blame, I was convinced that my car would blow up on the long, isolated roads from northern New Mexico to Texas and that I would be stranded for days.

We drank some coffee and waited. The tires looked fine. Finally, David referred me to a tire place on the highway not far from the ranch. I was there by 7 A.M. When Mr. Garcia arrived at 7:15 A.M., I was a bit calmer. He checked the tire pressure, told a few stories similar to what I was experiencing and sent me on my way. The red alarm light did not return and I survived the trip without incidence, feeling silly for the panic.

The early morning emotional stress exhausted my energy, and the last couple hundred miles were tiresome. I decided to rethink driving every year and mentally examined plane routes.

Once I arrived home and unloaded the car, I decided I was still good for another year. The Pecos cantaloupes were worth it.

25

Girlie party

While living in the middle of nowhere has its advantages, there are also some drawbacks, some of which I had not realized. I was recently invited to a Mary Kay party. The invitation promised a makeover, lunch and free gifts, a proposal much better than a shower invitation.

Not only did I reply immediately but I also called some of my bridge-playing lady friends and offered to drive them to the party. I knew the location, they didn't.

On the morning of the party, attempting to add some festivity to the event, I drove my Mercedes. It hadn't been off the ranch in over a month.

The hostess of the party was a friend with whom I attended high school in Houston years ago and whose relatives married my relatives. Emilie's home was quite fancy. The decorations were all in pink, tables set up with makeup mirrors and pink ribbons. We all chose a table and seated ourselves before a mirror that revealed more than we wanted to see. It was scary.

I had applied no makeup before leaving the ranch, only some eyebrow pencil and a bit of eyeliner. Being fair-skinned and fair-haired, I have light to nonexistent eyebrows. Many of the women had tattooed eyebrows and eyeliner. After four eye operations, I am too fearful to have anything done around my eyes, so I resort to the manual pencils and sticks.

After Emilie's welcome talk and revelations, we were all encouraged to cleanse our faces and buff our skin. That felt good. What really felt good was to look at each other in honesty and laugh at our vanity and wrinkles. There was no shame, only camaraderie.

We played with colors, foundation, eye shadow, lipstick, blush and moisturizers. And then we ate lunch. Emilie had prepared three different salads of fresh greens and chicken, peaches and cottage cheese and cakes and pies, all homemade. There was amaretto pie, strawberry pie, Russian black forest cake and fresh apple cake. One visit to the buffet was not enough.

Before leaving we received gifts from a large gift tub. It was a jolly grab bag confusion and laughter of ladies relaxing egos to be just girls once again.

We left Emilie's, clutching our purchases and gifts, made up to the nines or tens. On the way home, everyone agreed, "We need to have more girlie parties."

26

The rodeo

Pecos, Texas, claims the honor of hosting the first rodeo, but there are other contenders. Rodeo is alive and well in small-town Texas. Every year in the small town 20 miles from my ranch, a festival is held called Old Settlers. For fifty years, the old and young settlers have gathered in the park in Camp Wood. Two days of festivities are celebrated. The rodeo runs for two nights. It is not sanctioned and anyone can enter. Everybody does. The prizes are not significant. The crowd is. Families with small children congregate in the stands. Families sit together. The concession stand sells hot dogs, nachos and snow cones. The food is nasty. In the dark areas around the arena, the men stand smoking and drinking beer out of Igloo coolers. Restless horses stand tied to stock trailers.

The rodeo begins with the grand parade of riders. The pretty girls carry the flags of the United States and Texas. A tape of the Star Spangled Banner is played. Everyone stands with their hat off and their hand over their heart. Even the rodeo clowns remain still.

And then the fun begins. The clowns tell off-color jokes about bodily functions, and bad spouses. If the children don't get the jokes, they laugh anyway. Toddlers wear cowboy boots and sport plastic pistols.

Few riders remain on the bucking horses before the buzzer sounds. The mutton busting is a high point. Children under the age of six struggle to walk in the loose dirt of the arena. They are put on sheep and told to hang on to the wool. The child that rides the farthest and longest wins. It is hilarious. They fall under the hooves, are thrown for loops and arise dirty and smiling. The crowd cheers.

The team roping is the most popular event. Local cowboys team up in twos, one to rope the head, and one to rope the heels. Everyone cheers for their friends.

The clown continues with his antics. He blows off his pants to reveal polka dot undershorts.

The barrel racing features women and girls. The pretty and not so pretty girls circle the barrels. Some of the women are fast and professional. Some girls are very young, loping slowly. The crowd applauds for the slow ones as well as the speedy ones.

Bull riding is the final event. No one manages to stay on the bulls. Some of the spectators retire to the show barn for the dance. The families return home.

Another small town 45 miles away hosts an annual Fourth of July festival. The rodeo prevails for two nights. It is the same, a small-town rodeo.

Uvalde holds an even bigger rodeo. Contestants come from all over south Texas. Some manage to stay on the bulls before the buzzer sounds.

The small town of Rocksprings hosts a Professional Bull Riding Event, commonly known as the PBR. The PBR events are televised almost weekly on cable TV. Having watched Saturday night rodeos on TV, I wanted to attend a live PBR event. Rocksprings was close and the tickets were reasonable. I was disappointed. No one rode the bulls. The bulls bucked and twisted much slower than on TV. Watching at home was better. I didn't stay for the dance.

A ranch rodeo is different from the local rodeos, the PBR or anything I have seen. Ranches send their ranch hands to compete. In order to enter, the contestants must prove they are employed full time as ranch hands. There are events such as wild cow milking, where the cowboys on a ranch team must lasso and milk a wild cow and then run to the finish line with enough milk to deposit a few drops from a bottle. In another event, they must saddle and ride a wild steer to the finish line. The funniest event of all is dressing a goat in five articles of clothing and dragging it to the judges. The winning teams receive buckles.

Fat Stock Shows in Houston, Fort Worth, Dallas and San Antonio last for days. Every animal from chickens to pigs to rabbits to horses and cows is displayed. The competition is fierce. Famous entertainers perform in the evenings. Money is made and spent. Carnival rides are available. The food is outstanding. Everyone dresses Texas chic.

Rodeo is alive and well in Texas, but I prefer the intimacy of small-town rodeos.

27

The concert

I don't like crowds, cities or concerts. I've been to only a few concerts. The first concert I attended was back in the 70's outside of Huntsville. We were all drunk and chemically altered. I don't remember much, except that it was dusty and hot.

Back in the 90's, I attended a concert in Houston with my family. My cousin Lyle Lovett was the performer. It was elegant and entertaining, comfortable in the air-conditioned venue with cushioned seats.

Summers later, when my children and I were visiting my mother at her Colorado home, we attended yet another concert by Lyle. It was set outside in the dramatic red rocks outside Denver. The weather was delightful, the stone benches not so.

Still in the 90's, I attended an Elton John concert at the Woodlands, north of Houston. I was a reluctant attendee, but my girlfriend Barbara Sue had tickets and convinced me to go with her. We parked far from the site, locked our purses in the trunk and hiked to the hillside site carrying only a blanket.

After spreading our blanket, we discovered that drinks and food were available. Our money was locked far away, so we decided to make friends with fellow concertgoers and bum. It was no problem. Everyone was generous, buying us wine and passing cigarettes that were not legal.

The concert was simple. Elton John came on stage, on time, in blue jeans and a white shirt and sat down at the piano and played out his heart for two hours, no break. He sang my favorite song of all time, "Indian Sunset," and then concluded the concert with the song about Princess Diana. Everyone lit lighters or candles and cried. We were all one with Elton John.

Years later, I attended a Willie Nelson Fourth of July Concert outside Austin with my daughter and her boyfriend. It too was hot and dusty. The more beer we drank, the more we were forced to use the nasty Port O Cans. We left before we were too drunk to drive, but barely.

Roundtrip from Texas

My friend Linda, who is an excellent songwriter, was invited to perform in Uvalde at the Opera House with some other well-known songwriters. The performance was intimate and entertaining.

My travel agent, with whom I have established a friendly rapport over the years, called to announce that she and her husband had tickets to Lyle's concert in California. Since she had performed so many extraordinary favors for me over the years, I offered to obtain backstage passes. I succeeded.

She emailed me pictures and raved about the concert, noting that he would be in San Antonio the following week. I got on the Internet and called Linda. We purchased front and center row tickets and drove to San Antonio. Making the most of the trip, we arrived early and shopped at a large department store in the mall. I had not been shopping at a department store in over 10 years. I behaved like country come to town. I oohed and aahed over the displays of shoes and jewelry and clothes and made some purchases.

Linda had made reservations at the hotel across the street from the Majestic Theater. It seemed that everyone in the hotel had driven from somewhere else to attend the concert. My cousin Lyle Lovett is quite famous. If you haven't heard his songs and music, you should.

The concert was intimate, the entire audience perched on the edge of their seats. Linda met friends she had not seen in years. The occasion was festive. We visited with Lyle after the concert and drank champagne back at the hotel. I'm ready for another concert.

28

Election Day

The Screwup Fairy was in Real County. Election day had dawned cool and clear. A light wind was blowing. I planned on driving the 20 miles of winding roads to the small town of Camp Wood, population near 500, to pick up some cat wormer for our barn cat and vote in the elections, both local and national.

For company, I chose to pick up my grandson Theiss (pronounced "Tice"). Living on an isolated ranch, he always needs socialization. Dumping the weekly garbage and purchasing bread, yogurt and milk were also on the list. The plan was a good one.

As I stopped at my daughter's home in the creek bottom, her partner deposited the garbage in the back of the pickup.

After dropping some mail at the post office, I dropped off some surplus squash at a friend's house. Summer gardens in Texas produce more squash then needed. The rule is not to leave your vehicle unlocked or you will find a sack of squash on the front seat. The feed store visit went well, with the owner accepting another bag of squash. The GetNGo supplied the bread and milk, only they didn't have any regular yogurt, only the low fat.

The last stop was the County Nutrition Center, where I voted for the past four or five years after the polling place only nine miles from the ranch was forced to close due to noncompliance with the American Disabilities Act.

As I entered the small frame building and attempted to vote, I was told that I could only vote in Leakey, the county seat. That was another 25 miles of winding roads. When I asked why, I was told, "Due to the redistricting, you are now in precinct 6 and your polling place is in Leakey."

"Why?"

"There were not enough minorities in your precinct, so they changed the boundaries."

"But it says on my voter registration card that my commissioner and justice of the peace are in precinct 4 and my voting precinct is 6."

"It's all due to the census."

"Well I don't have the time to waste another hour driving to Leakey and back. I have just been disenfranchised. How fair is that?"

"Sorry."

"I'm not mad at you, just the system. I guess they don't want me to vote."

"You could have voted here early. It was in the paper."

"I don't always get the free paper, but come the next election I will make a point of voting early."

I was aggravated on the drive home, but my grandson enjoyed the ride.

Upon returning home, Israel, my daughter's partner, came up to my house to shoot the coon I had trapped after repairing the coon trap. The trap was now in working order.

On the list was to replace the battery in my smoke detector, unjam the door the coons messed up trying to get into my utility room and replace a light bulb in a kitchen ceiling light. Unfortunately, the light bulbs I had placed on the kitchen counter weren't the correct ones. The fixture required some round neon coil thing that Israel said was common. Maybe it was common if I lived near a Home Depot or Lowe's, but both of those mega-stores were 100 miles away.

My daughter had placed all my travel photos on some sort of device she called a passport or passbook; I don't know which. She said, "Mother, all you have to do is plug it into a port on your computer and follow the directions. You can post photos of yourself on your blog and Facebook sites."

"Easy for you to say."

"You can do it."

After going through my mail, I looked at the back of my computer. There were snarls of cords. I had to pull the computer from the wall only to discover moss and dust and a tangle of cords. It was dark. I went to the kitchen for my flashlight. It didn't work. The grandson had played with it once too often.

I couldn't find a port that fit the little square thing on the passbook. I did wipe up some of the dust and moss. I left the mess pulled away from the wall and called my daughter. She was cleaning house and didn't want to be bothered.

Disgusted, I sat down at the computer to check my emails. There was an email from Ticket Master in Calgary, Alberta, Canada, saying that my tickets for the events had been returned marked undeliverable. I checked the address. It was perfect. I emailed her back and asked her to mail them again.

Daughter called back, "How old is your computer?"

"I don't know. It works fine."

"Mother, you should consider buying a new computer."

"I like my computer."

"I can get you a discount on a new one, but in the meantime I think I have an adapter that will give you more ports."

"Let's do that."

"You need a new computer."

"Look for the adapter."

I shoved the computer against the wall, leaving the tangle of cords intact. I didn't want to mess up anything.

Another email came through. It was Cheryl at Ticket Master in Calgary. The message said that she could mail the tickets again or email them. I emailed her back to send them via email.

I went outside in the afternoon heat and re-baited the coon trap. When I returned the tickets had arrived. I printed them out, bar code and all and placed them in the folder with my email plane tickets.

Then I was reminded of the past week, when the U.S. Passport Agency did not have any record of my passport I had sent in for renewal. I attempted to track it online for a few days. Their website repeatedly said they had no record of having my passport. As a last resort, I called the toll-free number and was told that the passport had been mailed the previous day. I received it with a sigh of relief.

I still had seven large squash on my kitchen counter. The overhead light was flickering sufficiently to make me think I was having an acid flashback and I wished the Screwup Fairy would take a vacation or move somewhere else.

29
Canada and the East Coast

After trying to either find or lose myself, for whatever reasons, in the far reaches of the earth, I decided to visit eastern Canada and the east coast/New England states of America. My excuse, not that I needed one, was a bargain fare on a small cruise ship advertising the opportunity to view the colorful fall leaves. I admit it seems a bit silly to travel that far to see bright leaves when I could observe them on the cliffs of the ranch from the comfort of my living room.

When I consulted my computer for expected temperatures, I was overjoyed to find that my good friend, the colorful Navajo coat, would be my companion.

The flight from Houston to Toronto on Air Canada was not full. I was comfortable and dozed before landing, making a seamless connection for the short hop to Quebec City, Canada, where a French Canadian holding a sign with my name met me.

The airport was busy with tourists, many Orientals, who planned on taking one of the several very large cruise ships docked in the harbor, all destined to view the fall foliage.

The driver wheeled my one heavy suitcase to his black Lincoln and ushered me into the back seat. I had forgotten the luxury of a soft American car after driving pickups. The ride was nice.

I realized shortly thereafter that he spoke no English. Thankfully, the ride to the Hilton was short.

Not much was left of the afternoon when I checked into the hotel and surveyed the surroundings. The lobby was crowded with tourists of all nationalities.

I freshened up and went to the bar, hoping to meet some fellow travelers. The French bartender didn't pay much attention to me as I patiently waited to order a glass of wine that the bar menu advertised as costing $10. At least he filled the glass to the top. I then ordered salmon tartar and grilled veggies and turned to the man sitting next to me at the bar. He was a tour bus operator from Tennessee chauffeuring a rock band from the 1980's on a concert tour. After leaving Quebec City, he would escort the band to New Jersey, Virginia and Tennessee. We commented on the bartender's surliness and visited about the current mess in politics. The bill for two glasses of wine and dinner was $44, including the tip.

I returned to my room and noticed that the bottle of water, only half a liter, was priced at $3.50. Canada appeared to be an expensive place to live.

Following a puny breakfast buffet crowded with rude Asian tourists, I walked around the heart of the city, observing the fortress walls and gardens.

My instincts worked well when I returned the key card to the desk, I was not given a receipt, the cruise line having arranged for the hotel. A few minutes later, I was back in line asking for one. The lady at the desk printed out a sheet of paper, folded it three times and handed it to me. In an attempt to be courteous to those in line behind, I left the desk and sat in the lobby. When I examined the bill, the hotel had charged me for my room. I patiently returned to the line, waited my turn and explained that the cruise line was paying for the room. The desk clerk agreed, printed another sheet, folded it three times and again I gave up my place in line. When I examined the second bill, there were no charges due but my credit card charge was not shown as being reversed. Back in line, I received my third bill; this time I unfolded the paper before I left the line.

I was ready to sail. The harbor was a short ride from the hotel. The temperature was cool enough to wear the Navajo coat. I felt secure as I entered the ship and was given a glass of champagne and directed to the lounge, where a sandwich buffet was waiting. After light munching, I went to my room to unpack and relax.

I dined in the main restaurant with the social director and his wife, a retired doctor with his wife from California, and also another widow like myself from Michigan. The conversation was lively; everyone at the table was widely traveled.

The dinner was elegant. First and second course choices were elaborately described as follows: maple-glazed duck breast with cucumber, potato salad with a country mustard vinaigrette, seared tuna carpaccio, pickled artichokes and tapenade crostini, and oven-baked chicken and vegetable spring roll with chili dipping sauce. I chose the tuna and duck breast.

The main course was described: pan-roasted cod fish with creamy asparagus risotto and roasted mushroom sauce, seared shrimps wrapped in prosciutto, oven-roasted capon "Saltimbocca" with sweet garlic, grilled sirloin steak with braised beet confit and Lyonnaise potatoes, or the vegetarian selection, which was spinach and corn fritters, sautéed bok choy and Oriental stir-fry sauce. The steak was my choice. I don't have the patience to describe the dessert selection, just to say that I ordered fruit and cheese.

The meals continued to be pretentious but tasteless. I preferred eating at the grill out by the pool. There, I mostly ate lamb, grilled cowboy steak, that meant it had a bone in it, or pork ribs. I usually ordered sautéed spinach and a green vegetable. At least I could detect the flavor. The main menus I found to be fusion, the new rage in cooking. All the flavors are fused together so that no distinct taste is discernible. I am of a different ilk. I want to taste the meat and vegetables and have some good herbs and spices added. Sauces don't thrill me.

The first day at sea, the ship cruised through the Gulf of St. Lawrence, the world's largest estuary and the outlet of North America's Great Lakes via the St. Lawrence River into the Atlantic Ocean. The Gulf of St. Lawrence is a semi-enclosed sea, covering an area of about 91,000 square miles. Half of Canada's 10 provinces adjoin the gulf.

The gulf has provided a historically important marine fishery for various native nations who have lived on its shores for thousands of years and used its waters for transportation. The first documented voyage by a European in its waters was that of French explorer Jacques Cartier in 1534.

The scenery was breathtaking, with colorful forested mountains retreating into the gulf. The weather was cool. The Navajo coat was a comfort out on the deck.

Saguenay, Quebec was our first port of call. As I left the ship, Canadians dressed in native costumes waited on the dock, offering maple sugar on a stick and blueberry pie with hot tea. The atmosphere was festive. It was Thanksgiving Day in Canada. As I embarked on a tour of the area, the guide informed me that the population of Saguenay was near 150,000. Saguenay is located on Ha Ha Bay, which means dead end. The Saguenay area is known for farming and its aluminum production. Ore is imported from all over the world to produce aluminum. Blueberry production is so high that the guide warned us if we remained in the area for over three months, we would turn blue. Snowfall is high, 10 to 12 feet in the valleys and 15 to 20 feet in the mountains. Snow remains on the ground until May. Skiing and ice fishing are favorite sports, and there are over 35,000 glacial lakes in the 100,000 square mile province of Quebec.

As we drove through the outskirts, I observed agricultural fields, and was informed that 60% of the province is devoted to agriculture. My first stop was a visit to a sheep dairy farm. One hundred ewes are milked twice a day. Each ewe produces between one and two liters of milk per day. I learned that sheep milk contains two times the fat of goat or cow milk. The sheep are sheared every eight months. The dairy produces Brie, cheddar and other cheeses, all made from sheep's milk. The cheese was tasty and not available for purchase except to wholesalers. The two brothers who owned the farm were excellent guides and very passionate about their cheeses and sheep.

Returning to town, I visited a soap factory. Again, the owner was very funny and emotional about his soap. He demonstrated the process of soap making, emphasizing that his soap was all natural and the very best. He displayed soap to enhance male erections, soap to firm the breasts, and soaps for most any ailment. A small bar cost $7.95.

I walked next door to a glass-blowing factory and watched an Italian glassblower create a beluga whale of glass. The process was complicated and involved many steps. Many beautiful pieces of his work were displayed in the gift shop. I was tempted but left the shop empty-handed.

I returned to the ship in time for Trivial Pursuit. I joined a team of eight, some Australians and Americans. I learned that a female duck is called a duck and that a group of owls is called a parliament and that the natural occurrence that only happens at 40 degrees on the horizon is a rainbow. Our team came in second. The Captain's Dinner was served that evening. The prime rib was rare, as I prefer, and the squash curry soup was among the best I have ever tasted.

Day three was a day at sea. I attended a well-delivered lecture on Nova Scotia, which means New Scotland and was settled in the 1600's by the British and French. The French called the area Acadia. The French and English disputed the area for many years and the French Canadians still resent the British, as well as the French, for not making the territory French. It was interesting to learn that after the American Revolution, 30,000 Americans loyal to England immigrated to Canada.

Roundtrip from Texas

I spent the afternoon playing duplicate bridge. My partner was a woman from Sydney, Australia. We scored high board. It was a pleasant afternoon.

Earlier I had reserved a seating in the limited Restaurant 2, an advertised dining extravagance. I was seated with a couple from Australia. Fusion prevailed. The menu advised me that I was enjoying lobster martini, watermelon gelée, and vanilla froth as a cocktail. This was followed by artichoke salad, seared sushi tuna, black olive vinaigrette, crab with spinach pop, stir-fried shiitake mushrooms, bok choy, cured and roasted duck breast in mango and chili mint oil. The next course was lemongrass seafood presse, double-shocked shrimp, tomato and coconut cappuccino and a braised oxtail cigar. (No, the cigar was not the smoking kind.)

The main course was crisp sea bass, bean meli-melo, citrus fondue, barbecue-glazed short rib and seared *foie gras* and orange potato soubise. After reading what I ate, I can honestly say that I did not detect any individual flavor. Each concoction consisted of one or two bites, served on small saucers. While I ate everything served, I received no thrill from the culinary experience. The intimate atmosphere and the wine rescued the evening.

Halifax, Nova Scotia, was the next port of call. The weather in Halifax was windy and cold. I left with a guide to tour the city. As with all guides, he was full of information. Unlike most, he wore a kilt. Halifax is the capital of the province of Nova Scotia. The town of Halifax was founded under the British government by General Edward Cornwallis in 1749. Cornwallis settled the area by bringing 13 ships with 2,600 settlers. His purpose was to confine the French to the north. The French settled the area first. The founding of Halifax marked the beginning of Father Le Loutre's War, during which Indians and Acadians raided the capital region 13 times. The city was founded below a glacial drumlin that would be later named Citadel Hill. The outpost was named in honor of George Montague-Dunk, 2nd Earl of Halifax. Halifax was ideal for a military base, the vast Halifax harbor being among the largest natural harbors in the world. The harbor was well protected with batteries. Citadel Hill was used as a command and observation post. For this reason, Halifax was a very important port during both world wars, serving as a transit barracks, a sentinel on the home front, an anti-aircraft command center and a parting symbol for the thousands of troops who took ships overseas for the battlefields of Europe.

During the 20th century, over one million immigrants entered Canada through Halifax. Today the population is about 250,000. British influence was obvious as I walked through the Victorian Park in the central district. Many of the plants were tropical and in bloom. The guide informed me that it rarely freezes in Nova Scotia. Yet, the weather was quite cool. My Navajo coat protected me; the kilted guide did not seem bothered by the weather forecast, which he titled, "an episodic drizzle with embedded downpours."

During my visit to the park, I learned from my guide that many victims from the sinking of the Titanic are buried in Halifax. I chose not to visit the site.

From the park, we journeyed to the citadel, one of the most visited sites in Canada and the principal British naval station in North America. I strolled through the fortress, climbed the stairs and walked among the cannons aimed out to sea. The weather shortened my stroll. The warmth of the gift shop beckoned. I purchased some blueberry/maple coffee beans and a tee shirt for my grandson. I haven't yet tried the coffee.

After the visit to the citadel, I shopped along the docks at the port and returned to the warmth of the ship and another overly described meal. The inclement weather had forced the closing of the patio grill.

Earlier in the day, I spoke with my guide about the fate of the Acadians, the early French settlers who came in 1605 and farmed the fertile Annapolis Valley. They were ousted by the Treaty of Utrecht, which ceded Nova Scotia to the British. When relations between the British and French later deteriorated, the British suspected the Acadians as subversives and forced them to swear allegiance to England. Many of them refused, and in 1755, they were forcibly deported and their properties confiscated. Many moved south to the American colonies. A remnant survives to this day in south Louisiana, the Cajuns.

The East Coast

The rain continued as we cruised south to Maine and the United States. The day at sea was cozy as I attended a lecture on the east coast. The trivia team continued in second place while we learned that a group of unicorns is called a blessing, that a female gerbil is called a doe and that bagpipes originated in Italy. (I already knew that one.)

Roundtrip from Texas

After a light buffet lunch, I played bridge with my Australian partner. We scored next to last. The late rainy afternoon found me reading and cozy in my deluxe stateroom.

New friends from California who I had met on the ship invited me to a special dinner. They were on my trivia team, and in the course of the competition, we realized that we shared a love of raw meat, beef tartar to be exact.

John and his wife Betty arranged with the chef the preparation of beef tartar, preceded by escargot. Sautéed spinach completed the meal.

The food was perfect and the company enjoyable.

We docked in Bar Harbor, Maine, on a chilly rainy morning. I had arranged a tour. The lady guide was passionate in her love of the area. I learned that Bar Harbor is a resort town located on Desert Island, the third largest island on the east coast. The charming town boasts a population of 4,500 and is connected to the mainland by a bridge. Fishing, tourism and lumber are the primary industries.

In the early 1900's, artists and then the ultra-rich discovered the beauty of the area. The Astors, Vanderbilts and Morgans built summer mansions, referred to as "cottages." Most were destroyed by a fire in 1947.

Bar Harbor currently serves as a base for whale-watching boat trips and for visits to Acadia National Park, a mountain area of seacoast, crisscrossed by hiking and biking trails and great for bird-watching, climbing and cross-country skiing in winter.

The area became a national park in 1919, becoming the first national park east of the Mississippi River. All of the lands in the park were donated by the wealthy landowners who did not want the timber harvested. Three million visitors frequent the area per year.

Leaving the park, I visited a lobster hatchery. The host was a retired lobster fisherman who spoke with passion and knowledge. I learned that the young mother lobster carries the eggs for one year, part of the time in her body and part of the time outside her body. A young mother can carry 3,000 eggs; a mature lobster carries 100,000.

This hatchery, founded in 1986, is the only lobster hatchery in the world. The hatchery survives financially by teaching programs, not by the sale of lobsters.

Lobsters live four to seven years until harvesting maturity. Before they mature, they shed their exoskeleton nearly 20 times. They eat fresh food, not rotten, and they can go six months to a year without eating.

A license to fish for lobster allows the fisherman to have 800 traps, which are all tagged. Fresh herring is the commonly used bait. The female lobster is released and her tail is notched to identify her as a female.

I viewed young lobsters in tanks. A six-month-old lobster is the size of a mosquito and there are over 50 species of lobster in the world. The hatchery raises the baby lobsters and then sends them to be released all over the world where lobsters are endangered.

Coincidentally, I'd recently read a book published about the Somali pirates. The well-documented book stated that the beginning of the pirate industry began because of the invasion of Somali waters by the Thai, Korean and Japanese fishermen destroying the lobster industry.

From the lobster hatchery, I traveled to one of the cottages/mansions that had survived the fire, Cleftstone Manor, currently a bed and breakfast with 17 bedrooms and baths. The guide spoke of the "Gilded Age," when the wealthy hosted parties where the tables were covered with sand, disguising gems. The guests were given a bucket and shovel to mine for the precious gems that were theirs to keep.

I learned about Stokesbury Mansion, which had 80 rooms, 30 of the rooms devoted to the servant's quarters.

The drizzling rain persisted as I returned to the ship for a fresh lobster dinner in the main dining room. The scuttlebutt on the ship circulated that they had seen 400 live lobsters loaded on the ship. My dinner was delicious.

New England

The following day we cruised the coast of New England. I attended a lecture in the morning, faithfully taking notes.

New England is a region in the northeastern corner of the United States consisting of six states: Maine, New Hampshire, Vermont, Massachusetts, Rhode Island and Connecticut.

In one of the earliest settlements in North America, pilgrims from England first settled in New England in 1620 to form Plymouth Colony. Ten years later, the Puritans settled north of Plymouth Colony in Boston, thus forming the Massachusetts Bay Colony in 1630. Over the next 130 years, New England participated in four French and Indian Wars until the British defeated the French and their native allies in North America. In the late 18th century, the New England colonies initiated the resistance to the British Parliament's efforts to impose new taxes without the colonists' consent. The Boston Tea Party was a protest that angered Great Britain, who responded with the Coercive Acts, stripping the colonies of self-government. The confrontation led to open warfare in 1775, the expulsion of the British from New England in the spring of 1776 and the Declaration of Independence in July 1776.

The trivia team remained in second place. I discovered that the face that has appeared most often on the cover of *Time* magazine is the Virgin Mary. Our team had the correct answer. Most of the teams chose Jacqueline Kennedy or Princess Diana. And the Indian Ocean is the third largest ocean in the world. (I knew that one.)

Bridge did not fare so well. We placed in the middle, entertained by quarreling couples and mismatched partners.

The weather cleared and I dined with new friends at the grill out on deck. The grilled Nigerian shrimp/Tiger prawns were the size of small lobsters.

I arose well before dawn to experience the entrance to New York Harbor. I had flown over the city many times but never set foot in the city. The coffee and pastries were enjoyable as I selected a good seat to view the famous harbor.

I was enchanted as I saw the Statute of Liberty, Ellis Island and the towering skyscrapers of New York. The weather was cool and windy.

After the ship docked at Pier 90 and we cleared customs, I disembarked for a guided all-day tour of the city. My guide was a gentleman from Brooklyn. With my notepad in hand, I jotted down pertinent information.

New York traces it roots to its 1624 founding as a trading post by colonists of the Dutch Republic and was named New Amsterdam in 1626. Not having the population to colonize, the Dutch did not settle the area. Instead the city and its surrounds came under English control in 1664 and the area was renamed New York after King Charles II of England, who granted the lands to his brother, the Duke of York.

New York served as the capital of the United States from 1785 until 1790 and has been the country's largest city since 1790. Located on one of the world's largest harbors, New York City consists of five boroughs:

the Bronx, Brooklyn, Manhattan, Queens and Staten Island, with a total population of over eight million distributed over a land area of just 305 square miles, making it the most densely populated major city in the United States. As many as 800 languages are spoken in New York, making it the most linguistically diverse city in the world.

Our first stop appropriately was Central Park, consisting of 843 acres. I walked through a portion feeling quite safe. There were joggers, strollers, dog walkers and bench sitters. I did not feel threatened, though I remained near the outskirts.

From Central Park, I visited Soho, Tribeca, Little Italy, Greenwich Village and the lower East Side. Each neighborhood has an individual character. The streets, small cafés and shops were swarming with people.

I visited Rockefeller Center, one of the world's greatest urban spaces, consisting of a unified collection of commercial properties, gardens, theaters, a skating rink, breathtaking public artwork, including paintings and sculptures, and an underground concourse with a maze of corridors flanked by restaurants and stores.

Standing in line across from Radio City Music Hall, I felt the ground shake. At first, I blamed it on the days at sea. When the earth's movement persisted, I realized it was the subway below. I hoped it wasn't an earthquake. Finally, I entered an elevator that propelled me to the top of the tower. Once at the top, I felt the building sway. It was scary. I took a quick look at the view, snapped a few photos and returned down. When I discovered I was in the underground maze, I managed to get lost and ended up at the skating rink and kept moving to my right until I found Radio City Music Hall.

My tour continued among the many skyscrapers. I learned about the famous people who lived in them and how many millions they cost. This Texas lady was not impressed.

Lunch was a quick beef fajita taco at the harbor. No tables were available, so I sat with a couple from Chile. The taco was world class.

I spent the afternoon learning more about the early wealthy settlers. John Jacob Astor was a German immigrant who created musical instruments. He expanded into the fur industry and became famously rich. Cornelius Vanderbilt began his career with one ferryboat, purchased more boats and then railroads and made his fortune.

We stopped at the square with the Wall Street protesters. There was only a small enclave of people with cell phones camped in high-dollar tents. The crowd walking around the square was much larger. Vendors selling food and souvenirs were on the outskirts. The protest was surprisingly small, unlike that portrayed by the media.

The last stop of the day was at the World Trade Center. Barriers surrounded most of the area. The newly opened memorial was accessible only to those who had purchased tickets online. The tickets were free but had to be purchased before a visit. The new buildings were under construction. One was completed and occupied. My guide took me across the street to the second floor of the American Express Building. From there, I could view the memorial.

My guide recounted that on the day of the attack he was guiding a tour. Of his three co-workers, two were killed. The third had innocently taken the last elevator down to smoke a cigarette. She survived. He was emotional. The whole incident was incomprehensible. I can't say with honesty that I felt much of anything though. The city was overwhelming.

New York City was exhausting. Happily, I returned to the pier and the ship. I enjoyed an evening cocktail as we sailed from the harbor past the Statute of Liberty and Ellis Island.

Another leisurely day at sea found me attending a lecture on the eastern seaboard, Chesapeake and Delaware Bays. The first European expedition to explore parts of the Chesapeake Bay may have been by the Spanish explorer Lucas Vásquez de Allyón in 1525. Captain John Smith of England explored and mapped the bay between 1607 and 1609. He wrote in his journal that "heaven and earth have never agreed better to frame a place for man's habitation." As a result, there was a mass migration of southern English cavaliers and their Irish and Scottish servants to the area between 1640 and 1675.

The Trivial Pursuit team remained in second place. I learned that the disposable diaper was the invention that affected the decline in the use of the safety pin in 1946. I'd voted for the zipper. I was wrong.

My Australian partner and I placed first in duplicate bridge. We celebrated that evening at the patio grill, dining on lamb chops.

We docked on a warm sunny day in Norfolk, Virginia. I had signed up for a tour to Colonial Williamsburg. During the one-hour trip to Williamsburg, I was given the expected lecture. With pen in hand, I learned that Norfolk has a population of near 250,000. The greater area contains near 500,000. The city has a long history as a strategic military and transportation point. Norfolk Naval Base is the world's largest such base and the home of the world's largest military alliance, The North Atlantic Treaty Organization, NATO, has its defense headquarters here. I can't begin to describe the variation of ships I spotted in the harbor.

The trip to Williamsburg took me through Hampton Roads and Newport News. A short ride from Williamsburg took us to Jamestown, the first settlement in North America, founded in 1607. Jamestown was abandoned in 1699 when the seat of power was transferred to Williamsburg.

The pristine appearance of this 18th century town can be attributed partly to neglect and partly to the beneficence of a billionaire. When war with Britain erupted in 1776, Virginia's leaders decided that Williamsburg was vulnerable to attack and instead made the inland city of Richmond the capital. Although its buildings were left to decline, most survived. In the 1920's, John D. Rockefeller financed the restoration. Hundreds of the old houses, shops and taverns were renovated. Colonial Williamsburg, America's first historical theme park, opened in 1924. Everything possible was done to create an authentic picture of colonial life.

I spent the entire day touring the Governor's Palace, the House of Burgess and the Public Gaol. I visited a public tavern and was instructed in colonial dancing. I found the workshops of gunsmiths, cobblers, wheelwrights, blacksmiths, cabinet-makers and printers fascinating.

One of the most interesting facts I learned from my visit to Williamsburg was that the original colony of Virginia consisted of the present-day states of Indiana, Michigan, Wisconsin, Ohio and Illinois. Virginia was the largest of the colonies, thus explaining its predominant role in the American Revolution. Also, the Battle of Yorktown was in Virginia, where Cornwallis surrendered to Washington, thereby ending the Revolutionary War and giving America independence from the English.

Something else I learned was that the patriot Patrick Henry had 13 children by his first wife and 10 children by his second. He was a busy man.

While enjoying a veggie sandwich, I visited with a man from Pennsylvania. He spoke about the dog he had adopted from a shelter. He had the dog's DNA tested to determine the breed. I don't remember the results but I did think he might be a little nuts for doing so. After some light shopping, I returned to the ship, traveling past Langley Air Force Base.

Rain and storms rocked the ship during the night. I was lulled to a peaceful slumber before the last day of cruising at sea. I loafed through the morning. The final day of Trivial Pursuit beckoned. We won. One of the questions was why the domes of Russian churches are shaped like onions. The answer was to avoid the snowfall. I had the correct answer but was outvoted. We missed that one but won the day.

To end a splendid cruise we scored high at bridge. We dined in celebration.

South Carolina

A sunny day greeted me as the ship docked in Charleston, South Carolina. Again, the local guide was the source of information as we embarked on a walking tour. I walked the cobblestone streets, pen in hand.

Charleston was once the fourth largest city in North America. The city was founded in 1670 and named after Charles II. The climate suited the growing of rice, cotton and indigo. Slaves were shipped over to work the plantations.

Charleston's big moment came on April 12, 1861, when South Carolina troops fired on the federal garrison at Fort Sumter at the mouth of the harbor. It was the signal that the Civil War had begun. Even though Charleston was spared the destruction that Atlanta suffered during the war, hurricanes, the earthquake of 1886 and fires rendered the town into decay.

As I walked through the restored historic French Quarter with the lovely homes, my guide pointed out the bars on the gates and the windows, advising me that in the 1820's more slaves populated Charleston than whites. As a result, there was a slave insurrection that changed the city.

As I stumbled on the rough cobblestones and tried to write, the guide told me that Charleston was known as the London of the west, that in 1680 there were 180 art performances and that in the 1730's all religions were accepted. I thought that in 1730 my ancestors were still farming in Germany and Texas was inhabited by Indians.

Sonja Klein

Strolling among palm trees, blooming flowers and large oaks, we passed the only active French Huguenot church in the United States. The Huguenots were French Protestants.

The guide described the city. Charleston has a population of 125,000, has a rainfall of 60 inches per year, is a historic town with a drinking problem, and is a holy city with unholy people. More battles of the Civil War were fought in South Carolina than in any other state.

I learned that the porch ceilings were painted blue because wasps and hornets will not nest on blue and that blue repels bad spirits. As I walked among the beautiful restored mansions and homes, my guide informed me that from May to November the planters spent time in the city with their families to avoid the summer fevers.

By the time I finished with my multi-mile guided tour I was on the verge of a fever myself. But as we approached the dock, I mustered the energy to visit the market. There I purchased African spices: goolah blends for gumbo, shrimp and crab, rib rub and vegetable spices.

The ship was welcome home as I packed in preparation for disembarkation in Ft. Lauderdale early the next morning. For a change, the flight connections went well and I was more than happy to spy my daughter-in-law Carla at the baggage claim area.

We stopped on the way to her home for Mexican food, and the following day I drove the seven hours home to the ranch, this time not suffering from jet lag. What a relief.

In retrospect, I learned a lot from the trip. Most of all I understood Colonial America and the east coast. By the time they had achieved independence and were enjoying theaters, art galleries and a cultured existence, Texas was still a wild land.

People of the West are people of the land. We had no leisure time to enjoy the arts. We struggled for survival against the Mexicans, the Indians and the elements. There was no quarter given. Westerners, especially Texans, are different. I revel in the difference. I'm glad my ancestors chose Texas and not Ellis Island.

30

My new computer

I am averse to change, especially when it comes to modern technology. The television in my living room is over 20 years old. It still works.

When I purchased my second computer over five years ago, I was told, "You'll never need another computer. This one has everything you'll ever need."

My son Joe and his wife Carla have Macs, iPads and smart phones, and my daughter Molly is equally equipped. My cell phone is the $14.95 version. I can make calls and receive them. That's all I require.

Against my wishes, my daughter gave me a Kindle for Christmas. I gave her a list of books to put on it and she ordered them. On my next adventure, I took the little thing with me and was amply supplied with reading material. I thought it quite nifty.

Being a lover of books, I keep a running list of books to add to my Kindle in anticipation of future travels. I enjoy the physical sensation of holding a book and turning the pages more than holding a flat pad and touching the screen, but carrying five to 10 books on a trip becomes excessive and finding a fellow traveler to trade with doesn't always result in good reading material.

My daughter, who lives on the ranch, has WiFi. I don't. When I went down to her house to add some books to my Kindle, she said, "You do it. You have to learn."

The experience was humiliating. I felt like an idiot. But I managed to follow her instructions and download my selections.

Being an author, I have a website and blog and participate in Facebook and LinkedIn. After attending a seminar on book marketing, I realized that these skills were necessary to establish a platform for my books. I don't like it but will do whatever is necessary. After all, I'm German.

When Molly came to my house to download pictures to my computer, it crashed. One moment she was sitting at my computer and the next moment she said, "Your computer is toast."

I was in the kitchen. I was stunned, "What do you mean?"

"Mother, your computer crashed. It's *finito*. I've been telling you to order a Mac."

"It was working a minute ago."

"Well, it's not working now."

She stood and walked away from the desk, heading for the front door.

"You can't leave me like this."

"It's your own fault for being so hard-headed."

"It was working this morning. What did you do?"

"Mother, your computer is old, like you. You should have listened to me."

At last, she took pity on me and offered, "I guess I can take it down to my house and try to fix it."

"Please."

She disconnected a bunch of cords and took the box out to the truck, "I'll see what I can do when the baby takes his nap. I'm not promising anything."

The remainder of the morning was spent in shock. I was aimless, couldn't even read. My concentration was shot. Early in the afternoon she called, "I've got it up and running, but Mother, you need a new computer. It's just a matter of time before it crashes again."

"Okay, order me a Mac if you'll set it up."

"You need an iPad too, for when you travel."

"Okay, get one of those too."

"I'll call my friend who lives in Austin and works for Apple and see if she can get the employee discount and have it shipped here to the ranch."

"Just do it."

I was momentarily happy. She returned my computer, plugged in a bunch of cables and I was back in business but fearful of the days ahead. I would have to tell my old friend the computer goodbye and learn a new system. Molly had assured me that everything from my old computer would be transferred to the new one, that she would take care of it.

In the meantime, I was less than happy with the job performance of her partner. Israel was employed as my ranch manager but wasn't doing much of anything but drinking beer, talking on the phone with his children and using his computer. I fired him. The backlash wasn't very nice. Molly decided to return to school and complete her master's thesis and within two weeks they had moved back to Alpine, Texas.

The day before they left, she partially installed the new computer, transferring some of the data but leaving my old computer still operating until I could find someone to complete the process and give me some sort of instructions. Her parting words were, "Good luck."

Fortunately, I have neighbors a few miles away whose son is a webmaster and computer guru. I called him and arranged for him to come with his assistant and install my new Mac. I was greatly relieved but apprehensive.

Aron and his associate were here for three hours, but before they left I could turn it on and off and turn the iPad on and off and navigate a few necessary skills such as retrieving my email, logging in to the Internet and finding the word processing program called Pages.

I learned that I had a backup thing that saved all my data and that I now had WiFi and could order books on my Kindle. On top of that, my daughter had ordered a new camera. I now had a Kindle, a digital camera, an iPad and a new Mac. I had mastered the skill of being able to turn them on and off. In parting, my computer guru signed me up for a free 30-day trial on a program called Logmein, where he could log into my computer and help me. It wasn't very reassuring. I don't like asking for help.

In a moment of elation, I called my son and revealed that I was now set up with a new Mac. He offered to help anytime. Little did I know how much I would need him. He too subscribed to LogMeIn, having helped his in-laws with their new Macs.

My son came for a visit. He synchronized my iPad with my computer. He showed me how to download pictures from my camera, and how to post them on Facebook and on my blog site. During the day, he helped with some projects on the ranch and in the evenings, I learned about my new equipment.

About the time I was feeling halfway confident, he left. The following week I ordered Quicken, an accounting system for Macs. When it was successfully downloaded, I could not figure out how to make entries and start with a beginning balance. I called my son. He logged into my computer and showed me how. I was amazed.

One Saturday I cleaned my house, a job I had sorely neglected in the past month. I worked all day and completed a heavy cleaning of my modest home. Sunday morning I decided to reward myself and after feeding the sheep and chickens and watering the fruit trees and garden, I returned to my home, already sweaty and tired after two hours of moving hoses. The August heat was unforgiving.

While I was checking my email, the computer said it could not find the wireless keyboard. I changed the batteries and it worked for a few minutes. The same message returned. I changed the batteries again and it worked for a few minutes. I picked up the mouse and there appeared to be a battery cover. I opened it and found two batteries. No one told me the mouse had batteries, but after some thought it made sense. I changed the batteries and was back in business until the message appeared again. The green light on the wireless keyboard would not illuminate.

I called my son. He went online and found that others had the same problem. He told me to get some aluminum foil, wad it into a ball and put it in the bottom of the battery compartment to strengthen the connection. I did so and shoved it down into the dark cylinder. The keyboard still didn't light green. He asked, "Does the aluminum cover the whole bottom or just the connection in the middle?"

I looked, "It covers the entire bottom."

"Take it out and make it smaller so that it just covers the circle in the middle."

I put down the phone, retrieved an ice pick from the kitchen and tried to take out the mashed aluminum foil. Nothing moved.

Joe suggested, "Try a coat hanger."

The hanger worked. I then tried the rolled-up ball of aluminum; still no green light.

Joe asked, "Where is the nearest Apple Store?"

"Probably San Antonio."

I had an idea, "Look up the location."

He gave me two locations.

"Thanks, Joe. I'll just have to make a trip to San Antonio. Ugh."

I looked up the phone number of the nearest store on my iPad. It wasn't easy. Several weeks had passed since my iPad lessons. When I called, I was informed that the store was open on Sundays until 6 P.M. I returned to the iPad, obtained directions from MapQuest and walked out the door with my wireless keypad, still dressed in my grubby working clothes, jean shorts and a stained tee shirt from the Buddhist kingdom of Bhutan. I had not combed my hair. I had no eyebrows or makeup. On a hot Sunday afternoon, I drove 150 miles to San Antonio.

As I approached the high-scale complex of stores called La Cantera, I was overwhelmed. There was a Nieman Marcus, Nordstrom's, Macy's, Dillard's and a host of other stores.

After parking in a restricted area and being asked to move, I found a legal parking spot and entered the complex. It was not a mall but rather an open-air assortment of stores. I found my way to the Apple Store from a map posted along the walkway.

I had expected a quiet, small store. I was wrong. There were computers everywhere, people lined up, salespeople in blue shirts and a bank of technicians against the back wall. I approached a technician, who offered to help me, "I have a wireless keyboard that isn't working."

"Do you have an appointment with a technician?"

"No, I've driven 150 miles. I need my keyboard."

He punched some buttons on a handheld device and scheduled an appointment.

"How long?"

"About 15 minutes. Stay here and someone will take care of you."

Another salesperson approached, "Can I help you?"

I told him the story. He checked out my keyboard and agreed that it wasn't working.

My original salesperson, Oscar, returned. When the other employee confirmed the wireless wasn't working, Oscar asked for proof of purchase. Since it was a backdoor purchase, I told the truth. The supervisor came over and took the information. She spoke with the store manager. In the meantime, I had followed my son's advice and told Oscar that I wanted to purchase a keyboard with a cord and a mouse with a cord. Backup is important when you live in the middle of nowhere and the hassle factor has a high value. For $100, I now had backup.

The salesperson gave me a new wireless keyboard and I returned home in ample time to witness a pink sunset.

The computer found the new keyboard, I followed the instructions and was back in business by dark, feeling quite satisfied. I slept through the meteor shower that night.

Monday morning I was back at work, cleaning the ranch house after the workmen had left. My ranch hand and I moved a mattress and box springs and set up a bed in one of the bedrooms. I watered the trees and garden, fed the sheep and chickens and vacuumed and mopped the floors. We moved a table and some chairs around, arranging the rooms.

I quit early in the afternoon. I was tired and hot and took a shower. The shower restored my energy a little. I sat down at the computer to check emails. The skies were gray and there was thunder in the distance. The electricity clicked on and off. The computer was without power. I turned it back on and a screen appeared asked me to set up my mail. My mail server had been knocked out by the power outage.

I called Joe. He logged into my computer and went into this thing called Time Machine and restored my email account. He is so capable and patient, something he didn't learn from me. He advised me to turn off the computer while the storms passed to the north.

My friend Eric called. He lives about 12 miles from the ranch. The power outage had fried his computer. It wouldn't turn on. He was devastated. I don't blame him. I would be too. He later called and said a neighbor's son would work on it for him. We were both relieved and optimistic.

And then it occurred to me—What next?

31

Creatures of habit

When I realized that I always parked in the same area at Walmart in Uvalde, I began to take notice of my habits. At the grocery store, I did likewise, always parked in the same vicinity. Then I rationalized; I park consistently so that I am able to find my vehicle. Good reason.

On Sunday I found my regular space outside as well as inside the church, second pew on the right. I usually purchased gas at the same place. On trips off the ranch, I made the same gas and rest stops along the roads of Texas, rarely venturing into new spaces. I questioned, *Is this part of growing old, being predictable?* Not a very good thought and I didn't like it one bit.

For the last four years, I have driven in July to my brother's ranch in New Mexico. The same man at the fruit stand in Pecos sells me watermelon, cantaloupe, peaches and any other fresh produce.

Hundreds of miles down the road, the gas station in Vaughn, New Mexico, where the gas pumps function interminably slow is familiar. I always purchase the same thing, a bean burrito and some bottles of Carrizzozo raspberry and cherry cider.

Every year my brothers, their wives and I drive into Las Vegas, eat the great northern New Mexico food seasoned with green chilis, walk around the square and stop for an ice cream cone at the old-fashioned drugstore before returning to the ranch.

In an effort to combat predictability, I now park in a different spot. I've had a few anxious moments trying to find my vehicle but haven't lost a pickup or a car.

Instead of eating at the same Mexican restaurant in Uvalde, I have tried two others. The food is quite good and instead of always ordering beef enchiladas with onions and chopped jalapeños, I have tried steak quesadillas and fajita tacos.

I even visited a beauty salon for a haircut rather than having a friend or my daughter trim the ends.

Sonja Klein

I have a new camera, an iPad, a Kindle, a new Mac computer but not a new phone. Enough is enough. I'm having trouble just assimilating the new devices with their cords, chargers and paraphernalia.

I ordered a new scent, new makeup, a bedskirt to replace my 25-year-old one and two ottomans in orange leather.

A friend cleaned my guns and my son insisted that I fire them. I did. I'm even thinking about tattooing my eyebrows and eyelids.

I've added quinoa, chia seeds, walnut oil and garlic-flavored rice vinegar to my pantry. However, I have no plans to kayak in Iceland, climb glaciers in a national park or parachute.

Perhaps I'm a bit of a contradiction. I think nothing of stepping on a plane and flying to Bhutan or Kazakhstan or Vladivostock or the Seychelles. For me that is adventure. Maybe adventure is my habit.

32

Turning seventy, ugh

For nearly a year my daughter Molly had been saying, "Be careful, Mother, you're 70."

My reply had been the same, "I'm not 70 yet."

Daughters stick in the knife and twist it viciously. My current boyfriend was 60. I hadn't discussed age with him. When we were having dinner with my daughter, she mentioned that I was turning 70. I almost died of shame.

I was so embarrassed about turning 70 that I booked a trip to east Africa for Christmas and my birthday on January 2. I never leave home for Christmas or New Year's, but turning 70 was a good reason to leave the country. Maybe I could regain some years when I crossed the international dateline.

I spent the holidays dancing and having a good time without the benefit of being around those who knew I was 70. I kept the secret, a total illusion.

Reflection is part of every birthday. I decided I would babysit, write books and gradually shut it down. I traveled to most every place in the world I wished to visit. I've been married enough, had many boyfriends and published a book. I even went ziplining, rappelling, jetboat riding, whitewater rafting, snow skiing, marlin fishing and whatever else lay in between. I've been to Willie's Picnic, the Terlingua Chili Cookoff, the opera in Santa Fe, the wine country, the rain forest, the Kentucky Derby and Mardi Gras. I've seen the Grand Canyon, the redwoods and sequoias, Old Faithful, Las Vegas, Branson, Disney World and the Statue of Liberty.

For the months following my January birthday, I ate a lot, gained five pounds and vegetated. I could not get over the hump of being 70. It was an impenetrable barrier.

Turning 30, 40 and 50 wasn't too bad. Sixty was a bit shaky, but the promise of Social Security and Medicare spurred me onward.

But life would not let me off that easy. I was romanced, had red roses for Valentine's Day and delivered a speech that I think has changed my life. The romance was unexpected. The exhilaration of captivating an audience with my words put me so high I don't think I'll ever come down. It was such fun. I must do it again.

Just when I thought I had done and seen enough, life jumped in my face and said, "Oh, no. You're not done yet. There is a lot more out there. Come on. You bought the ticket. For God's sake, ride the ride."

My new career is that of speaker, which will enhance the sales of my published book and the books I am currently writing. The main thing is that I now know there's a lot more out there and my job is to find it so that when I do die, I'll die while I'm alive.

33

Guns

Most Texans are familiar with guns. Everyone in my family hunted and killed. We ate what we killed unless it was a pesky varmint. My brothers allowed me to go hunting with them if I carried the game and cleaned the animals. It never bothered me. I was happy to be included.

My first husband was from Louisiana. He preferred to collect guns and not kill anything except my love and respect for him. He purchased collections of guns, a set of commemorative pistols, an antique pirate pistol and handguns. He proudly showed them to anyone who visited our home.

I cautioned him that valuable guns invited robbery, but he ignored my advice. Two brothers who were casual acquaintances burglarized our house, stole the collection of pistols and robbed a bank in Willis, Texas. Following our bitter divorce, it took me three years to regain the pistols from the FBI.

My second husband was from Louisiana also. He was no stranger to violence. He kept a few pistols around the house. He purchased an elegant rifle for our son Joe. I think the gun was capable of killing an elephant.

My third husband fished and played golf. I don't remember him having a gun. I had accumulated a few over the years: Joe's rifle, a pistol, the pirate pistol, the collection that had been stolen and a .22 rifle that was my father's. The .22 rifle was stolen from my home on Lake Livingston and the pirate pistol disappeared when my children were teenagers.

When I discarded my third husband and finally found the right man, he was from Texas and familiar with guns. He agreed that guns were an invitation for robbery. I sold the pistol collection, gave my son his powerful rifle and kept one pistol for defense. John recovered a rifle from his childhood. I don't remember the caliber.

As time moved on, I acquired my mother's double-barreled shotgun and purchased a .357. I never fired them or killed anything. John used the guns we owned to kill rattlesnakes, hogs, deer, coons and pests.

John died. After his death, some friends of his came to the ranch to hunt. They managed to jam the rifle and break all the rules. I ordered them to leave and prepared to repair the damage. I took the rifle to the gun shop in Uvalde. Weeks later I went to Uvalde with a girlfriend. We went in my pickup because she planned to pick up a sofa that she had left to be reupholstered. Imagine our surprise as we drove to the upholstery shop to discover a pile of burned rubble. We saw the charred remains of her sofa.

When I suggested we stop at the gun shop to check on the rifle, she agreed. The owner of the shop explained that the man to whom he farmed out some of his work had a fire in his shop. Over 30 of his customers' guns had burned, including mine. He had no insurance. I obtained the gunsmith's phone number after being assured that the man was declaring bankruptcy and the gun was a loss.

I went home and thought about it. Not to be deterred, I called the man and received directions to his home, determined to salvage something. At first, he was defensive, I flirted a bit and he opened up. He did have the barrel and part of the gun that did not burn. I convinced him that I would pay to have the gun restored. He said, "Call me in a month."

When I called him a month later, I stopped by his home and joined him for a cup of coffee. He asked my opinion on painting his house. He introduced me to his son. I encouraged him to work on the gun, giving him the reason that my husband had died and saying I wanted to give the gun to his son for his birthday.

Every few weeks, I would call him or stop by his home to keep the project alive. I resolved to not give up, even if I had to kiss him. I would go no further than that. Finally, I brought the rifle back home and I never had to kiss him.

John's son committed suicide before I could give him the gun. I still have it.

My son Joe and his wife Carla are avid gun enthusiasts. She is small and petite, works at a hospital and has a license to carry a gun. My son has an armory. When they come to the ranch, they shoot at targets. I can't recall Joe or Carla ever shooting a living thing.

My daughter and her partner Israel moved to the ranch. He is from Louisiana and is a crack shot. He brought his guns with him. He commits the killings on the ranch. Israel kills goats, sheep, deer, coons and possums. He processes the meat in the barn, cutting steaks, grinding meat, stuffing sausage and even tanning the hides. Molly and I help him.

He even has paint-ball guns and dart guns. I'm surprised he doesn't yet have a slingshot or bow and arrow. Maybe that will be next.

I recently viewed a special on TV about guns. The premise of the show was that the United States will never be invaded by a foreign country. The facts cited were that Michigan registers several hundred thousand hunting licenses, West Virginia another couple hundred thousand and Wisconsin also registers a couple hundred thousand. In only three of our states, there were over half a million trained hunters with guns. That doesn't count any of the other states. In other words, America has a formidable citizen militia in addition to our armed forces. The message is 'Don't Mess with America.' We are armed and ready.

34

East Africa and the Indian Ocean

After spending many grueling intercontinental flights curled up like a sausage, I had discovered business class, better yet the tax deduction available once I published a book. A bonus in the Houston airport was a special line for navigating security offered to business and first-class passengers.

As I boarded the plane via a special line for those of us paying a premium, three United States agents stopped me and asked, "How much cash are you carrying to Dubai?" My answer was considerably less than the $10,000 allowed.

I never heard the safety speech or an announcement from the captain, and at some point in the flight, I ventured a guess that the plane was being flown by robots.

The 16-hour flight was one of unaccustomed luxury, my own pod and seat that reclined into a comfortable bed, complete with blanket and pillow. The meal was light and tasty. I had a choice of appetizers, either classic ceviche with lightly poached prawns marinated in a lemon and cilantro vinaigrette and served on a bed of roasted pepper and onion salad or Arabic mezze, a traditional selection that included fresh vine leaves, creamy hummus, baba ghannouj and tabouleh with an assortment of pickled vegetables and a fresh lemon slice. I chose the Arabic mezze. It was delicious. The soup was roast pumpkin and carrot, again delicious. I skipped the common salad and chose the grilled veal chop with classic cafe de Paris butter, a creamy celeriac puree, grilled asparagus and portobello mushrooms. I skipped the variety of rolls and garlic bread, as well as the offered desserts. I read a book that my daughter Molly had downloaded on the Kindle that she had given me against my wishes for Christmas. Rather than carrying pounds of books for my avid reading habit, Molly had downloaded 10 books, the titles of which I had provided.

Several hours later, I declined the offering of a light snack. The choices were tempting: a delicatessen sandwich of smoked turkey and

Brie cheese, hot lamb shawarma, Singapore noodles or chili con carne and tiramisu cake for dessert.

My pod partner across the high partition was an Arab. He snored loudly and drank wine and worked on a computer when he wasn't sleeping. He even took his computer with him to the bathroom following breakfast and stayed in there longer than was mannerly. We never spoke but exchanged smiles when I left my lounging area to walk a bit and use the bathroom.

The breakfast was just as elaborate—fresh-squeezed orange juice, fresh fruit, yogurt and a choice of scrambled eggs served with salmon and asparagus, a fresh mushroom omelet, an apple-and-cranberry pancake tart or a breakfast deli platter.

The sun was setting in hues of scarlet and orange as we landed in Dubai. The lights of the city seemed to extend for miles.

As I sat in the Emirates Airline executive lounge, 12,000 air miles away from Houston, many hours and a day later and observed the dark, swarthy male passengers, I once again asked myself, *What the fuck am I doing here?* The obvious answer, *Off on another solo adventure, dummy.*

It was 7 P.M. Dubai time. My connecting flight was scheduled to depart at 2:35 A.M. The quiet elegant airport that I remember from four years prior was now huge and bustling with every nationality imaginable. The lounge covered a full acre and the amenities available were buffets of gourmet prepared foods, coffee bars, quiet areas with lounge chairs, computers with Internet service, newspapers in every language, and a spa offering massages, facials, manicures and pedicures. After a quick walking tour of the lounge, I settled at a computer terminal to email my children that I had arrived safely. I then went for a manicure and received instant service.

A young lady of undetermined origins escorted me into a cubicle and gave me a nice manicure. I peppered her with questions.

"Are you from Dubai?"

"No, I from India, Mumbai. No Dubai people do this work. Dubai people work for government or banks."

"How long have you been in Dubai?"

"Eight years."

"Have you been back to India for a visit?"

"No, I going next year to visit mother, three brothers and three sisters."

"Are you married?"

"No."

"How many days do you work?"

"Work six days from 10 until 10 at night."

"Where did you learn English?"

"India."

"Do you have a cell phone?"

"Yes."

"Do you have a computer?"

"Yes."

"Do you speak Arabic?"

"No need. Everyone speak English."

Her skin sparkled as if she had spread glitter on her face and arms. I gave her a $5 tip. She was quite nice to tolerate my questions.

The buffet was my next stop even though I had been fed three meals on the plane. The buffet offered pumpkin curry, grilled fish, vegetable ratatouille, lamb navarit, various salads and quite a few tempting desserts. I tried the curry and the lamb. It was tasty.

The bathroom was next. The attendant motioned to the cubicle for me to enter. Being contrary, I entered the adjacent one. The toilet was Asian, flush with the floor. I left. The attendant smiled. I entered the one she had first indicated. Flustered, I left the restroom without brushing my teeth.

With five hours left of my layover I went to the newspaper stand in the lounge and picked up every English paper available and settled in a lounge chair with my feet up and with a glass of water and read them from cover to cover. I discovered that Iran and Russia signed a billion dollar deal to develop an Iranian oilfield, that Israel formed a crack military team to combat Iran, that Pakistan was growing very anti-USA, that the Taliban was establishing an office in Afghanistan so the Afghanistani government can find them, that protests were increasing in Nepal, that the Arab countries were fearful of Iran and advocated the overthrow of the Syrian government and that the international community was very critical of U.S. politics getting in the way of economic reform. Another hour passed.

I settled into a recliner and meditated for an hour and then began to read a book, becoming so engrossed that I almost missed my plane, not realizing it was a 20-minute walk to the gate. The airport was bustling at 2 A.M. The shops were open and doing a brisk business. I was among the last of the passengers to board the plane, feeling very stupid for being a so-called seasoned traveler. I should have checked the distance to the gate. I blamed it on the newfound luxury of the executive lounge.

Business class on this five-hour flight was not as elaborate. I wasn't in a pod and my seatmate spoke a language that sounded like Russian. He snored and drank and turned his sour breath toward me. I faced the window for the entire flight and slept a few hours.

As the plane approached the landing at the airport in Mahé, Seychelles, the thunderclouds rose like mountains above the lavender sunrise. I was ready for a shower, clean clothes and a bed. It was 7:30 in the morning.

The airport was modest. I exited the plane directly onto the tarmac and walked to a metal Quonset hut. The air was hot and humid. After retrieving my one bag from the carousel and having my passport stamped, I engaged a taxi for the 30-minute ride through the town of Victoria to a hotel on the ocean. The hotel was both French and African. The lobby was open, had no walls and was covered by a thatched roof. The sea breeze was warm and the view was astounding.

I approached the desk and was asked, "Where are you from?"

"Texas."

A blank look followed. I changed my answer, "America."

"Ah, America." A smile.

For the second time, I'd managed to find someone who had not heard of Texas. I knew I was in for a good trip.

After the smiles faded, I was told my room would not be ready until 3 P.M. but that I was welcome to wait in the lobby and eat in the restaurant. There was nothing to do but sit in an upholstered chair and pull out the Kindle and people watch. There was no one about. The hotel seemed deserted. I couldn't board the cruise ship until the following afternoon. It was time to be creative. I walked over the terraced grounds and beside the swimming pool. The thunderclouds were threatening. A rainstorm was comforting. The lobby was cozy.

A taxi deposited a couple, obviously American. They approached the desk and I surmised were given the same answer about their room not being ready until that afternoon.

I waved and invited them to join me. We exchanged greetings. They were from Philadelphia. We commiserated on the trip to the Seychelles, long flights, layovers and now a wait for a bed. In the course of the conversation, we shared return arrangements as difficult as the arrival.

Richard, the husband, suggested to Diane, "Why don't you call Tami and see if she can arrange a day tour when we reach Mauritius since our plane doesn't leave until late."

I ventured, "Tami from Oklahoma?"

"Yes."

"She's my travel agent too. What a coincidence."

As we visited the morning away, we discovered that we had stayed at the same hotels in Cusco, Peru and in Erfoud, Morocco, and agreed that both were among the best.

The lobby soon filled with travelers waiting for rooms. At 11 A.M. I was called and told my room was ready. The rain was falling in torrents as I was escorted to my cabana. An umbrella shielded us as we made our way along the path. My room was spacious, much more than I needed, three rooms with all the amenities. I took a shower and snuggled into the comfortable bed and slept until late afternoon.

The rain had stopped when I made my way to the downstairs bar overlooking the ocean and swimming pool. I sat next to a single lady and ordered a glass of chardonnay and exchanged greetings. I joined her and found she was also traveling solo, was an attorney from Ireland and a seasoned traveler. After she left I visited with a couple from Mexico City. The wife is the daughter of the author who wrote the book from which the movie, "Treasure of the Sierra Madre," was filmed. We shared stories. I looked forward to embarking on the ship. My fellow passengers would be interesting.

I indulged in the buffet breakfast, joining Mary from Ireland and returned to my room to read before checking out and traveling to the ship. I was a bit dismayed to find that the two glasses of wine and breakfast buffet cost $67. Mahé, Seychelles, was not a cheap destination.

I boarded the ship about 3 P.M., was shown to my stateroom and introduced to my butler, Bo, a young Chinese man from northern China. He opened a bottle of chilled champagne and we visited, talking politics. I quizzed him on the situation in Tibet. He was not proud of the Chinese government's treatment of the Tibetans.

After unpacking, I walked to the pool deck and had a glass of wine at the bar. I visited with a man from Scotland traveling alone as the ship left the port.

Following a welcome cocktail party in another lounge, I joined two couples for dinner as the fog and drizzle returned. I dined on duck pate, spinach ravioli and pork tenderloin wrapped in prosciutto.

The Seychelles

The following morning the ship docked in Praslin, the second largest island of the Seychelles, measuring about nine by four miles with a population of near 5,000.

About 42 of the 115 islands of the Seychelles are granitic while the remainder are coral. The total population of the Seychelles numbers about 82,000. The French settled the islands in the late 1700's; then the British conquered them in 1814. Languages spoken are English and French as well as Creole.

Primary exports are tuna, fish and cinnamon bark. The government is a constitutional democracy and the literacy rate is 98%. The Seychelles are an exotic destination for French and British tourists. Prince William and his bride honeymooned in the Seychelles, and the beach scene in the movie, "The Castaway," with Tom Hanks was filmed in the Seychelles.

When the ship docked in Praslin, I visited Vallee De Mai, the smallest UNESCO World Heritage Site. During a guided walk into the magical rain forest, I followed the paths that made the coco de mer accessible. The endemic coco de mer palms, some of which grow up to 90 feet tall, are unique to the Seychelles. The fruit grow up to 40 pounds and are uniquely double-cheeked. Other botanical species were in evidence in the tranquil setting, and the fronds of the palms offered some protection from the light drizzle. The air was hot and humid.

After a drive along the coastline to observe the beaches, I returned to the warmth of the ship in time for Trivial Pursuit. My Irish lady friend joined the team of eight and we scored second. I was the only American on the team and certainly felt dumb.

La Digue, Seychelles, was the next port of call. La Digue is the fourth largest island, 3 miles long and 1.8 miles wide. Transportation is limited, truck or oxcart. The island's population of about 2,000 resides either in La Passe or Reunion. I visited a copra kiln, a traditional coconut-oil mill and a plantation house. Copra is the term used for cooked coconuts. While on the plantation I learned that 35 kilos of coconuts produce 10 liters of coconut oil. The coconut palm is known as the tree of life. The husks are used to stuff mattresses and the shells are used for fuel.

As we walked through the plantation, I observed vanilla vines growing on acacia trees. The vanilla flowers are hand pollinated and the plant is a member of the orchid family.

I rode an oxcart back to the pier and boarded the ship to attend a lecture about the Seychelles.

The Seychelles are the smallest country in Africa, comprising 260 square miles. They lie 93 miles off the east coast of Africa and were discovered by Vasco da Gama in 1742.

The country has a democratic government.

The following morning the ship docked off the coast of Silhouette, the third largest island, where the original nature of the area is preserved. Silhouette Island is a sunken remnant of the mountains of a former ancient continent, Gondwana. There are no roads or motorized vehicles on Silhouette. Today the population is 147. The human impact on the island has been insignificant, and as such, it has one of the richest biodiversities in the western Indian Ocean. The Nature Protection Trust of Seychelles manages conservation on the island and has a breeding center for giant tortoises.

Unlike its neighbors, the island is of volcanic origin and is named after an 18th century dignitary. Coral reefs make it difficult to land. Most visitors arrive by helicopter or boat.

Legends of buried treasure abound in the Seychelles because pirates used the islands as a hideout. Captain Kidd and Olivier Levasseur, "The Buzzard," were among them. Medieval graves of passing Arab sailors are common in the Seychelles as well.

Before leaving the safety of the Seychelles, the captain gave a safety speech and a handout was delivered to every stateroom. British security officers had boarded the ship in Mahé and were seen walking the decks with binoculars in hand.

The safety speech informed us of the ship's five-whistle blast sounding the alert for pirates. Instructions were to sit or lie on the floor as the ship would undertake a zigzag operation. All curtains were to be drawn at dark and the upper decks would not be illuminated.

Many of the passengers were alarmed at the announcement obviously not being aware of the danger. I jokingly remarked, "Don't worry, pirates don't want to deal with a bunch of old people on medication. They prefer cargo ships with more valuable cargo and a small number of crew."

A portion of the written announcement told the story, "Once we leave the Seychelles archipelagos heading toward Africa, the ship will be navigating into the open part of the Indian Ocean, which along with the Red Sea, the Gulf of Aden, Gulf of Oman and the Arabian Sea, has been designated by the International Maritime Organization as a High Risk Area. Acts of piracy reported in this region by Somali Nationals have been affecting the ships transit in this geographical part of the world."

Continuing on, the directive read, "Naval forces from several countries have deployed ships and helicopters to patrol those geographical areas, supported by the Maritime Security Centre Horn of Africa, the United Kingdom Maritime Trade Organization, the European Union Naval Force and the United States Maritime Liaison Office. This has created the safest way to navigate in those areas."

The following morning as I walked the deck at sunrise, I noticed a navy patrol boat moving along side the ship. On the front deck was a man standing behind a mounted machine gun. There was an identical boat on the other side of the ship. As I closely examined the escorts, I realized that the men behind the machine guns were manikins.

Kenya

As we entered the harbor of Mombasa, Kenya, larger patrol boats joined our escorts. The dock was full of officials and native costumed dancers, fat and lively. I later learned that we were the first cruise ship to dock in Mombasa in over a year. They were happy to see us.

The smell of Africa was one of woodsmoke and unidentified spices. Most of the Kenyans were thin, hair buzzed short. Toyotas dominated the dock area.

Vendors were lined outside the secured area, selling carved wooden bowls, statues, jewelry, items made from bone and horn, and musical instruments. Armed guards patrolled the dock area. Hostility pervaded.

Sonja Klein

I boarded a small coach for an excursion to Tsavo East National Park. In addition to the driver, two guides provided information, "Jambo" is Kenyan for hello. Africans are gifted by nature for adapting to the heat. Their skins are black and their hair is curly to retain moisture.

As we drove through the crowded city on a road that was merely a suggestion, I observed stick-thin Africans standing along the road with no sign of hope. The women seemed busier, walking slowly in the heat with bundles balanced on their heads. The traffic was chaotic, mostly trucks going every which way, dodging potholes deep enough to break an axle. There were no boulevards or flower-lined sidewalks.

The 62-mile drive to the park lasted three hours. We passed fields of sugar cane and villages with one-room thatched or tin-roofed huts. Cattle and goats grazed the fields. Male herders stood close by the livestock. Piles of trash littered the road. People picked at the trash. The scene was one of despair.

As we passed through small settlements, there were no traffic lights, only speed bumps. Sisal plantations dotted the hillsides. Domed roofs covered the Masai houses.

Tsavo East and West National Park makes Tsavo one of the world's largest game sanctuaries. Situated about halfway between Nairobi and Mombasa, the park spans approximately 8,036 square miles.

The vegetation is savanna grassland with thorny bushes and some swampy marshland near the Voi River. The main river that passes through the park is the Galana River.

Following a comfort stop, we switched into a specially adapted safari minivan, entering the park through the Bachuma Gate. There were five us in the van in addition to the guide and driver. The roof was open. We could stand or sit, whichever was best for viewing or photographing the African wildlife.

Before lunch, we sighted oryx, a bustard, a cheetah lying in the shade of a tree, Coke's hartebeest, Kirk's dik-dik, zebra, waterbuck and elephants.

We dined on a buffet lunch at the Ashnil Aruba Lodge, situated in the heart of the park. The lodge features a large watering hole that attracts the game.

That afternoon we spotted gerenuk, ostrich, baboons, monkeys, water buffalo, gazelle, guinea, impala, giraffes and kudu as well as many more elephants.

The long drive back to the ship lasted even longer because of the evening traffic. I was glad to be in the back of the coach. I didn't want to see the large trucks we dodged on the way back to Mombasa.

The guide lectured most of the return trip, relating the details of his country. Kenya has a population of about eight million. There are 32 native tribes, Kikuyu being the most numerous. Swahili and English are the predominant languages. Swahili is a mixture of Arab and Bantu. There were no schools until the missionaries arrived. The first eight years of schooling are free and uniforms are required.

Kenya became independent in 1963. Mombasa is the largest port on the upper east African coast. Durban, South Africa, is the largest on the entire east coast. Unemployment is high. Elections are held every five years.

Indians were imported to build the railroads. Many of them stayed and intermarried. When we journeyed through the Indian Ocean, I was surprised to see such large numbers of Indians.

As I returned to the ship, I shopped with the vendors in the port. I soon learned how they love to barter. As I approached one man he said, "Lady, here, I give you this necklace as a gift. Do you have a fountain pen to give me for my son who is in school?"

The necklace was modest, a few beads on a heavy cord. I fished in my bag and handed him a pen, "Here, this is for you, a gift."

He handed me three more necklaces, similar to the free one. I took them. He said, "Do you have $5 for these necklaces?"

"No, I don't have $5 for the necklaces."

He returned the pen to me, "No, the pen is a gift. You keep it."

I walked away with the first necklace traded for a Bic pen.

The rumor circulating on the ship was that the Kenyan police had raided an apartment in Mombasa and arrested some terrorists and found bomb materials, supposedly destined for our ship. In spite of that, the ship hosted a deck barbecue with music and dancing, the reasoning being that we were safe from attack in port rather than being illuminated on the open ocean. I viewed it differently. We were sitting ducks, anchored dockside and all out on deck eating and dancing. Nothing happened.

The following morning I left the ship to tour the city of Mombasa. I learned that Mombasa can be traced back to the 11th century. Settlements thrived due to the excellent deep-water harbor and its protected position. In an effort to consolidate their hold on the European trade with India and southeast Asia, the Portuguese built a formidable fortress, Fort Jesus, in the late 16th century. Several changes were made after the Omanis conquered the fort at the end of the 17th century. Today the impressive structure still dominates the harbor.

The first stop was at a Hindu temple for a guided tour. From there, we proceeded for the photo stop near the enormous aluminum elephant tusks that spanned the main avenue.

The most exotic part of Mombasa is the Old Town. Here, narrow alleys lined by mosques and cramped old houses slope down to the bustling harbor filled with boats called dhows. The Arab influence is obvious. As we walked the cobbled streets, vendors called out, advertising their wares and asking if we were from the ship. Evidently, the arrival of the ship was big news.

After visiting Fort Jesus we drove to the Akamba Woodcarving Factory. Nothing could have prepared me. In a jungle setting were many thatched shelters. There was no electricity. Under the shelters in the darkness, men sat on bare ground, carving wooden statues, bowls and artifacts with ancient hand tools. Most of the workers were thin and aged. They were members of a union. They work when they want and sign their number on their work, which then goes into the large modern union building where the artwork is offered for sale. As their work sells, they are given a portion of the proceeds. It was beyond primitive. I purchased several beautifully carved bowls.

The ship sailed at sunset. A naval gunboat accompanied the ship to Zanzibar, another exotic destination.

Zanzibar

Years earlier I shopped in a huge used-book warehouse in Dallas, purchasing several boxes of travel books. One of them was written by the daughter of one of the many wives in the harem of the Sultan of Oman, who owned Zanzibar. The book, written in the 1800's, was a fascinating account of a young girl growing up in the Sultan's palace in Zanzibar. Later I came upon a book titled, *The Zanzibar Chest.* So Zanzibar was on my list.

A lecture had prepped me on the facts. Zanzibar is a semi-autonomous state of Tanzania, formerly Tanganyika. The archipelago is comprised of over 50 islands, three of which are inhabited. Zanzibar lies less than 30 miles from the coast of Africa and composes about 950 square miles. At one time Zanzibar held the largest population in east Africa. Today the population is near one million people comprised of African, Arab, Persian and Indian origin. The state gained independence in 1963. Today, spices, raffia and tourism are the main industries.

The Persian traders settled in Zanzibar and there is a Zoroastrian temple as well as mosques on the island. The Sultan of Oman conquered the island, transferred his seat of government to Zanzibar in 1840 and exported ivory and slaves. Over 60,000 slaves per year were exported from Zanzibar. From 1890 to 1913, the islands were a British protectorate.

I arose before sunrise to feel the ship dock on the island of Zanzibar. As the ship approached, I detected the smell of spices for which the islands were famous, and taking a spice tour gave me an understanding of why Zanzibar and spices are synonymous.

In the 19th century, the Sultan of Oman introduced cloves to the island, which today is among the main exports of Zanzibar. We left the pier, and drove past the house where Dr. David Livingstone stayed while planning his explorations into the interior.

We visited the ruins of Maruhubi Palace, built in the early 1800's by Sultan Barghash, the third Arab sultan of Zanzibar. He used the building to accommodate his wife and concubines. The sultan himself lived in a separate palace in Zanzibar Town. In 1899 fire destroyed the Maruhubi Palace. The palace contained 14 bedrooms, that same amount of toilets, and running water. There were many pools for bathing. Giant mango trees lined the drive to the palace. I could only imagine the idyllic life in such an exotic setting.

Leaving the palace grounds, we drove through fields of cassava, yams, mango trees, jack fruit trees, breadfruit trees, grapevines, banana and apple trees and fields of eggplant. The soil was red and fertile.

The coach stopped in an off-road region. We walked the next few hours through a fascinating spice world. Khatib was our guide.

As we stepped into the tropical forest, an assistant met us. He cut a banana leaf, trimmed it and rolled it into a large cone, like an ice cream cone. He then secured the loose sides with a toothpick-like splinter that he sliced from a limb. There were 12 of us. We were each given a cone and instructed that before the tour was over we would have 10 spices in our cone.

The first stop was a tree with fruit similar to an apricot. The guide picked some leaves from the tree, crushed them in his hand and passed them for us to smell, asking, "What is this?" None of us knew. He picked a fruit, cut it in half and revealed a nut in the middle. The nut was nutmeg. One went into my cone.

We approached a tree with small red blooms similar to a honeysuckle. Again, we had no clue what it was. The red blooms dry and become cloves. The cluster of flowers dropped into my cone.

Crushing the leaves on the next tree did not help. The bark was the spice, cinnamon. The roots are used medicinally. The bark was third into the cone.

The next tree had small clusters of what appeared to be tiny green peppers. Pepper was correct. The green peppers mature to white, red and black; thus green, white, red, and black pepper all from the same tree. We learned that at one time white pepper was as valuable as precious stones because it disguised the odor and flavor of rotten meat. I dropped the green pepper bouquet into my cone.

Grass followed, lemon grass, used for tea, ground for seasoned powder; the stalks are used in soup.

Ginger, I recognized. I learned that ginger is a six-month crop. The plant dies and the roots are replanted. Ginger is made from the root. I learned that ginger kills bacteria and that Coca-Cola produces ginger ale in Zanzibar.

Turmeric was a mystery. I had never seen the plant. Ground turmeric is made from the root. It is a nine-month crop and is replanted.

Coffee plants grew in the forest too. The beans were turning red. Our guide showed us the plant. I snuck a few of the beans into my cone.

We stopped at a tree the guide called a lipstick tree. He broke open a seedpod. Inside was a thick bright orange-red juice. Some of us women rubbed it on our lips and cheeks. We were going native.

Cocoa was the eighth spice. The bean was round and green. The seed inside produces the cocoa, but the flesh of the fruit surrounding the seed is edible. Two crops of cocoa are grown per year.

The vanilla pod I recognized from my tour in the Seychelles.

The last spice was a cluster of small seeds within a pod. This I guessed correctly, cardamom. The rain fell lightly throughout the spice tour. The hours had been enchanting.

The coach returned us to a modern world as we toured Stone Town, a UNESCO World Heritage Site. Here the cultures mix to make Zanzibar a unique destination. It was one of the most enchanting and exotic places I ever visited. The moment was defining. Perhaps I made it so.

The Indian Ocean

The following day was spent at sea. I attended a lecture on the Indian Ocean and learned more interesting facts. The Greek word aphrike means not cold and could be the origin of the name of Africa. I learned that in 600 B.C. the Phoenicians sailed around Africa in a *trireme*, an ancient vessel with three rows of oars on each side. I learned that Stanley crossed from Zanzibar to the Atlantic Ocean in 999 days and that he was the first to do so. I learned a Tuareg saying, "Kiss the hand you cannot sever."

"Scrambling for Africa," the title of the lecture, was presented in four segments: the slave capturing period prior to the 1870's, scrambling to colonize from 1876 to 1912, the Cold War from the 1950's to the 1990's and China seeking resources from the 1990's to the present.

The lecturer stated that the Muslims took more slaves than anyone else and that the Portuguese captured 4.6 million. The European countries were not kind to Africa. King Leopold of Belgium owned his own country and killed 10 million Africans.

The Indian Ocean was the center of trade for the world and enabled the European cities to develop and prosper. Printing, the compass and gunpowder all arrived in Europe from China via the Indian Ocean.

The Indian Ocean is the third largest of the world's oceanic divisions, covering about 20% of the water on the earth's surface. The Indian Ocean carries a particularly heavy traffic of petroleum and petroleum products from the oilfields of the Persian Gulf and Indonesia. An estimated 40% of the world's offshore oil production comes from the Indian Ocean.

Following the decline of the British Empire, India and Australia dominated the Indian Ocean. Fishing fleets from Russia, Japan, South Korea and Taiwan now exploit the Indian Ocean for shrimp and tuna. The indiscriminate harvesting off the coast of east Africa is one of the underlying causes of the current pirate outrages.

Sonja Klein

I received an invitation to sit at the captain's table on New Year's Eve. Elaborate festivities were planned and I dressed for the occasion, wearing a silver squash blossom necklace and a large turquoise ring and bracelet which accent black silk pants and a turquoise silk blouse

The evening began with a cocktail party in the large lounge. Entertainment with singing and dancing followed. From there the party moved to the main dining room. I was escorted to the captain's table and pleasantly surprised to be seated next him. Also seated at the table were the ship's chief engineer, the social director and some other women. The captain and chief engineer were Italian but spoke English. The initial conversation focused on my necklace and jewelry. None of the guests had seen or heard of a squash blossom necklace or pawn jewelry, defined as old southwest handcrafted pieces, signed by the artist. Most of them did not recognize turquoise even though the Mid-East is known for its lovely turquoise.

The dinner was elegant, with many courses and consumed the better part of the evening. Near midnight, the band began to play and I danced with the captain and chief engineer. They were not accomplished dancers. The music switched to rock and roll and everyone gyrated to the music. At midnight, noisemakers drowned most of the music and we sang "Auld Lang Sine" and innocently kissed everyone. I can't recall a nicer evening.

The following morning the ship docked at Nosy Be, an island just a stone's throw off Madagascar's northwest coast. The fertile island is the center for the production of perfume essence from the yiang-yiang trees.

I left the ship to visit the town of Hellville, named after a former French governor. The town features a few old colonial buildings, a busy market and shops. I rode into the countryside to a yiang-yiang plantation and a coffee plantation. The road wound through the hills among sugarcane, pepper and vanilla plantations.

I declined making the trip to Nosy Komba, a tiny island nearby known for its lemur preserve. These arboreal primates, with their large eyes, soft fur and long curling tails, have lived unharmed for centuries. I had seen lemurs in the arms of vendors in Hellville.

Following the drive through the countryside I stopped at Andilana Beach, enjoyed some refreshments and listened to children singing native songs. The island is poor, with a diverse ethnic mixture. I learned that the culture is one of taboos and animism and that there were no jobs since the rum factory shut down. The natives were black, African and spoke French and Malagasy.

Somehow I managed to join a tour where no one spoke English, not all bad but difficult to obtain information. The guide spoke French and some English. He lectured on the meaning of taboo, but it was hard to follow. The pouring rain drove me back to the ship, where I attended a lecture on the violence that has permeated African history and the Indian Ocean.

The lecturer stated that suicide bombing originated in Sri Lanka with the Tamil Tigers. The Portuguese traders terrorized the Arab sailors in the Indian Ocean. In 1502, Vasco da Gama captured 800 Arab crewmen and cut off their hands, noses and ears. The Arab traders were unarmed and had been sailing the waters for years. The authorization of such violence originated with the Catholic popes.

The ship sailed to Reunion Island, located about 480 miles east of Madagascar. Reunion is the largest of the Mascarene Islands. The archipelago consisting of Rodrigues, Mauritius and Reunion was named the Mascarentes following its discovery in 1512 by the Portuguese navigator Pedro de Mascarenhas. The French decided to settle Reunion in 1642. Since 1946, France has administered Reunion as an overseas department, with St. Denis as its capital. The facilities are comparable to any major town in metropolitan France, and looking about, I could have been in France. Phone calls to France were local. The island was modern and the roads were excellent. The European Union funded the coastal roads and highways on the island, spending millions of Euros. The Europeans on the tour were not very enthused about their tax dollars being spent on this remote island far from the European continent. I found it ridiculous.

The island is volcanic, about 50 by 70 kilometers in dimension and hosts a population of over 800,000. It is the highest point in the Indian Ocean. With such a large population, food and water are of utmost importance. Chicken and sugar cane are raised. Electric power is generated from ocean currents. Hospitals and universities are modern.

I visited the most popular place on the island, the Volcano Piton de la Fournaise, a massive basaltic shield volcano rising more than 8,632 feet above sea level. The volcano is one of the world's most active, an eruption occurring almost every year. I wasn't too comfortable hearing that information.

Arriving at the summit, I viewed a nested caldera created by two eruptions. Clouds veiled the active crater, and the panorama was spectacular. I relaxed somewhat as we descended the volcano to dine on a traditional Creole lunch, spicy chicken and fish.

The trip was ending. The ship docked in Mauritius. The large island gained independence and in 1982 became a republic. Indians, imported to work, dominate the population. I spent the afternoon visiting the Pamplemousses Botanical Garden, which dates back to the French period. In 1736, the French governor resided around the present gardens and years later, vegetables, fruits and flowers from all over the world were introduced to the gardens. The gardens faced difficulty under the British rule, but were revived in the mid-1800's.

The weather was uncomfortably warm. I strolled among many species of palms and saw giant lily pads floating in waters. Leaving the gardens, I visited a sugar museum, tasting grades of sugar and sampling rum.

I traveled across town to the Eureka Colonial House, a restored French plantation home. The view was nice and the grounds lush.

The day was long. I was ready to return home. My flight to Dubai was not scheduled to leave until 11:30 that evening. I spent the remainder of the day people watching at the Bagatelle Shopping Mall. It was vast and busy. Young people dominated the food court. The people were mostly Indian. It was difficult to comprehend the contrast between poverty and affluence seen in that mall.

The flight home was without incident, the layover in Dubai nominal. Reflecting on the adventure I decided it was one of the best. The diversity of fellow travelers, the intimacy of a small ship and the contrast in port destinations was extremely stimulating. The future of Africa with over 50 separate countries does not look good. I was told that cell phones have improved the information base, but the infrastructure and poverty encourage despots. The people suffer immensely. I have seen poverty but never before as severe as in Africa. I will never forget the lack of hope and despair on the faces of the stick-thin Africans. Scenes of them rummaging through piles of garbage with long sticks will remain.

Roundtrip from Texas

I could never live on an isolated small island in the middle of the ocean. I'm glad and thankful to be an American and live in Texas.

35

Grandmama day care

With only three of us managing a ranch, the workload is shared. We share duties according to ability, but as the senior resident, I usually preempt the easy jobs.

Since my daughter Molly is currently working on her master's thesis and her partner Israel does most of the hard labor, the task of taking care of Theiss, my 20-month-old grandson, is my first choice.

I don't think I have ever loved a human being except for my children as much as I love that little boy. Not being his mother gives me the opportunity to adore and spoil him to the nth degree.

We have such fun together, cooking and playing. He loves to play with a flashlight, pots and pans, empty oatmeal cylinders and pillows. We laugh together. He is so alive. He knows every object in my home. I tell him stories about the origin of each item, "This is the abalone shell that Uncle Joe brought back from California. This is the seal your mommy bought in Dunedin, New Zealand. This is the picture of the serpent your beautiful, famous grandmama purchased in Bhutan. This is the trophy your beautiful, famous grandmama won for her excellent writing. This is the award your beautiful, famous grandmama was awarded for her great pecan pie. She is a wonderful cook."

He knows every object and story. When I ask him, "Where's the picture of the cowboy on the horse?" he points to it. He knows the location and description of every picture on my walls, and there are lots of them. In fact, my walls have very little open space. There are ornaments from Mongolia, Turkey, Uzbekistan and other exotic destinations hanging from the ceiling fans. Woven tapestries from faraway places surround my doorways. There are tiles from Mexico, rugs from Peru, animal skins on the backs of the bar chairs, a Ferris wheel of skeletons celebrating the Day of the Dead, a metal horny toad, a wooden porcupine with sharp toothpick-like quills and a cuckoo clock. The minute he enters the house he goes to the base of the cuckoo clock and waits for me to pull the metal chains and set the pendulum in motion. On the hour and half hour, it chimes a song and cuckoos. He dances to the chimes and his mouth makes an O and his eyes light in wonder every time the clock makes a sound. The minute he leaves, I stop the pendulum. The thing drives me crazy.

The weird thing about the cuckoo clock is that my husband John hated it and it stopped ticking at 9:15 on the day he died, September 15, 1997. I hadn't activated it since then and was sort of surprised when I did so to entertain Theiss. I know if I died tomorrow, he would forever have a cuckoo clock in his memory.

He loves to watch me cook as I pick him up and show him what's simmering in the pots on the stove. When I cut up vegetables, I set him on the counter carefully and he takes a bite of everything I give him: sliced peppers, onions, garlic, squash, fresh spinach leaves, beet greens, raw potato. If I eat it, he eats it.

Usually around noon, he takes a nap. He gets quiet and falls asleep in the playpen that won't hold him much longer. Molly, his mother, says, "He never naps at our house. He only falls asleep at your house because he's bored." Of course, I know better but say nothing.

When he naps, I lie down on the sofa and read, welcoming a break.

When the phone rings, he discovers all sorts of forbidden places that he normally ignores. Sometimes he hides. One day he discovered the rattan shelf unit that holds the hard liquor. In the course of my phone conversation, I found him fingering a glass bottle of vermouth. It was a close call.

He loves the baby bracelet that was mine. I almost waited too long to fit it onto his small wrist. It's just perfect. He drinks from the two small silver cups that were mine as a baby and smiles every time he picks one up. I only put a small amount of water in them, no reason to take a chance and have a sticky mess on the floor. Actually, he does quite well with the cups.

We don't watch TV; instead, we read books. He loves books. I read to him and point out the pictures. He likes that. When my children were small, I would put them in their beds for a nap and give them books. I told them, "As long as you stay in bed, you don't have to sleep as long as you have a book." To this day, both of them read before going to bed. That was one of the things I did correctly. God knows, I made my share of mistakes. I tried. With Theiss, I try harder.

36

The speech

After receiving delivery of my first published books, I asked myself, *How am I going to sell 1,000 books?'* I didn't know.

I emailed everyone I knew. I sold about 50 books. I held book signings. That was scary. I sold a few more. I sent copies to Texas newspapers and magazines. Nothing much happened. I emailed and called libraries, offering to host more book signings. The Barbara Bush Library in north Houston was interested. In May, they asked if I would be the keynote speaker at their 35th anniversary the following March. I agreed and immediately began to worry about public speaking. Most of the time, I tried to forget the commitment, but it was there in the back of my mind when I lacked anxiety.

Six months before the deadline, I wrote a speech. A month or so later, I refined it.

At the three-month mark, I worried. I rewrote the speech, practiced it and was relieved to find that it took 18 minutes to deliver. Twenty minutes had been allotted. I was good with the time. I began to practice, reading the speech on the front porch pretending the audience was before me. About the tenth time, I was bored. I didn't like it. So I let it rest.

Not wanting to waste a road trip, I arranged to attend a writing seminar in Johnson City on the way to Houston. Then I loaded the agenda with an evening of bridge with my brothers and sister-in-law. Not to be deterred I made an appointment with my attorney for some estate planning and a conference with my CPA about my income tax. I figured if I stayed busy, I wouldn't have time to worry about the speech. As usual, I was wrong.

The afternoon before the speech my heart threatened to jump out of my chest. I took some aspirin and meditated for an hour. It didn't help much. My son drove to the library and carried the books to the display table where I would sign and hopefully sell them to all the hundreds of people lined up to buy an autographed copy.

Roundtrip from Texas

The library was huge. The event was festive. There were drinks and snacks, a scavenger hunt for door prizes and a picture of me on the program with a brief biography. My brothers and their wives, nephew, niece, son and daughter-in-law sat on the front row. I was certain that I would fall over from a stroke as my heart again threatened to leave my body.

When I was introduced and approached the podium and saw that the room was not only crowded but also there were people standing along the walls, something happened. I don't know what, but I stood up there and delivered the speech of a lifetime. As I looked upon the sea of faces, I felt a sense of power that was the highest high I have ever experienced. They hung on every word. They laughed, they smiled and they were mine.

I ad-libbed, I gestured, I was passionate.

37

Bush Library speech

"Congratulations on your 35th anniversary. The Friends of the Library play an important part in the programs designed to serve the community and I am honored to be here.

I remember when there was no Cypresswood Drive. Most of this land on which the library rests was a heavily wooded swamp and Louetta was a dirt road.

I have been asked to speak about growing up in the Klein community, so this is about my family.

My theory of how the area became known as Klein is quite simple. My great uncle, Charlie Klein, was the rural mail carrier.

In the 1850's, my father's family, the Kleins, immigrated to Texas from southwestern Germany.

My mother's family, the Theiss' emigrated a decade earlier. The other branches of my family: the Haudes, the Mittelstedts, the Wieds and the Klenks, arrived during the same period along with the Stracks, Muellers, Hildebrandts, Hasslers, Holzworths, Hiedens and others. Through marriage, I am kin to most all of the early German settlers in this area.

They had large families. My Grandmother Theiss, maiden name Haude, was one of 13 children. Her husband had 10 siblings. My grandfather John Klein was one of eight.

My mother's family farmed. They were poor but ate well.

My mother's mother, Grandma Theiss, was the only grandparent I ever knew. The rest of them died either before I was born or when I was too young to remember them.

Mother was one of eight children, six girls and two boys. Her father worked on the farm and in the sawmill nearby. She was born in 1920 and grew up during the Great Depression. She never forgot those days. She was always proud to have been in the first high school graduating class from Klein High School.

She married my father when she was 19. He was 46 and a veteran of World War I. They both grew up in the Klein community. He also was one of eight children, five boys and three girls. Their families knew each other and my mother's aunt had married my father's brother. The Kleins were also farmers.

My father was educated at Trinity Lutheran School. His education consisted of primary school. They spoke German and English. I remember as a young child attending church in the old wooden building near the present Trinity Lutheran. The service was conducted in German. When we were children, our father often sang songs to us in German, and when he was with his brothers and sisters, they spoke German. Most of their spouses did not speak German. I always thought they were telling secrets not to be heard by the children or in-laws. They probably were.

I grew up in Houston, but our family spent most every weekend and summer at the farm, land that my father had obtained from his father's estate. Daddy was a weekend farmer. He loved to plant. He planted a pecan orchard that still exists on Spring Cypress. After his retirement, he planted over a million pine seedlings on the sandy prairie. We grew corn, peanuts, sugar cane and vegetables.

I think I was quite young when he put me on the Ford tractor to steer while he and my brothers followed, stripping the ears of corn and throwing them in the wooden trailer behind the tractor. When we reached the end of the row, I stepped on the brake and clutch. Daddy made the turn and we worked the next row. I felt important.

His work ethic was strong. We dug peanuts, shucked corn, picked up and shelled pecans and helped our mother process the produce. Daddy always had a few cattle and some horses. Every fall we butchered a calf. My job was to drag the guts to the upper pecan orchard for the buzzards. After the animal was skinned and quartered, Mother and I drove to Tomball to Klein Grocery and left the meat before returning weeks later to wrap the meat as the butcher cut the steaks and ground the meat.

On the day we butchered, Mother would scramble the brains with eggs, chicken fry the heart and liver and boil the tongue in spices. I ate it all except the brains. I never could eat brains.

I especially remember one time we had a barbecue. I don't recall the occasion. My mother's Uncle Lawrence Theiss was in charge of the barbecue. He dug a pit and he and some of the relatives stayed up all night drinking beer and telling stories. They called him Uncle Windy. His stories were ethnic and funny. The next day they played washers, using silver dollars. It was an exciting weekend for me.

Rarely were we allowed to have fun. Work always came first. Once our work was complete, we went fishing at the pond or rode horses. As my brothers grew older, they hunted rabbits, squirrels, frogs and ducks. We cleaned and ate everything we killed. The ducks were plucked and pillows were made with the feathers.

Up until a few years ago, I slept under Grandpa Klein's feather comforter. He died before I was born. Before my mother died, she periodically asked, "Are you still sleeping under Grandpa Klein's comforter?"

I always replied, "Yes, of course."

"Don't you think it's time for you to get rid of that old thing? Those feathers are older than you."

My answer was always the same, "No, Mom, I'm not going to get rid of it. That comforter is my friend."

After weekends at the farm, we Sunday visited. Sometimes we drove to Spring to visit my father's sister, Aunt Ella Doering. I loved her a lot. Her food was good, especially her chicken and dumplings. There was always a game of 42 dominoes.

I remember when Aunt Ella's daughter was to be married. We were all sitting in the wooden church at Klein. The organist kept playing the music. Uncle George Klein was sitting behind us and I heard him say, "What if the groom doesn't show up?"

The groom didn't show up. We left the church and returned to Aunt Ella's, where the band played and the food was served. We could hear the jilted bride crying in the upstairs bedroom. The bride's brothers went looking for the groom. It turned out he was already married.

Occasionally, we visited Aunt Mathilda Arp. Mother's family always said, "Better go see Aunt Mathilda. She's been sick." She was always in bed. She lived to her 90's. Or we would stop to see Aunt Elizabeth Lemm and her mother, my great grandmother, Louisa Mittelstedt Theiss. She was in her 90's when she burned to death from a stove fire.

Other times we stopped at Uncle Adam's, who lived next to the farm. His farmhouse was white with a big porch. Lyle Lovett now lives in that house. Adam Klein was his grandfather.

Uncle Adam dressed in overalls and chewed tobacco. Aunt Amanda was always in the kitchen. She was a good cook. Uncle Adam's sons ran a dairy behind the house and farmed. As children, we always ran to the dairy to see the cows. Country music played and my grown cousins would set us children on the cows as they were being milked. I loved the attention and the smell of the dairy barn.

I remember walking to the dairy barn. I never wore shoes. The dark green clover in the path was burning grass. My feet turned to fire. I probably cried.

I remember the reception at the house when Uncle Adam's youngest son was married. There was a band and dancing in the yard, food and beer. When the bride and groom prepared to leave for their honeymoon, all the male relatives stood outside the room where they were dressing and banged metal. They called it a chivaree. I thought it was exciting.

Tomball was included in our Sunday visits. I loved Uncle Alec. He was Daddy's brother and had nine children. He was in charge of the Klein Grocery Store. They lived in a large white frame house on Main Street. Uncle Alec smoked cigarettes and sat in his recliner telling stories. I remember sitting on his lap and listening. He was a great storyteller.

A few times a year, Daddy would drive to Christian Strack's farm on Louetta and honk the horn as he parked at the yard gate. I was always embarrassed by the honking horn. Daddy bought smoked sausage from him. It was good.

Many Sundays on the way home from the farm we visited my Grandma Theiss. I remember turning off Stuebner Airline onto the rutted dirt road that passed the McDougall farmhouse and then the farm of Mose Mueller. I think he was kin to my mother in some distant way. Then we drove across the rickety cattle guard to Grandma's.

One time after a rain, the boards slid together as we crossed. The front tires fell below the surface. Daddy was not very happy. My brother walked to Grandma's, and Uncle Pete came with the tractor and pulled us out.

Grandma's dog was called Youknow, so if you asked what his name was, the answer was, "You know." He always followed us off the farm to the cattle guard. There he stopped and returned home.

When we visited Grandma's, Uncle Pete was usually sitting on the top porch step, one knee propped up and smoking a cigarette. We went to Grandma for a kiss and said hello to Aunt Myrtle, my mother's oldest sister, who never married due to a congenital heart condition. She sewed and stayed with sick people for money.

My mother and all of her sisters sewed. When I was small, my mother sewed my dresses and delicate lace-trimmed batiste panties. When I was in high school, she made my dresses. When I went to college, Aunt Myrtle sewed my wardrobe, including a wool coat. She sewed Uncle Pete's shirts. She died in the 1960's. She was in her 40's.

One year I stayed at Grandma's when she and her sisters quilted. I was thrilled to be included and taught to quilt. Two of my mother's sisters still quilt.

My mother tried to teach me to sew. I must have been about 11 or 12. She started me out with pillowcases. If the seam was crooked, I had to rip it out. I wanted to sew clothes for myself. I never mastered sewing. I didn't inherit that gene.

Uncle Pete lived on the farm. He never married and took care of his mother and sisters. When my Grandpa Theiss died, the youngest child was nine years old.

Once we said hello, we went outside to chase the chickens or play under the house in the sandy soil. Daddy usually stayed outside and talked with Uncle Pete about the weather.

The visits were not prolonged but always before we left Grandma would fix us a bread and butter sandwich with home-canned pear, fig or peach preserves. She wore an apron made from scraps or flour sacks. She wore her long hair in a bun and was bent over from hard work and a weak back. She was a kind, sweet person and called me Sony Rose, not Sonja Rose.

During the summers, we were sent to Grandma's for a week or two. I remember the kerosene lamps along the wall of the wooden farmhouse her husband, William Theiss, built. It was set back off Theiss Mail Road. The Theiss's were always handy with building. My father was not.

The house plan was simple and functional, a long, wide hallway with three large rooms on either side. The left side contained bedrooms, the right side was one bedroom followed by a connecting dining room and kitchen. The back porch was screened.

On the back porch was a washstand with a towel, basin of water and soap. Uncle Pete's razor strap hung beside the back door.

Behind the house was a well with a bucket and rope and hand pump. Off to the side was the smokehouse, and behind that were the barn, cattle pen and water trough. Farther behind the smokehouse was the chicken yard and in the far back corner of the chicken yard was the outhouse, a two-holer. The boards were weathered and gray. It stank and the door was hard for a child to open.

We worked the summer weeks we spent at Grandma's. We arose at daylight, drank coffee milk and rode or walked to the field behind the sled pulled by two mules. I recall picking peas, dragging a sack tied around my waist. We dug sweet potatoes that Uncle Pete uncovered with the mule-driven plow.

Uncle Pete topped the corn stalks with a knife. We picked up the tops and loaded them into the sled to be fed to the livestock. We gathered eggs, washing the dirt and droppings with a soft rag dipped into a vinegar and water solution. We then scaled them to determine whether they were small, medium, large or jumbo and put them in the appropriate crate.

Returning from the field mid-morning, we ate lunch, usually fried chicken, mashed potatoes, cream gravy and fresh vegetables, always with bread, butter and preserves. Uncle Pete always covered a slice of bread with cream gravy and dark molasses. I imitated him. It was good.

After lunch, as the day heated up, everyone took a nap; that is everyone except us kids. We played in the dirt under the house, usually under Uncle Pete's bedroom. If we were too noisy, Uncle Pete would say in a deep voice that instilled the fear of God, "If you kids don't keep quiet, I'm going to get my razor strap after you."

Those were the scariest words we ever heard. In later years, we spoke of our fear of Uncle Pete. He never laid a hand on us or that strap in our presence. I think I was in my 40's before I realized what a kind and gentle man he was.

Following nap time, Grandma, Uncle Pete and Aunt Myrtle drank coffee and ate something sweet like homemade coffee cake. We drank milk. Uncle Pete poured the hot coffee into the saucer to cool it and then picked up saucer and drank from it.

Often we returned to the field or would sit on the front porch and shell peas, lots of peas: blackeyes, crowders, purple hulls or cream peas.

Saturdays, we bathed. Grandma would heat water in a black pot over a wood fire in the chicken yard. She carried the hot water to the washtub either on the back porch or in the back yard near the well. We all bathed in the same water. Dirty clothes were boiled in that same pot.

When Grandma pulled the head off a chicken, we watched in wonder as the headless chicken thrashed. After gutting the bird, she dunked it in hot water before picking the feathers.

Some afternoons we were sent to the corn crib in the barn to shell corn for the chickens. We first shucked the dried ears of corn and then fed them into a hand-cranked sheller. When the bucket was full, we scattered the kernels in the dirt of the chicken yard.

The evening meal was light, usually leftovers. We went to bed early with the chickens. The mattresses and pillows stuffed with chicken feather were soft.

As the years progressed and I grew older, I remember electricity and a refrigerator coming to Grandma's. In the evenings, after supper, Uncle Pete would sit almost on top of the radio and listen to the weather and news. On Saturday nights, we stayed up late to listen to the Grand Ole Opry.

The son-in-laws helped Uncle Pete install indoor plumbing on a portion of the back porch. An electric fan found its way to the dining room. A washer and dryer were put in the smokehouse. Uncle Pete drove a tractor. A TV and window air-conditioning unit appeared in the dining room. A seven-party line was installed. Everyone on the line had a different code of rings and eavesdropped. Uncle Pete watched the Grand Ole Opry on television.

In 1992, my mother took us four children to Germany. We visited the small towns where the Theiss and Klein ancestors were born. On the trip, we also played tourist. On one occasion in the town of Trier, we stopped to view a cathedral and some Roman ruins. It was a Sunday and my brother Allan was driving. He parked in front of a grocery store that was closed. The sign in the parking lot read that the spaces were reserved only for customers. As Allan parked the car, our German friends who were with us protested. They said we could not park there, that it was forbidden. Allan replied that the store was closed. The Germans insisted we move. Since my mother's mobility was limited, the two of us got out and waited while my brother parked the van quite a distance away. As we were reunited, I made the comment, "I'm glad our ancestors made the right choice." The four of us agreed.

Roundtrip from Texas

Grandma was in her early 80's when she died. My father died that same year. He was 80. My mother died three years ago. She was 89. I miss them all. My memories, I keep,"

As the speech ended, they stood and clapped. They clustered around me as if I was famous. My brothers lauded my talent, the same brothers I have spent my life trying to emulate.

The library staff wants me back. People lined up to buy my book. I now know the addictive nature of fame. It was marvelous. The library presented me with a framed print of a beautiful mural in the Children's Section of the library, along with a thank you note and a check for $100, my first paid speaking gig.

A bottle of wine and some cheese and crackers at my son's house enabled sleep. But the next morning I was still soaring. I sold some books in Old Town Spring and drove to my brother's ranch in Crockett, had dinner, attended a concert and sold some more books. I even sold one to a lady at a gas station on the drive home.

Three days later, I was still high and sent a press release to the local newspapers touting my successful publicity tour and offering my services to speak for local community groups.

Still floating, I signed up for a seminar in Austin on marketing and arranged to attend a concert and sell more books.

On top of that, I came home energized with so many ideas for essays that I found myself waking at 3:30 A.M. wanting to write and sitting at the computer, fingers flying.

Every time I think it's time to lie back and relax for the rest of my life, the universe throws the most marvelous experiences in my path. I'm ready and willing to catch every one of them.

38

Two weeks with Theiss

Having sworn never to be a babysitting grandma, I became one. Almost two years had passed since Theiss was born and my daughter and her partner left on their first vacation since his birth.

I was both apprehensive and elated, apprehensive that something might happen to him on my isolated ranch and elated that I would have him all to myself.

Being brilliant and sharp, as all grandchildren are, he would be a challenge. I figured I had about another year before he could outsmart me. I was determined to outthink him and minimize my dumbness.

We started out well with no problems. I established a routine: lunch at noon, nap at 12:30 and bedtime at 8 P.M., smooth as silk.

The first trip into town was fun at first. We walked into the bank. He held my hand. He charmed the tellers and customers. When it was time to leave, he threw himself on the floor and refused to walk. I dragged him kicking and screaming to the truck. The next stop I left him tightly buckled in his car seat and ran in the store to buy milk. Fortunately, I left a window open just in case. It was the right decision. A honking horn disturbed the store patrons. I noticed right away it was my truck. My first thought: *Something is wrong with the truck. It's going to blow up.*

I ran outside. He was safely buckled in his car seat. My car keys, which I had left on the middle console were missing. I went back into the store and looked all over, thinking I had taken my keys with me and dropped them. Everyone helped me look. Then I went back to the truck and examined it closely. No keys.

Next thought, *Someone tried to steal the truck but when they saw the baby in the back seat they changed their mind but took the keys anyway.*

By then everyone in the town of 500 was helping me look for the keys. We found them tucked between his legs in the car seat. Embarrassed does not sufficiently describe my feelings. I was relieved to leave town and return to the ranch, where I was on familiar ground.

Roundtrip from Texas

Fearing that Theiss might lock the bathroom door from the inside, I taped the pointed thing that locks the door. The tape was transparent, so I didn't notice he had removed the tape until he locked himself in the bathroom. A letter opener saved the situation. I kept it handy.

I certainly did not teach that child the word, "Ow." He must have discovered it at Walmart because he kept yelling it as I pushed him up and down the aisles. Fellow customers eyed me suspiciously, as if I was hurting him. I merely smiled and kept moving.

Determined to triumph, I met friends for lunch. Theiss was well mannered. He sat in the highchair and ate all the French fries, never threw anything on the floor or off his plate. He was quiet and attentive. As we left the restaurant, he held my hand and charmed the public. My friends remarked, "He is such a good child, so well behaved."

The kicker came when I picked him up to put him his car seat. He erupted with a blood-curdling scream and his body became as pliant as an earthworm's. He twisted and turned like a corkscrew. I was exhausted when I finally buckled the monster in his car seat. The best news was that his screams were not as loud as I thought.

When I returned to the ranch, I stopped at my daughter's house to retrieve something from her refrigerator. I left him buckled. As I left their yard, closed the gate and approached the truck I noticed that Theiss was not in it. His car seat wasn't there either. First thought: *Someone has taken him and the car seat too. I* am a writer. I have a vivid imagination. I'd gone to the wrong truck, the ranch truck. My truck was six feet away.

By the second week, my senses were finely tuned. I was aware and totally in the moment. There was no time to pay attention to my worry list. Theiss had my utmost concentration. I watched him like a hawk. I knew his every move. He still tricked me a few times a day but with less success.

I was sad to see his mother and father return and missed him, but not for very long. I had to eat my words. I am still a babysitting grandma.

39

The scapegoat

Mostly, I enjoy writing about positive experiences. I shun negativity for the obvious reasons, but on a recent trip, I encountered the familiar scenario of guided small group trips where one or more travelers are singled out because they weren't like everyone else.

As the scenario developed, I watched, remembering the trips and the scapegoats I had met, my favorite people, those I had befriended and remember fondly.

The first was a red-haired lady from California. She was flamboyant, dressed colorfully and closely followed the guest hosts who were on board the ship to dance with the unattached ladies. She knew them all. All of the other women talked about her every waking moment, "Look at her; she's dining with the guest hosts again."

"Did you see that outfit she had on last night? Ridiculous for a woman her age."

"She must be at least 60."

"The hosts are only supposed to dance one dance at a time with a passenger. Last night I saw her dance twice with Ron."

"I think someone should tell the social director."

I sat next to her on a shore excursion. She was sweet and kind. Her story was typical. She lived in a small southern town, was married with two sons. She worked at the courthouse, had an affair with the sheriff, then divorced and moved to California with him and her children. They owned some franchise businesses, the new husband fell dead of a heart attack, the restaurants were sued and money was lost.

She signed up for ballroom dance classes, met a contractor and married him. A month into the marriage, he hurt his back and never worked another day. She divorced him and found her way back to financial stability.

I liked her and we became traveling friends. How could I judge her, or anyone else, for that matter?

A trip to Asia found another scapegoat, a woman again. She was a schoolteacher from up east. She wore clothes that should have been in the rag basket and left them at the various hotels. She left bras with broken straps, dirty panties with holes in them and blue jeans with broken zippers. Her wardrobe was held together with safety pins. As her suitcase emptied, she purchased everything in sight using her credit card. Everyone talked about her and watched her every move.

When we arrived at a small rural town, the accommodations were short, and those of us traveling single were asked to share a room. No one offered to share with her. I did. I liked her and heard her story. She had taught school for years, was near 60 and had had an affair with a married man for 30 years. He died. She had waited her entire life for this man, who then left her with nothing.

On a long journey across Russia, a woman from Germany became the scapegoat. She was forgetful, often disoriented and lost, and regularly late. On one occasion, as she entered the coach late, the group booed and hissed at her. She was confused and hurt by the treatment. I stood up and asked her to sit with me. She was kind and sweet and probably in the first stages of some sort of dementia.

I later told the group, "Whether you like her or not, she's part of this group and instead of being cruel to her, we all need to take care of her and look out for her. What if she were your mother? Wouldn't you want someone to watch out for her? "

It worked. Everyone changed their attitude. The trip was more pleasant.

On a river barge trip, the scapegoats were a couple. She was a tall beautiful blonde from Venezuela traveling with her live-in boyfriend from Florida. He had teenage children. She was in her late 20's. She shopped with casual splendor. He was quick with the money. Phone calls were exchanged with the teenagers, crisis after crisis. She drank a lot; so did he. Everyone watched them, commented on her scanty provocative clothes with her beautiful body and long blonde dyed hair. The two of them were often observed more than the passing scenery.

Of course, I chatted with them every chance. He was in real estate, had published a book on divorce. She was a travel agent. They were planning on marriage. They were young, colorful and intelligent, but most of all different from the over 60's drab, retired and boring.

Along the Silk Road in central Asia, a couple in their 80's caught the small group's attention. They ate lots of supplement pills and power-walked every spare moment. They were both retired professors with doctorate degrees and let everyone know they were obviously superior in mind and body. No one cried when they both came down with dysentery. I left them alone. They had each other.

A unique lady from the east became the center of attention on a trip to Asia. She was in her 70's, had translucent pale skin, coal black hair and wore rhinestone jewelry of every color. Her outfits were straight from Hollywood and she was not ashamed to display bare arms or mid-torso. She was loud and outrageous and she became my best friend. I let her shine. She had traveled alone for years because her husband had Alzheimer's. He was in a condo next to hers with a nurse. She had left him in good hands. She was a master bridge player and an instructor. She took courses at a nearby university. She was intelligent and one of a kind. We rode an elephant together, we rode a bicycle taxi together and even sat in the back of an oxcart in a thunderstorm on the way to a Buddhist temple in the jungle. We had fun. Everyone watched us, which actually made it more fun.

When the trip was over, she commented, "This was the best trip ever." I replied the same. We weren't like anyone else, by choice.

If you are really intent on criticism, the swimming pool of a small cruise ship is ideal. On one such cruise, the focus of attention was on a Russian lady built very squarely with short spiky orange hair. She could have been anywhere between 30 and 60. Her bikini left nothing to speculation. She overflowed the fabric and walked with the assurance of someone familiar with her skin. She drank vodka most of the day. She was very happy, danced often and was loud.

Of course, I attempted to befriend her. She was different. Her replies were, "Only Russian." I persisted. Soon I was receiving smiles and waves. We became friends nonverbally. Our pantomimes became eloquent. Since I have always maintained that words are the lowest form of communication, this was an interesting experiment.

After the first week, our eyes met often and we exchanged expressions indicative of how things were going. We parted friends with a hug, having never exchanged a word.

Only once can I recall a scapegoat being thrown off a trip. He was an attorney from Atlanta, a short, heavy-set man who insisted on a massage at every hotel and then related lurid details that no one believed. He spoke obscenely with every woman he met, including the guides, waitresses, hotel employees and pretty women on the street. He was reprimanded for his behavior but continued to act as before.

Finally, in the middle of Asia, in Uzbekistan, he was put on a plane to Frankfort, having been told that his behavior was not acceptable and he could no longer continue on the trip. He deserved exactly what happened. He was responsible for his bad manners. I, of course, tried to be nice to him. It was difficult. His story was not all that bad, the usual, a wife who no longer cared. I can see why.

Imagine a mother and daughter on a trip with twenty seniors. The Texas pair was colorful, experienced, educated, curious, intelligent and lovely, but most of all fun loving and outspoken. Their fellow travelers paid more attention to them than the lectures or sights. The gossip was nasty; every word misinterpreted. Never has the contrast between living on an isolated ranch and a condo in the urban east been so apparent. The culture of the civilized east and the frontiers of the west clashed on the edge of the Caribbean. Only one befriended the pair, a survivalist who lives on an island in Michigan. No surprise there.

40

Tennis shoes

The glory days of America have passed. When citizens stand in line all night for the privilege of buying a pair of bizarre illuminated tennis shoes for $240 and the media covers the event on national television, I am inclined to lose all hope. And when a police force numbering near 100 is called to disburse the riot that ensues when the doors of the shoe store are opened, I shake my head.

Are these people informed voters? Are they following world events or sitting home at their computers anxious to purchase the latest consumer offering? Do they spend major bucks to attend sports events where the athletes are paid millions? Do they pay $10 to park and $10 for a hot dog, beer or soda?

The extended news coverage of the event justifies the consumer madness by adding that buying a pair of the shoes is an investment, that the lucky buyer can sell the shoes for up to $3,000. Is this the mind-set of America, investing in illuminated tennis shoes?

The world of the 1950's, the days of Ozzie and Harriet, "Leave It to Beaver" and "The Ted Mack Amateur Hour" is gone. Today, nothing is sacred; no bodily function is ignored. Rather it is displayed on the big screen for all to see, children not excluded.

Thanks to Bill Clinton, every child knows about blow jobs. And he was the President of the United States.

The War on Drugs ignores prescription medications. The majority of Americans are on some type of medication, driving, making decisions and present in the workforce. It's amazing that the country functions at all.

We pay more for bottled water than we do for gasoline when our water supply is completely safe. How was that hoax perpetrated on the public, the myth that we must drink bottled water? If it is that critical to our health, why not fill a bottle of water and carry it with you rather than pay for it?

Restaurants are now charging $2 or more for a glass of iced tea. Before long, they will be charging the same amount for water. And then there are the coffee houses, $5 or much more for a small paper cup of coffee or latte or espresso or cappuccino. Don't forget to stand in line, too, for that privilege.

What has happened to common sense and thrift? They have died along with the courage and spirit of the American people.

41

The sorority

My cousin Ida called, "Sonja, would you like to attend our sorority reunion in Fredericksburg?"

"When is it?"

"Not till the first weekend in May."

Fall had just approached the Hill Country. I had no plans for the following May.

My answer was simple, "Sure, I'd love to go. Send me the info."

"I thought we could share a room."

"That sounds great. I'll put it on my calendar."

As time approached, I began to think about my sorority days at The University of Texas. For the first two years of college, I was active in the sorority that two of my cousins had joined. When I hitchhiked through Europe the summer following my junior year, I left the sorority behind and was not very active. I had learned to fly with my own wings and had become quite critical of all the sister shit, even to the extent of believing that sororities were unnecessary. I was wrong.

The weekend in Fredericksburg was well planned. Cocktail hour was celebrated before a Mexican buffet near the hotel. I did not recognize a single one of my sisters until I read their name tag and noticed a faint resemblance.

A few glasses of wine encouraged comfort. Memories flooded.

"Who was our pledge trainer?"

I had forgotten we *had* a pledge trainer.

"Who was your big sister?"

I remembered Penny.

"Who was your little sister?"

"I don't have a clue."

"Ida, can you remember your big sister?"

"No, but I remember my little sister."

Someone asked, "Do you remember Judy, our choir director?"

"What choir director?"

"She was merciless when we had to compete against the other sororities in the singing contest."

"Oh, I remember that vaguely. Did we ever win?"

"I think we came in third one year."

Memories returned. I had forgotten the tiny room that three of us shared in the sorority house. There was one bed, three tiny closets and a desk. The sleeping porch accommodated the rest of us. There were no assigned beds. At sleepy time, we each picked a bed. There must have been close to twenty of us on the sleeping porch.

We spoke of the study hall, a tiny room where the pledges were required to spend a specified number of hours per week. I had to walk across campus to put in my time.

Following that first night's dinner we attended a theater presentation celebrating music and later adjourned to the hospitality room on the third floor. The hospitality room was equipped with tables, sofas and chairs, and most of all, wine and beer and snacks.

Someone had brought the group pictures of the years. I was in all of them, from my first year to my last. In the pictures of the early years, I appeared pretty, young and naïve. In the last year's picture was someone who knew everything, someone who had become awakened in that final year before graduation.

We shared life stories until the morning hours. I was amazed at the accomplishments of my sisters. And it was then that I realized the strength of the sorority. The sorority had made us into sisters. I never had a sister, only three brothers; I was never a girlie girl.

That bond from years ago had never broken. Again, we were sisters, covering each other's backs, accepting without judgment. I cannot describe that feeling, but it was an unsuspected revelation. We shared business cards and networked, and it seemed that we realized the significance of the sorority experience, a lifelong bond. Somehow, I had missed knowing how important we all were to each other. I know it now.

The dialogue was hilarious.

"Do you realize we couldn't be seen on campus without socks? I was out of college and married when my husband, who was a fraternity boy, remarked that I could quit wearing socks."

"We couldn't go on campus in pants either."

Sonja Klein

"Yet we could smoke in our rooms, but we couldn't smoke standing up. We could only smoke sitting down."

"And anyone could buy cigarettes."

"Remember during finals we would lower an envelope off the balcony and the fraternity boys would furnish us diet pills?"

"There weren't any drugs except the diet pills."

"I don't ever remember drinking wine. We only drank beer."

"None of us ever got in trouble."

"I hear that now you can have a roommate of the opposite sex in campus dorms."

Saturday morning after a chatty breakfast, we boarded a coach with a guide and drove through Fredericksburg and learned the history of the town. From there we drove to Luckenbach. I learned that Luckenbach, Texas, today is a "Texas state of mind," where you can kick back, relax and get away from the hustle and bustle of life, a step back in time. This hamlet was established as a trading post in 1849, making it one of the oldest settlements in the county. The Post Office/General Store/Beer Joint was first opened in 1886 by August Engel, an itinerant preacher from Germany, whose daughter Minna chose the name Luckenbach in honor of her fiancée, Albert Luckenbach.

The Trading Post catered to pioneer farmers and Comanche Indians alike. By 1885 the community boasted a steam-powered cotton gin, a blacksmith shop and a school.

In 1970, the town was for sale, having been owned continually by the Engel family. A collection of Texas characters purchased the town and it began its second life under ownership of Texans with overactive imaginations.

When Jerry Jeff Walker came to Luckenbach in 1973 to record an album, the music scene embraced the town. The album went gold. In the following years Gary P. Nunn, Ray Wylie Hubbard and Willie Nelson recorded and performed in Luckenbach. Today Luckenbach reflects an eclectic mix of its early history and an unrivaled legacy of great music. Wedding receptions, birthdays and corporate parties are booked each year, keeping the dance hall alive almost every weekend.

From Luckenbach, we drove the short distance to the Wild Flower Seed Farm, which is owned by the brother of one of my sorority sisters. Mistakenly, I had assumed that the facility was a typical tourist business. Wrong again. The Wild Flower Seed Farm is one of the largest in the

186

country, maybe even the world. Her brother John drove us through the fields of wildflowers, explaining the cultivation and the process of harvesting the seeds. I was fascinated by his inventions of seeding road right-of-ways across America and by his method of cleaning the seeds for market. The green carpet of grass seeds seen beside road construction areas was developed by this man in Texas and is used nationwide.

Following lunch, we visited the Lyndon B. Johnson ranch and home. I was impressed by the beauty of the ranch and realized how much the president loved the land. The Texas White House was modest, but I could tell that it was a home. Some of the anecdotes about the former president and the family pictures in the home revealed the humble life they lived. They were Texans and inherited a love of the land.

Upon returning to the hotel, we invaded the hospitality room, eager to share stories and more memories and some refreshments. Each one of the women had a story, even a book. I promised them a chapter.

Sensing the end of the journey, we returned to the Wild Flower Seed Farm for a private party with a band and a chuck wagon barbecue. We promised to return in five years. My cousin Ida was designated to be in charge. I can't wait. I promised to help her.

42

Cuss words

I never heard my parents curse, especially my mother. Once or twice, I think my father might have said, "Damn." As a child I thought it was exciting to hear that from my father because he was perfect, my mother too.

Even in high school, I don't remember any cursing, not even in college either. But as I grew older, the words, "Shit, Damn and Hell," occasionally entered into the conversation. Cursing was not cool, not ever. No one cursed in mixed company.

As I reached my 20's and was married, my father retired and my parents moved to the farm. When my father's nephew and his wife Isabel moved onto the adjacent property, my mother teamed up with Isabel. They played bridge. Isabel's favorite word was shit.

Once my mother slipped and said, "Shit. Oh, dear. I've been hanging out with Isabel too much." We laughed.

Today cursing is accepted in movies, in public and from the mouths of children and it's called cussing, not cursing.

The F word is everywhere and more proper than the N word. There was a TV series called "Deadwood." Every other word was the F word. Somehow I don't think the cowboys used that word. I rather like the term that Gus used in the movie, "Lonesome Dove." He used poke.

In fact, I wonder what terms were used for cussing in ancient times. Do the hieroglyphs, ancient tablets or sheepskin scrolls contain obscenities?

When Jesus cursed the money changers in the temple, what words did he use? Did the founding fathers of our country use curse words off the record? And what were they? And what did the defenders of the Alamo say when they saw all those Mexican soldiers outside the walls?

I know what I would have said, "Oh, shit. What the fuck do we do now?"

43

Cuba

What is it about Cuba? I've traveled to over 70 countries in the world and yet the allure of Cuba is never absent. Has it been because it is forbidden, mysterious or just unobtainable without risk for an American passport holder?

When cultural exchange visas became legal for Americans late in 2011, I was among the first to sign up for a visit to Cuba. I wanted to visit Cuba before the country was ruined. My daughter wanted to join me and when her partner Israel said he would keep Theiss, I booked the trip for the two of us.

It would be my second visit to a Communist country, though I would soon find out that Cuba is not entirely Communist, whatever Communist really means. In my reading prior to the trip, I discovered that Fidel Castro was from a very wealthy family and that his father owned thousands of acres. Fidel attended law school in Havana and was indulged by his father, who bought new cars for him. He honeymooned in New York City and purchased a new Lincoln there. Two of the books that I read before my trip were very informative, *Trading with the Enemy* and *Telex from Cuba*.

I flew to Miami only to discover that Miami is Cuba just as Uvalde, Texas, is Mexico. The mood was set. I spent the night at a hotel near the airport and attended an introductory lecture by the American guide who was to be our companion.

She has been traveling back and forth to Cuba for the last 30 years and appeared to be quite informed. She was born in Cuba. After a welcome, a few facts and some instructions concerning the morning flight to Havana, she introduced the lecturer, who was a Cuban/American and also the first Cuban woman to be elected to the Florida state legislature. According to our speaker, Castro visited the United States shortly after the revolution to establish relations. The U.S. turned him down. The timing was important. The Cold War was at its height and the president's advisors were adverse to any relations with Cuba, even though at the time of the revolution Americas owned 70% of Cuba.

Castro was snubbed, so he antagonized America by going to Russia, the next great power.

The lecturer stated that the Cuban government is the biggest employer in the country and that people stand around because they have no reason to be productive. She cited that a dental hygienist runs out of supplies by noon, goes home and gets paid the same salary no matter how long she works, but that change is occurring. People want to be productive.

I had been warned that the charter air service terminal that flew to Cuba would be crowded and hectic. It was. I arrived hours before the scheduled flight and stood in line with Cuban-Americans pushing dollies of bubble wrapped bundles protecting everything from pillows to piñatas.

The paint job on the ancient plane was not reassuring and the Russian lettering on the back of the seat in front of me confirmed my fears. The flight was short, less than an hour. At last, I arrived in Cuba. Customs was simple. My passport was stamped.

My senses were assailed as we rode through the city of Havana to the landmark Hotel Nacional de Cuba, built in 1930. A Cuban tourist guide spoke as we motored the smooth wide streets. There was little traffic, lots of old cars, gaudily painted to accommodate the tourists. I learned that two million people live in Havana, that Cuba has a total population of 12 million and that there are 15 provinces. Since it was April, the trees were in flower, all colors.

Billboards along the way proclaimed, "Love the Island" and "Socialism or Death." I even saw a car that displayed a sign in the rear window, HONK IF YOU WANT SEX, ironic since my first book was titled, *Honk If You Married Sonja*.

We passed a large sports complex where baseball, the national sport, is played. I soon noticed that everyone in Cuba wears baseball shirts, no matter their age.

After driving through the Plaza of the Revolution and the university grounds, we dined on the top floor of a modern building in the center of Havana. The view was lovely. The pattern was set for most meals. We received a welcome drink, usually a mojito or rum and coke. A smelly suspicious fish soup was served. Our choice of entrées was fish or chicken. Salads were mostly cucumbers, carrots or cabbage. The chicken breast was dry, the fish filet tasteless. Dessert was almost always ice cream. The Cubans love ice cream and line up in the city plazas for the treat.

I was not surprised to later learn that Cuba imports close to 80% of its food and that the chicken is purchased from Tyson in the USA, paid in advance with Euros because we have no balance of trade with Cuba. This is possible due to an executive order that allows us to sell food to Cuba on humanitarian grounds because a hurricane rained destruction on Cuba. The tilapia filets are imported frozen from South America. A favorite quote of the Cubans, "The three failures of the revolution are breakfast, lunch and dinner." Following lunch we arrived at the hotel, perched on a hill overlooking the Malecón, the ocean boulevard, and the Straits of Florida. The Hotel Nacional is a colonial masterpiece. The circular drive was crowded with taxis and colorful old restored American vehicles. I had to smile.

Since check-in time is usually around 3 P.M., we strolled the grounds with the hotel historian. The place was crowded, the bars were busy and the lobby was grand central station. I observed three coaches of American tourists arriving. It appeared that the floodgates allowing American tourists are open.

Following the walking tour, we relaxed in the celebrity bar, where we received our welcome drink, the famous mojito. I observed pictures of every famous person who has visited the Hotel Nacional. Pictures of everyone from Errol Flynn to Ernest Hemingway adorned the walls and ceilings. It was a walk into the past. The mojito helped.

After being assigned my room and freshening up, I took the elevator down to the lobby to exchange my dollars for the Cuban Convertible Peso, also called the CUC. For $100, I received 80 CUCs. I was told that upon leaving Cuba I could reverse the exchange and recover the 20% tax. The Cubans use the Cuban peso but are also allowed to have CUCs. Salaries are paid in Cuban pesos.

Instead of being free for bar time, we attended a lecture in one of the many hotel meeting rooms. Our lecturer was a retired architect and urban planner who is now a consultant.

He was an excellent speaker and included a Power Point presentation with his talk. I scribbled rapidly in my notebook that one third of the population in Havana is native and that the remainder are from other parts of the country. After the collapse of the Soviet Union in the 1990's, a severe recession occurred and migration to Havana increased 10 times. But in order to obtain a job, a person has to have an address. Homelessness is against the law, not allowed. Housing is crowded and shantytowns have developed on the outskirts of the city. The squatters are called Palestinians because they have no land.

In addition, three houses in Havana are crumbling per day and the average age of the homes is 75 years. According to the speaker, 90% of the homes in Havana are now privately owned. This is possible only since November 2011 and owners can buy and sell homes. A transaction tax of 4% is added, with no capital gains tax or real estate commission paid. The state owns the land. The property owner leases the land for 99 years.

Foreigners can now own property in Cuba. Separate laws apply to foreigners. Our speaker said the Canadians are building a multi-million dollar resort condo complex along the coast and as Cuba opens up, the land grab will be frantic.

Tourism and not sugar production is now the main industry of the island, with over a million visitors last year. Now that U.S. citizens can visit, I expect that number might double.

I learned that Cuba is known as the Key of the Gulf because of its geographic location, causing the waters of the Gulf of Mexico to embrace the Atlantic Ocean to the north and the Caribbean Sea to the south. The Cuban Archipelago is made up of 4,159 small keys and islands. Cuba is part of the islands formed by the Greater Antilles and the Lesser Antilles. The island of Cuba is long and narrow. Eighty rivers enter the sea.

Havana is the most important location in the Gulf of Mexico because of the Gulf Stream and the protected deep-water bay of Havana.

The lecture continued with a brief history. The Spanish built aqueducts in the middle 1500's. Three fortresses were also built in that same time period, one of them being the oldest fort in the Americas and the other being the largest fort in the Americas. I might add that at 9 P.M. every evening the cannon is fired from the El Moro fortress.

I learned that walls were built to surround the city and that it was one of the most fortified cities in the world. In spite of that, 28,000 British arrived in the 1760's and captured the city, bombarding it from the hills above.

Once the British took charge, the Cubans could trade with America. Under Spanish rule, trade was restricted to only Spain. Fortunately, the

British remained less than a year. Yellow fever and malaria drove them to more desirable territory. Our charming speaker exhibited some Cuban humor, "That's why Cubans don't wear Bermuda shorts or drink tea. The British were not here very long."

When the early Spanish explorers discovered Cuba, the indigenous population was poor with a simple culture of eating fruit and fishing. Disease soon wiped them out. Cuba was then settled by the Spanish and French who formed their own society, that of the Creoles. Their children were educated in Europe and returned with exaggerated tastes, building baroque palaces and later palaces in the Neoclassical style and later the eclectic followed by American modern after World War II.

The goals of the present government in Cuba are to reduce the 1.5 million government employees, to encourage the opening of small private businesses, to foster leasing the dormant agricultural land for production and to develop the real estate market for foreigners, to allow private ownership of homes and to encourage tourism. He mentioned that Havana has a shortage of hotel rooms, and with the increase of visitors, new hotels will be built.

He ended with a quote I will always remember: "The human being is the only animal that stumbles on the same stone."

We dined in the open-air restaurant on the grounds of the hotel and were given our welcome drink, the familiar mojito. The sea breeze and Cuban music floated through the pavilion. The rice and black beans were tasty, the shredded pork well seasoned and ice cream finished the meal.

The following morning the hotel served a complete buffet breakfast. I had been looking forward to the famous Cuban coffee. I didn't find it. Breakfast coffee was from one of those machines where you punch your choice and put the cup under the spout. The Cuban coffee was served after meals in small cups and it was good.

We motored to the Patranato Synagogue and Jewish pharmacy that serves the community. A short lecture revealed the history of the Jews in Cuba. Beginning in 1906, many Jews came from Europe to Cuba. Before the revolution, there were approximately 15,000 Jews in Cuba. Today there are only about 1,500 and several synagogues. The Jewish community has good relations with the present government and receives no financial support. No kosher food is available and there is only one kosher butcher in Havana. As a result, many of the Jewish ceremonies are not practiced. A rabbi from Chile visits periodically.

We visited the library at the synagogue and deposited our donations of over-the-counter cold and pain remedies as well as toothbrushes, toothpaste, soap, shampoo and hand sanitizer.

Colon Cemetery, established in 1871, was the next destination, a beautiful, peaceful place with acres and acres of carrera marble statuaries. Columbus was buried here, but later his remains were moved to Seville.

A wide boulevard runs through the cemetery and we were treated to a walking tour with a cemetery guide, who pointed out the meanings of the carved monuments. An obelisk covered with a shroud is the symbol of death and a broken column with a wreath symbolizes a short life interrupted.

Our American guide spoke of her personal history with the Colon Cemetery. When she was four, her seven-year old brother died. Every weekend the family would picnic in the cemetery at his grave. She found the cemetery restful.

I found it every bit as stunning as the famous cemetery in Buenos Aires, the Recoleta, where Evita Perón is buried.

We lunched in old Havana on the plaza near the Cathedral de la Havana. The enormous structure built in Spanish baroque style once housed the ashes of Christopher Columbus's son, Diego. We spent the remainder of the afternoon exploring each of the four plaza squares and strolling through the book market. That evening we dined at El Aljibe, a historic open-air patio restaurant. The welcome drink, music, chicken, fish and ice cream were familiar.

That evening when I returned to my hotel room, I found a note, "Hello: My best wishes to your and your family. It is a pleasure for me to be at your service. Have a nice trip tomorrow."

On the following day, we ventured from Havana to the Guanabacoa region, rich in many religious influences. We visited with a family in a nice home surrounded with walls and broken glass. The house was airy and clean, with a patio and fountain in the back, where we were seated and served the tiny cups of Cuban coffee. The lady of the house sat in the doorway while we asked all our questions. From the session, I learned that her father was a pediatrician and was given the house when the attorney who owned it fled Cuba after the revolution. Her family has lived in the house for 50 years. Her daughter works as a tour guide and her husband served with the military in Angola. He now is a private worker with a car repair shop.

When asked if she had family who had fled Cuba, she admitted that her sister left with the group of Cubans who stormed the Peruvian embassy and achieved asylum. She said that she was shocked by her sister's actions. Her sister has visited once and she has met only one of her sister's children. From the way she spoke, she regrets being separated from her family. We learned that the mail is not censored and that people bring goods from the USA.

For pleasure, her husband fishes and rides bicycles and she jogs and does aerobics. Their home has been robbed 10 times.

When her brother joined the conversation, he admitted that he wishes to visit the USA and see a major league baseball game and would like to have more information on baseball in America.

From her home, we walked to the Museo de Guanabacoa, where we took a guided tour. We viewed exhibits of the Afro-Cuban religion, Santeria. Following the tour, we witnessed a dance and musical performance. The music and dancing were quite sensual, and at the end, the audience was encouraged to join and make fools of themselves. Most of them did.

Later we visited the village of Regla and the church of the Black Madonna. Practitioners of Santeria sat under the shade trees outside the church. For a few dollars, they would read your future. Of course, I paid and an earnest woman told me I was a strong person and had sadness in my life, but everything was now okay. She looked deeply into my eyes as she spoke. I liked her and gave her a generous tip.

Following the typical lunch and welcome drink, we drove to Callejón de Hammel, a unique avenue devoted to Santeria artwork and murals. My daughter Molly purchased a few small paintings. On the way back to the hotel, we spent some time in a craft mall and purchased many Cuban mementos, mostly for the grandson: some tee shirts, a baseball with his named burned into the leather and a white Cuban shirt.

A free evening allowed us to sample the food at a palador. Paladors are private restaurants in people's homes. We chose Vistamar, located in the Miramar section of Havana. The house was on the ocean. We were escorted to a second-floor dining room with a terrace overlooking the water. A swimming pool at water's edge lay below. After a welcome drink, we dined on rabbit and lamb. My daughter said it was the best rabbit she had ever eaten. My lamb stew was tasty. The appetizers were also good. It was the best meal we had eaten in Cuba. The price of the meal was about $20 per person.

The taxi ride back to the hotel made the evening. The taxi driver entertained us with stories of his car, which he called the monster. It was Russian and he had been driving it for 26 years, after having bought it second-hand. He was allowed to purchase a car because he served in Angola, out of the country, for two years. His brother was a doctor in California. He joked about the conditions in Cuba and said that if he wanted to buy another car he would have to drive the monster into the ocean.

The motor coach in which we traveled was made in China. It was new, air-conditioned and had a bathroom. Rental cars were available for tourists and there were new cars on the streets. However there was little traffic because there are not many cars. Many Cubans ride the free busses.

Thunderstorms were forecast as we again left the city and drove to the San Lazaro Church and hospice, named after Saint Lazaro, the saint of the poor, health and dogs. Next to the church, we visited a hospice that specializes in skin diseases as well as diabetes and AIDS. Che Guevara was instrumental in organizing this facility. Che Guevara, the Argentine doctor and revolutionary who treated lepers in South America, is a national hero of Cuba.

Rain was pouring down as we ran through the streets of the facility to a reception room, where a very short, serene nun dressed in full habit met us. From her talk I learned that 200 to 300 cases of leprosy are treated there each year. Last year nine children were treated. The reason for the occurrence of leprosy in Cuba is slow diagnosis in outlying regions and failure to follow the doctor's orders. Leprosy is curable if diagnosed early.

The hospice has 200 beds, 30 nurses and 15 doctors. Some of the patients live at the hospice for social reasons. Their families don't want them. The World Health Organization donates medicines and the hospice cooperates internationally in research.

Only six nuns are currently at the hospice. During the revolution, they were not allowed to be part of the hospice and instead worked on the premise as assistants, cooks and cleaning women. Today they are allowed to practice their religion at the hospice.

We stopped in the small, simple church, lit candles with all the other visiting pilgrims and left in the rain to visit the Finca La Vigia, the Hemingway Farm. Nobel Prize winner Ernest Hemingway lived here with his third wife Mary for 30 years before being ousted from his land by the revolutionaries. The consensus was that he committed suicide because of depression and the loss of his beloved farm.

It was obvious why he loved the place. The property was on a hillside, covered with large trees and pathways. The quiet and solitude would appeal to any writer. We walked the grounds, peered in the windows and viewed the interior as it was when Hemingway lived there, his personal belongings still intact. I found it remarkable that every room was filled with volumes of books. He was an enthusiastic reader as well as a writer.

Also on the grounds was his beloved Pilar vessel, which he used to patrol the Caribbean waters, looking for Nazis. The boat is featured in his novel, *Islands in the Stream*. It was a beautiful wooden boat, much larger than I had pictured when I read the book.

We returned to the hotel for an early evening lecture on religion in Cuba. The lady speaker was quite interesting. From the lecture I learned that Cubans consider themselves a bit Latin American, a bit Caribbean and a little of something else that makes them Cuban.

She said Cubans are not religious but are believers and pray when they are faced with a crisis. Cubans are only nominally Catholic because the Catholic church had no mission in Cuba. There were no natives to convert; there was no advanced civilization and no riches/gold. In addition, the Catholic church held a celebratory mass when the national poet/hero of Cuba, José Marti, died. The lecturer also added that the Cuban culture was the most advanced in Latin America and they didn't embrace the Catholic religion since it aimed at the poor. I believed her because the first night in Havana performances of opera, ballet and symphony were held in three separate venues.

The speaker went on to add that there are now many religions in Cuba. There are the basic Protestant religions as well as 1,200 Greek Orthodox Christians. She stated that the first president of Cuba in 1902 was Protestant.

Sonja Klein

I found it interesting that 50,000 Arabs came to Cuba and married Cubans. There are no mosques in Cuba but 3,000 Cubans claim to be Muslim. The Jehovah's Witnesses number about 80.000. Our guide admitted that she found it odd that the Cuban government says there are 30 Mormons in Cuba. She said she didn't believe it because she doesn't know a single Cuban who doesn't drink coffee, enjoy rum and believe that marriage is for life.

The most popular religion is Santeria, a form of Spiritism, one of the many Creole African religions. Other New Age religions exist in addition to Yoga, Buddhism and Rastafari.

I was amazed to learn that 30,000 Cubans were Masons and supported the revolution, just as our American forefathers were Masons and supported our revolution.

In closing, she added that 15% of Cubans consider themselves religious, 15% are atheist and 70% are a mixture, whatever that means.

She commented that Cubans always overreact, but 50 years of living against the most powerful country in the world, the U.S., has not deterred the Cuban people. They are still here. She was a powerful speaker.

For our last evening in Havana, we dined at the Oriente. Still fighting the rain, we sloshed across a plaza to the second story of a former palace and enjoyed a Cuban meal in luxurious surroundings with music of course. The appetizer was salmon done quite nicely and the main course was beef. I can only say the meal was adequate; the atmosphere was lovely and the music was loud.

The note in my room read, "i hope on the next trip you stay more time with us and come back soon. Have a nice trip. With love, your chambermaid. God bless you. thank you." Her notes were perfectly printed. Of course, I left her a generous tip. She most likely receives more per month than a doctor.

The Cuban sun was shining as we departed Havana in our Chinese bus. The highway was empty as we drove on the four-lane highway, our destination being the Bay of Pigs. The orange, mango and banana orchards were well tended and full of ripening fruit. Much of the land was fallow. Cubans on horseback or driving carts used the same expansive road.

Our destination was Playa Girón and the Bay of Pigs Museum. We passed through the province of Matanzas and its capital by the same name. The Cuban guide informed us that Cubans recycle and that the government protects species of plants and animal as well as the natural resources. As we entered Zapata Park, a protected swamp and wetlands, I observed monuments along the road honoring the 170 Cubans who died in the invasion at the Bay of Pigs.

Approaching the coast we eased through the small town of Australia, where Fidel Castro commanded the resistance to the invasion. The road was littered with the smashed remains of hermit crabs. I was disappointed when I learned they are not edible.

My first vision of the Caribbean from the Cuban coast was remarkable. I instantly knew where the Havana blue originated. The waters were the prettiest blue I have ever seen. And I have seen a lot of water.

The small coastal village of Playa Girón is the site of the historical 1961 clash between the Cuban forces and American trained rebel forces that the Cubans called mercenaries, the historic Bay of Pigs Invasion.

The museum tells the story of the invasion and the 72-hour battle. Maps, pictures and artifacts, including a Sea Fury fighter aircraft were impressive. I found the pictures of the individual soldiers moving.

We dined at a beach resort near the museum. French, Russian, South American and German tourists were enjoying the waters. We were told we could not snorkel or scuba dive or swim on the beach because our visa was cultural, not tourist. We were allowed to swim in the hotel swimming pools.

The buffet lunch was the best food so far served at a state restaurant. At last, vegetables were served—okra, cabbage, carrots, beets and green beans. Pork, fish and chicken were also offered. The pork was the tastiest. And of course, they didn't forget the welcome rum drink or ice cream for dessert.

Our bus continued to smash hermit crabs as we drove to the coastal town of Cienfuegos. We stopped at the main plaza of the town of 100,000 and attended a private performance of the Cienfuegos Gospel Choir, called Los Cantores de Cienfuegos or Cantos Novinus. The young men and women sing a cappella and won a first place for an international performance in France. There were 10 of them: four sopranos, four altos, two baritones and two bass. Their rendition of "Shenandoah" was moving. It was obvious why they won. They practice many hours a week, are not paid and have other jobs.

We walked past monuments in the main plaza to a Chamber of Commerce area and enjoyed a welcome drink on the breezy patio.

Our home for the next few days was the Hotel Jagua, overlooking the harbor waters. The lobby of the multi-storied modern hotel was busy with tourists. We dined that evening at an early 1900's Arabian-style palace on the hotel grounds. The intricately carved wooden panels and décor were lovely, but the still air and humidity caused me to eat my swordfish, rice and potatoes as quickly as possible before escaping to the cool evening breeze. I requested some hot sauce for the flavorless fish and was given a bottle of German spiced ketchup. It was awful but at least changed the flavor of the dry fish.

During the meal, a hoarse-voiced Cuban lady playing an out-of-tune piano, serenaded us. Several of us shared a bottle of wine. It was South American and cost 22 CUCs. The wine was nice.

The following morning we traveled to Trinidad, an hour away from Cienfuegos. But before we left for Trinidad, we visited the Beny Moré Art School, where we met with faculty and students. The school was an amazing place. The school provides training in music, the visual arts and dance. The music students begin their studies in the third grade. Dance students begin in the fifth grade. Students remain at the school through the 12th grade before attending the University of Fine Arts in Havana. At the completion of their university education, they are eligible to join any of the cultural institutions as a career. Students from all over the province are eligible to attend the school.

To be accepted, students throughout the province are tested and examined by a board of professors who recognize talent. Every province in Cuba has an art school.

The Beny Moré Art School in Cienfuegos currently hosts 231 students. Many of the students from the outlying areas board at the school and some commute. Meals are furnished. Those who board are allowed to visit home on the weekends.

Two months of vacation exist during the summer. The students' days are long. They begin at 7 A.M. And end at 8 P.M. Half of the day is spent studying their artistic talent and the other half is spent on scholastic studies. Any course failed causes dismissal. There is a very low dropout rate. The school is free.

The students were polite and dressed neatly in uniforms, according to their level of education. We were treated to a dance performance by eighth grade girls. They were excellent. A third-year student then played two songs on the guitar. A young man played a piano solo.

We visited the visual art studio and met with the professors, who were themselves artists. My daughter purchased a wonderful oil painting in the style of modern obstructionism, whatever that means. The colors were nice. I liked it.

We limited our art purchases after being advised that all paintings were subject to a tax at the airport. The guide mentioned that it was about $25 per painting, a good reason to limit purchases.

As we left the art school, I again was amazed by the high cultural level in Cuba. The arts are encouraged and very important.

We made our way by a large cement factory in Cienfuegos on the road to Trinidad, a UNESCO World Heritage Site with a population of 50,000. Trinidad is a colonial gem. We left the bus to walk the narrow streets of the town founded in 1514. After a better than average buffet that included an unusual kale salad, fish and the familiar welcome drink, we strolled to the Plaza del Mayor in the heat of the day. My daughter and I had our picture taken with an old man smoking a cigar on a donkey. He was affectionate and hugged and kissed us, and we gave him five CUCs.

We then visited a home built in the 1700's that was once quite grand. The owner, Señor Tayaba, related his story. He now works as an accountant at the hospital and makes about $25 a month. His family owned the house since 1920. He was one of 10 children. His father was quite wealthy and owned 400 hectares of land. A hectare is more than an acre. The family also owned a cement factory, a cigar factory and seven beach houses. At the time of the revolution, all belongings were confiscated without compensation. All funds in the bank were also taken. The Cubans were allowed to keep the equivalent of $200. The family was allowed to keep only part of the house. The remaining rooms were partitioned and given to others. To supplement his income, he rents out three rooms to tourists, charging 25 to 30 CUCs per day. He also offers meals. Breakfast is five CUCs. Dinner ranges from 12 to 15. Most of his tourist renters are European: Russian, Italian, French, German and visitors from the United Kingdom.

The Cuban government charges him a tax of 200 CUCs per room per year for the privilege of indulging in private enterprise and he pays a

10% tax on the net profit. He advertises on the Internet but Internet use costs 60 CUCs per hour, very expensive.

Señor Tayaba related that one of his brothers was residing with his family at one of the beach homes during the revolution. A military truck with soldiers arrived and the family was given five minutes to vacate the home with no belongings. I personally cannot imagine someone driving up to my ranch and giving me five minutes to leave. I would have to resist with violence. As for confiscating my bank accounts leaving me with only $200, I might go postal.

His mother died from cancer at the age of 52 because the drugs to cure her were not available. He said that things were better now. You could leave property to your family. The family land that was confiscated has lain fallow since the government took possession.

Returning to Cienfuegos in the late afternoon we traveled through another UNESCO World Heritage Site, The Valley of the Sugar Mills. The valley was once the site of 50 sugar mills during the peak of the sugar industry. Sugar production was a lucrative industry until the collapse of the Soviet Union. When Russian money ceased supporting Cuba, the Cuban economy collapsed. There were food shortages and the people suffered. According to people with whom we spoke, things are much better now, especially with the rise in tourism.

We visited a sugar mill, where my daughter turned the wheel to grind the sugar. We relaxed on the terrace overlooking the fields of sugarcane and sipped our welcome drinks.

We returned to the Hotel Jagua for a concert by yet another a cappella choir and that evening dined in a courtyard adjacent to the hotel for the best state meal imaginable. The setting was under a canopy of large trees. The Cuban band serenaded us during our welcome rum drink. The breeze off the harbor was pleasant and the smell of a roasting pig hand-turned on a spit was inviting. The buffet was fabulous. I dined on roast pig, white sweet potatoes, yucca, pumpkin, carrots, black beans and rice. The meal was local and very Cuban.

Following the meal, my daughter and I went to the pool bar for a final drink. Even though the evening was still early, I was ready for bed. My daughter found a companion to visit the disco in the hotel.

The following day was one I had anticipated for years, a visit to Santa Clara and the Che Guevera Monument and Mausoleum. We made our way to Santa Clara, the provincial capital of Villa Clara, founded in the 1600's. The current population is 700,000. We first visited a senior citizen center and met with local Cubans over 60 to learn about their lives and activities. They demonstrated the dramatic dances, their artwork and told of their excursions and community participation. They were lively and fun. At last, I danced Cuban dances with a handsome Cuban gentleman. Then I played a game of dominoes with three Cuban men. I won, being a domino player of great repute. They were much more fun than the senior citizen groups I have encountered at home. They also sponsored and mentored Cuban children. They were awesome.

The meals were better in the provincial towns. A buffet lunch was served at a resort complex on the outskirts of Santa Clara. More vegetables were available and the local pork was good.

At last, I had the opportunity to visit the Che Memorial, which features unique historical pieces from one of the revolutionary leaders and chronicles the events of an era. The mausoleum is the resting place of this interesting individual who was a doctor from Argentina. Che Guevara is one of my heroes, though I do not espouse Communism or Socialism. I admire him because he dedicated his life to the needs of lepers and the poor and believed in his cause, no matter the politics. He gave his life for what he believed and I find that admirable. No judgment on his beliefs.

I collect Che memorabilia from tee shirts to dolls to magnets to playing cards to even a Che hat. I've read every biography and chronicle by him, including his letters. It's my thing.

My daughter looked askance as I became teary-eyed, "Mother, cut the tears."

"I'm not necessarily crying for Che; I'm crying for all the people I loved who are dead. Leave me alone. This is what I do."

At the memorial, I learned for the first time that Che, in command of revolutionaries, captured a train of soldiers and ammunition in the town of Santa Clara on December 28, 1958. This broke the supply line to Batista and the dictator fled on January 1, 1959, never to return. The revolution succeeded. Che continued his cause in Africa and South America until the CIA killed him in 1967, which of course has been denied. Instead, they claim the Bolivian army executed him.

His children live today. Of his two daughters, one is a doctor and the other is a veterinarian specializing in dolphins. His sons are a doctor and an engineer. His legacy lives.

Weird as it may seem, one of the men in the group was a Peace Corps worker in Bolivia at the time of Che's execution. He stated that he was sent to Bolivia, but when he arrived, there were no instructions or plans for their Peace Corps project. It was very disorganized. He added that the CIA had a very impressive presence there at the time. Where is the truth?

We walked that evening to a restaurant across the street from the hotel, the final dinner. Nice comments were invoked. The meal was a typical state dinner. The welcome drink was offered. The music played. We left early, almost to the point of being rude. I despise goodbyes.

I welcomed the note in my hotel room, "Hello. My name is Silvia. I'm your chambermaid. It's a pleasure for me to be of service. I hope you enjoy the decoration of the room and that you enjoy your stay in our hotel. Best Wishes and Good Luck. Your Chambermaid." I left another generous tip.

Early morning found us at the airport in Cienfuegos. The airport was my favorite kind, small and convenient. As Molly and I approached the desk, the cute young lady looked at Molly and asked, "Do you remember me?"

Molly smiled and answered, "Of course. I danced with you and your husband at the disco."

She smiled, didn't bother to weigh our overweight bags and assigned us seats in the front. How you could you not love Cuba?

Once we cleared security, we declared our paintings and discovered that the fee was only $3 per painting. We gladly displayed our art purchases and were directed to a window to purchase the stamps for $3. We returned to security with the stamps. The customs officials photographed the paintings, pasted the stamp on the back of the paintings and happily waved us onward, back to the United States.

Normally after a mind-changing trip, I wait for parts of myself to reconnect. As for Cuba, I was happy to leave those parts behind. Why don't we as Americans embrace the Cubans? They are doing some things right. After all, they are our neighbors.

44

Used to be

Travel used to be simple. Drive to the airport, buy your ticket and walk onto the plane. No longer true. Today, you spend hours in lines at the airport just so you can arrive in the holding area an hour before the plane is scheduled to depart; that is, if it flies on time.

There was a time in our history when no passports were required. Customs inspection was nonexistent. You could take out or carry as much cash as you wished and bring back antiques and jewelry with no limit. No visas were required. Freedom reigned for the travelers.

With the European Union, travel between countries in Europe requires only a passport, much simpler. South America varies from country to country. I recently paid $235 for an expedited visa for Brazil. In Asia and the Middle East, visas are usually required.

When I visited the "Stans," in Central Asia, visas were required for all of the five countries. I was without a passport for several months while obtaining $750 worth of visas. When I complained about my passport being gone, a fellow savvy traveler told me, "You can apply for and obtain a second passport so that you can travel while you're getting visas. Diplomats and business people do it all the time."

Returning from wherever I had gone, I went to my trusty computer, logged online and printed out the request form for a duplicate passport. I filled it out, included more recent pictures and mailed it off with the money order and my old passport after being assured online that I could track the progress that would take up to 30 days.

When I received the priority mail envelope, I ripped it open to find a new passport. But my old passport was not in the envelope, the old faithful passport that I had sent off for more pages, the one with all the exotic stamps. Then I noticed that the envelope seemed to have been opened. I panicked, certain that someone had stolen my old passport and that I would not be able to travel when I reported it missing.

Several days passed before I courageously called the United States Passport Office and informed them about the missing passport. The government employee laughed, saying, "You should be getting your other passport any day. We have a policy never to mail two passports in the same envelope." The following morning, my passport was in the mailbox.

Every year my brothers, their wives and my solo self spend a week at my brother David's New Mexico ranch. From Houston, they fly to Albuquerque and then drive two hours from there to the ranch.

Common sense forces me to drive. For me to fly to New Mexico, I must drive three hours to San Antonio, arriving at least two hours before the flight, fly to Dallas, where I need sufficient time to change terminals and hopefully make the connecting flight to Albuquerque. In the same amount of time I can drive through west Texas in the comfort of my car, stop along the road, buy fresh produce and arrive before my brothers. I then have my car to leisurely visit my cousin in Santa Fe, prolonging the trip.

My Canadian friends, a world-traveling couple, recently arrived for a visit at the ranch. Over a glass of wine, we spoke of our travels. They had just returned from Vietnam, Laos and Cambodia. Together, we commiserated on the efforts of traveling, agreeing that it used to be much simpler. We shared our fears that intercontinental travel may someday be restricted. I remarked, "Perhaps we don't appreciate that we are free to travel, even though we pay for passports and visas. Remember, the Chinese, North Koreans, Vietnamese, Cubans and Laotians are not allowed to travel, except in neighboring and Communist countries. I would hate to think I had to live on the island of Cuba all my life, pretty as it is."

Our conclusion: Choose your destination wisely and suffer through the vagaries of the journey. It's all part of the trip.

45

Trespassers

John and I lived at the ranch only a short while before we encountered our first trespassers. The ranch had been vacant for years and the three houses, if you could call them that, were in poor repair. The main house up on the hill enchanted us from our first glimpse. The white house with its flat roof sat snugly on the high hill overlooking the flowing creek. What came to mind was a Buddhist monastery.

The reality was quite different. The roof leaked. The asphalt floor tiles were cracked. The parquet flooring in the living room was splintered. The dark green drapes kept out the light of the canyon. The kitchen was a disaster. A stovetop under a window was coated with grease. The window was just as bad. There was no air conditioning, just a non-operating swamp cooler on the roof. A propane unit supplied the heating, and to make matters worse, the propane tank sat square in the front yard.

As for water, it was supplied, untreated, from a submersible pump in the creek. However, the plumbing worked, thanks to the God to whom you pray.

We addressed the roof first. The drapes, we tore off the walls, letting the Texas light into our lives. One ceiling fan worked. It helped.

The doors and windows were kept open. We heard every noise. The Axis deer trumpeted in mating season. The turkeys gobbled in the morning. The birds and insects created a symphony.

Life was good and one day as we worked toward a common purpose, the familiar sounds were interrupted by voices down below.

John walked out on the porch with the binoculars and commented, "There's a truck and trailer parked down below the dam. A bunch of people are unloading canoes."

Ever the activist, I replied, "Go down and run them off. I can't believe this."

He continued to look through the binoculars, "You should see this. Look. They're dressed in Orvis fashions."

"Go down and ask them to leave."

Sonja Klein

"No, I'll wait until they have unloaded and set up before I drive down."

"Great idea."

When John later returned, I asked him, "What was their story?"

"They claimed it was a navigable river."

"What fools."

Over the years, trespassers invaded on a predictable basis. Most of the time, they came during spring break or in the summer months. Their excuses were inventive, "We just want to take pictures of the cliff."

"We didn't know this was private property."

"Can we fish?"

"Can we swim?"

The answer was always, "No." Liability is always an issue.

After John died prematurely of cancer at the age of 52, it was left to me to patrol. Depending on my mood, I was sometimes nice and sometimes not quite so nice.

Motorcyclists have discovered these hidden canyon of beauty in Texas. They ride the fabled three sisters, Highway 335, 336 and 337, aptly named the Twisted Sisters. My ranch, Ambush Hill, lies off Highway 335. A few adventurous riders branch off onto Ranch Road 2631 until they arrive at our heavy metal bump gate.

Some turn around but if they come through the gate they usually stop at the dam, observing the long cable dangling from the cliff over the clear creek. They see it as an invitation to stop and swim. I see it as an invitation to vent repressed anger.

Fifteen years of living alone provides the opportunity of freedom. I write, I travel and I don't welcome intruders in my yard or playing in my sandbox.

During the spring and fall, my doors are open. One such day I heard voices down at the dam. Forgoing the binoculars, I drove my pickup down the hill. There were three motorcycles parked at the dam and three men in their underpants were swinging from the rope into the creek. I parked the truck, walked to their motorcycles and found their keys in the bikes, their wallets on the saddles and yelled, "You are trespassing. You have to leave."

They were shocked and embarrassed, caught in their underpants, "Okay, we're sorry." Fortunately for them, their clothes were on the

208

ledge. They hurriedly dressed with their backs to me and returned to the dam.

I was waiting, "You're lucky I'm in a good mood. I could call the sheriff and have you arrested for trespassing, take your keys and wallets, shoot the tires on your motorcycles or simply punch out the tires with the ice pick I have in the truck."

They were apologetic, chagrined and humble, "This is ranch country," I advised them, "You are welcome to ride your bikes on our roads. We are happy to have you here. Don't stop on the road and trespass. Most of the ranchers are not so friendly." We parted with smiles.

Adjoining my ranch is an abandoned Girl Scout Camp. With the permission of the owners, I patrol their acreage. After returning from a trip to Houston, tired and road weary, I came upon a couple sitting in the creek in their lawn chair with a cooler of beer and fishing. I stopped on the low-water crossing, observing them downstream. I yelled over the rushing clear water, "You are trespassing. You must leave."

Slowly, they folded their chairs and walked up the creek to the road on which I had parked. I asked them, "Don't you realize you are trespassing?"

"No."

"Who do you think owns this land?"

"I don't know."

"Is there a sign that says public park or state park?"

"No."

"Well, then. Who do you think owns it?"

"I don't know."

"Would you like for me to park my car in your yard and picnic and fish?"

"No."

"Has it occurred to you that someone owns this land?"

"We thought the river owns it."

"Does this look like a navigable river?"

"No."

"Please leave and respect property rights."

"Yes, ma'am."

Later that same month, the sound of four-wheelers disturbed me. There were three of them. By the time I drove down to the dam, they had unloaded and were swimming in the creek with small children.

Again the familiar admonishment, "You have to leave. You are trespassing."

"We're just here to swim."

"This is private property."

"Why can't we swim?"

"I can't be liable for you and your children."

"You aren't being very nice."

"You are trespassing. I repeat. This is private property."

They were surly as they left.

Over the years, I've been confronted with the familiar excuses. They don't know it is private property. When I ask them, "Who do you think owns this property?" they act dumb, as though it never occurred to them that someone owns the land. It seems that because they are in the uncivilized wilderness, they surmise it is free range.

Being a fifth generation Texas, I cannot imagine invading the property rights of anyone. Never would I assume to walk on someone's territory. I'll continue to keep them off mine.

46

Four pages

At a recent family gathering, one of my sisters-in-law made a comment, "A friend of mine read your book and asked a question. He wondered why you devoted only four pages in your book to the husband to whom you were married 15 years."

"That's a good question. I'll give it some thought."

Actually, I didn't realize I devoted only four pages to Raleigh. Perhaps it was because I started a book on his life and abandoned the project because either I was reluctant to face the truth or it was too painful.

The story of Raleigh deserves a book. I entered his life at the age of 31. He was 34. He swept me off my feet after a marriage with a philanderer who gave me a sexually transmitted disease. Raleigh appeared when I had the lowest self-esteem. He wined and dined me and I married him because he made me feel good. I really can't explain any more than that.

Though I knew he had a nightclub with girls and gambling, I somehow justified that in my creative writer's mind. I saw him as a big shot wheeler-dealer and I liked it. He dressed well, had good manners and was a master criminal. Because of his generosity, I balanced that with the bad. He gave people money, always had a big wad of cash in his pocket and helped everyone. When we entered a bar, he purchased a round for everyone in the place. He was noticeable. I felt like a queen being with him.

Raleigh helped me adopt my two children. He encouraged it. And then I was too busy raising a five-month-old and an 18-month-old. I didn't have time to realize who he was or judge him. He was home perhaps only two days out of ten. He came and went. When he came, he was polite and gentlemanly. Sex was never his concern. I didn't have time to think about it. I was preoccupied with my children. He never interfered.

Sonja Klein

Only in later years did I realize he could not read or write very well and had little comprehension of the written word. He relied on conversation and handshakes. For him, it worked.

His life as I later pieced it together was a great story. He quit school early and took to the streets, becoming a boxer known as Killer. It was tattooed on his upper arm. At 18, he married an older woman who supplied him with a liquor license and opened up a nightclub. I think she was a hooker.

They divorced and he married another woman, another hooker, and had a nightclub in New Orleans where he connected with the Mafia and became an enforcer in the French Quarter.

He then moved to Lafayette, Louisiana, robbed a bank and used the funds to purchase land and open a nightclub next to the racetrack, Evangeline Downs. That was when I met him.

Only after we were divorced did he tell the story of robbing the bank. I was appalled. He even admitted, "Thieving is the thing."

That's when I remembered all the antiques, jewelry, paintings, crystal and silver that he brought home. They were stolen.

Our life on a plantation was idyllic. I purchased only three acres, but the grounds were beautifully sloping to the banks of the Bayou Teche. We had a swimming pool, two guesthouses, a huge work building, a party boat, fish pond, rose garden, gazebo, horses, chickens, rabbits, dogs, cats and a complete life.

When he went to prison for 10 years, I remained busy with the children, never admitting to myself that I was married to a sociopath. How can you tell yourself that you have been such a fool?

He was diagnosed with kidney cancer while serving a 10-year prison sentence. He was released after serving three and a half years. Once the cancer was in remission, I divorced him and moved back to Texas. He continued to call me almost daily, even when I married my third husband and then fourth husband. We remained friends.

When my fourth husband died, he continued to call. I hadn't seen him in years. I traveled with my son and his wife to New Iberia for the Sugar Cane Festival. We connected with Raleigh and had dinner. He invited me to spend the night with him. I refused. He offered cocaine and weed. I declined. He still looked good; his charm was appealing. He was the same old Raleigh. I had nothing left for him.

Shortly before he was killed in a car accident, he came to the ranch for a visit and asked to share my bed. I denied him. He slept on the sun porch and left after a week, uncomfortable with the isolation.

In retrospect, I suppose I remained married to him because he left me alone. He didn't necessarily pay his way, but he didn't bankrupt me. When he was home, we dressed the children in their best and went out to dinner. He always wined and dined me. I was a sucker for loving it.

What he did when he was gone, I never asked and he never told. I believe that he treated me with respect. He was a lousy lover, but was a great cook, always clean and neat, dressed well and somehow he made me feel good. I guess it was about me and not him. I was selfish.

I did realize over the years that he never had a bank account. He held a longshoreman's card from his years in New Orleans and he filed an income tax form. I never saw it. I never probed deeply into his affairs. I must have sensed the violence below the surface.

He was killed in a car accident. At his funeral, three adults appeared claiming to be his children. Two, I knew about. The third one by my math was conceived during my marriage. I can't begin to describe how that hurt. Later DNA tests revealed none of them were his. Somehow, I was not surprised, even though I was aware that he contributed to the support of the ones I knew.

And again, I ask myself, *Why did I marry him and why did I remain his wife for 15 years?* I really don't know. I was stupid. I have forgiven myself. I have two children and a grandson. I would not hesitate to do it again, but I don't know why.

This is not even four pages, but I hope it answers the question. Perhaps there is no explanation. That's just the way it was. There are no answers for some questions.

47

Garage sales

I love garage sales and once read that if you wish to help the American economy, rather than buying Chinese and other foreign-made products at Walmart, visit a tattoo parlor, a whorehouse or a garage sale instead. Makes sense.

Garage sales are cleansing and much fun to get rid of unused items. Preparations include cleaning out drawers, garages and closets. I cling to the theory that if you don't use it, lose it. For me the pleasure is not the money, it's the absence of stuff.

The most important part of a garage sale is getting rid of the leftover items that do not sell, the first thing you line up before the sale. In the case of the most recent garage sale in which I participated, Hospice was the destination. Once I discovered that they were open on Saturdays, the sale was set.

The sale was at my friend Linda, the singer/songwriter's house. I live too remotely and lack sufficient goods to justify a sale.

Of course, there is the aspect of wanting some of your friend's stuff. We trade out, a puzzle for my grandson, some Legos for him when he is a little older. I purchased a child's saddle. She took a suitcase and a sweater. We make our meager piles of each other's stuff and stash it to the side.

We were ready at 7 A.M. The people came. Linda always greeted them with, "Is there anything special you are looking for?" It usually worked. Chatting with the consumers is important. You can't just sit there drinking a cup of coffee and expect to sell anything.

That's when you realize that people are starving for conversation and socialization. They will stand and chat and tell their life stories or share experiences for a long time. If you listen, they will eventually buy something.

What they don't buy much are decorator items, tablecloths and napkins and nice clothing. They do buy shoes and small tables and lamps, glasses and functional items. Video games, music and movies are best sellers, as well as computers and electronic items.

By 11 A.M. It's about over. The visitors dwindle as the day progresses. The best part is loading the remainder in the pickup and taking it to Hospice, returning and counting out the crumpled dollar bills stuffed in our pockets.

The best news of the day is that I returned home with less than I left and a few dollars in my pocket.

48

New York City

The first time I was in New York City, I didn't get it. I was on a cruise ship traveling down the east coast of the United States from Quebec to Ft. Lauderdale to view the fall foliage. I was focused on the east coast, contrasting it to being a fifth generation Texan and being a frontier-type person. I was confronted with the culture and east coast money.

The short time I was in New York City, I took a city tour that moved me through the districts and pointed out the high-rise buildings where the celebrities live, took a walk through Central Park and visited the Rockefeller Center, as well as Ground Zero.

I realized how different Texas was from the east coast. As the ship traveled down the coast, I visited Williamsburg and Charleston and felt a bit intimidated by their ancient history, old by Texas standards.

When my girlfriend Linda called and asked if I would like to fly to New York City spend a few days and learn about pearls, I easily said, "Yes." The choice was an easy one.

I specified, "I want to stay at the Waldorf Astoria." She arranged the hotel reservation and we flew from San Antonio through Dallas and landed at La Guardia early in the afternoon. By the time we retrieved our baggage and engaged a taxi, we were starving.

The taxi driver was all I expected. I have seen so many movies of New York City taxi drivers that I anticipated a character. I was not disappointed. His name was Felix; he was from the Dominican Republic and had recently retired from being a trash collector for New York City.

Linda's research revealed that the taxi fare from La Guardia to the Waldorf would be about $40. It wasn't. The fare was in the $20 range. We were welcomed at the Waldorf and entered the elegant busy lobby. The Waldorf has over 1,000 rooms, several restaurants and bars and was full of inappropriately dressed tourists in shorts and flip-flops.

Our room was outdated. The carpet was old floral, the bathroom was bare necessity. There was no countertop for cosmetics or even a toothbrush. It was clean. Since we were starving, we dumped our bags and headed for the street. The doorman at the Waldorf hailed a taxi. I asked, "How far is it to Chinatown?"

"Very far."

The trip took 20 minutes and the fare was less than $20. That was when I discovered that far in New York City doesn't really mean far. In Texas we know what far means. I drive 60 miles one way for groceries. That is classified as maybe far.

Our taxi driver was from Ghana and spoke tolerable English. He left us in the heart of Chinatown. We wandered the street, reading the menus on the various restaurants until we reached one that appealed to our senses. Remembering we hadn't eaten since early that morning, we were anxious to eat. The time was 4 P.M.

The Zagat restaurant rating on the door was favorable and there were white tablecloths. The restaurant was not busy. We were escorted to a small table and handed one of those six-page menus with pictures. Hungry as we were, we wanted to order everything right away.

Both of us settled on a picture of a heaping bowl of snails for starters. We ordered the snails, a small bottle of sake, some shrimp in a dumpling and crab and pork cakes. We sipped the warm green tea served as we were seated. It was soothing but did not satisfy our raging hunger.

Linda asked the waiter, "We've just flown in from Texas and haven't eaten. Is there anything you could bring us right away?"

Since the restaurant wasn't busy, they were very obliging. Within minutes, we were served a bowl of soybeans and a bean sprout salad. The soy sauce we poured over the dishes was light and unique.

Between the tea and the sake, we were quite mellow by the time the bowl of snails and other mild dishes arrived. And then our problems began. Somehow we didn't realize when we ordered that the snails were attached inside their shells. I think we must have expected escargot. We poked, prodded and sucked. Not a snail was released. In our frustration, we summoned the nice young waiter. He advised sucking. It didn't work. He offered toothpicks. After digging and fumbling, we managed to get one out. It looked like a toasted maggot or grub worm. The flavor was good. We were determined to conquer a bowl of about 50 snails.

I never felt so stupid. We imagined the staff laughing at us. But Texas girls don't give up. At one point, I debated sending them back to the kitchen, not to be wasted. We got better, but not adept. After finally managing to eat that bowl of snails, we ordered the sea bass. It was a winner, very fresh and delicately seasoned. The bass was served on a large platter and the waiter made a dramatic display of giving us each the cheek meat.

Hours after entering the restaurant, we called for the bill. By then the entire staff had become our best friends. After presenting us with a bill that approached $100, the waiter served us dessert, compliments of the house. A bowl of pink liquid consisting of tapioca, red beans and coconut was before us. It was not very good. We ate it out of respect. I don't think the Chinese are big on desserts.

As we left the restaurant, Linda asked our new best friends, "Where can we buy knock-offs, fake Rolex, Louis Vuitton purses and Gucci wallets?"

"Just walk down the block. Someone will contact you. They are everywhere."

With that vague instruction, we entered the busy streets of Chinatown. I was limping due to a trip and fall on the steps to my bedroom. After two blocks, we were a bit discouraged, but then a young Eurasian lady walked past us and said, "Watches." She was walking so fast Linda had to almost run to catch her. I limped behind. It took about a block and a half before Linda caught up with her. By the time I arrived, the young lady was on her cell phone, "Follow me," she instructed us.

Around the corner, she stopped and said, "Wait here."

We waited and soon a young man appeared, "Follow me."

Around another corner he stopped, "Wait here five minutes."

Another young man appeared with two sheets of well-worn glossy paper. The watches on the worn pages were Cartier and Rolex. We pointed to the ones that were interesting. He disappeared. The young lady returned, "Follow me."

We returned to one of the original waiting spots, next to a black Suburban with darkened windows. A young man appeared with a black plastic bag. He fished out some watches. We selected the ones we liked and asked, "How much?"

"Seventy-five dollars."

"How about $50?"

"Okay."

"The band is too big. The watch is loose on my wrist."

Roundtrip from Texas

He pointed to two men at an open-air stall not 50 feet away, "Go there, he'll fix it."

Linda asked, "What about the purses?"

"Wait here."

I walked to the stall and gave the man my watch. He said, "Three dollars." I gave him the money while he removed the excess links from my Cartier watch.

When I returned to Linda, she was looking at glossy sheets picturing Louis Vuitton purses. She selected several and again we waited. Another man appeared with a black plastic bag. The purses were in it. Linda selected two nice ones, bargained for the price and we completed the transaction before Linda had the links taken out of her new Rolex for the $3 fee.

Feeling quite successful, we walked a few blocks to a busy street and hailed a taxi. The west African driver delivered us to the Waldorf, where we cleaned up, dressed up and set out for yet another adventure. The bars in the Waldorf were not busy. We wanted action. As we walked out onto the streets of New York City, we asked the doorman, "Where is a good place to have a drink?"

He directed us around the corner to the Kimberly, where we took the elevator to the top floor and entered an outdoor rooftop bar. The Chrysler Building stood illuminated in the evening air. After taking pictures and examining the menu, we discovered that a martini was $14. So was a glass of house wine, "What the hell. We're in New York City."

The crowd was too young and the music not to our liking. Linda remarked, "What we need is a nice piano bar with an older crowd."

"Look on your cell phone and find one in the area."

The Russian Vodka Room looked promising.

After a light rain shower that sent the staff hustling to roll out the awnings, we summoned the waiter for the bill. The price for the two martinis was $37.60, which included tax, title and license.

The taxi driver from Bangladesh left us at the door to the Russian Vodka Room. So far, most of the taxi drivers had been Muslim.

When we entered the Russian Vodka Room, we knew we had come to the right place. The piano player was playing classical music. The room was dark and the bar had two empty seats. The crowd was our age, seasoned. The price was right. A two-ounce shot of vodka was $7. I ordered the garlic and pepper vodka. Linda ordered the ginger vodka.

Before long, we were exchanging tastes with our fellow patrons. Linda switched to grapefruit vodka. I stayed with the garlic and pepper. After all, I did not plan on kissing anyone.

Seated next to me were two young women, one from Moldavia and one from Virginia. Next to Linda was Ignacio from Argentina. He was a screenwriter. Vladimir from Novosibirsk was with him. The bartender was from Kazan. Both Siberian cities I had visited. The conversation was lively and global. Feeling the vodka, I ordered a plate of herring, very Russian. It was tasty and cost less than a martini. It prevented a hangover.

Our taxi driver at 2 A.M. was Egyptian and talkative. While the Waldorf's bathrooms need updating, their beds were feather soft and the pillows plush.

By 9 A.M., we were back on the streets, looking for breakfast. The breakfast buffet at the Waldorf was over $20. We found a nice restaurant a block down the street and for $6, ate eggs, toast and coffee, much more to our liking.

Sri Lanka was the home of the taxi driver who took us to the Pearl Factory on Park Avenue. We strolled past famous stores, De Beers and Tiffany, and entered a skyscraper, gave our names, showed identification and were ushered through a turnstile. Linda had scheduled an appointment with the owner of the Pearl Factory, guaranteed entry past the guards to the elevator.

Again, there was security, as we were buzzed into the modest offices and led to meet Eddie. While we were seated in front of his desk, he explained nacre, the thickness of the pearl, luster and the roundness of the pearl. In order for the pearl to be round, it is required to be within 2%. We learned that weird-shaped pearls are called baroque. Linda was interested in black Tahitian pearls. While their color was similar, there were different shadings called peacock, green and gray. There were strands and loose pearls displayed in the glass cases below his desk.

Eddie showed pictures of the oysters that produce the Tahitian pearls. The oysters were two feet across. I would never have believed oysters grew that large. Eddie is the third-generation owner. His grandfather came from Israel and started the business. His brother and mother also worked with him.

Eddie explained that the Japanese have perfected the art of cultured pearls. Once the human hand touches the oyster, the pearl is considered cultured. A pearl bead is inserted into the oyster to stimulate pearl growth. An eight-millimeter pearl requires two years to mature. A larger pearl can take up to five years.

Linda purchased a strand of lovely baroque Tahitian pearls. The price was modest. The case was lavish, red leather. Satisfied, we left the Pearl Factory and visited some other jewelry stores, where the black Tahitian pearl strands were three times the price.

We walked into Henri Bendel's and had a makeover, purchasing some very expensive makeup that would make us look younger. The sales girls were knowledgeable and good marketers. We were in New York City.

Hunger encouraged us to dine at Katz's Delicatessen. The taxi driver was Muslim. The famous deli, where the movie "Where Harry Met Sally" was filmed, was crowded. We patiently waited in line, observing the size of the sandwiches. We split half a Reuben. Even a fourth of a Reuben was huge. The sandwich was as good a Reuben as I have ever eaten and the deli pickles were tasty. With two bottles of water, the bill was $25.

We were getting quite adept at hailing taxis. This driver was Latin and dropped me at the Waldorf before taking Linda back to the jewelry stores. When she returned, I had showered and dressed. She did the same, and again, we set out for another expensive meal.

After the most expensive martini yet in the lounge of the Waldorf, we hailed a taxi and ventured into the Theater District and Hell's Kitchen. We walked the street, passed Broadway Joe's and settled on a small Italian restaurant with white tablecloths. Linda has a thing about white tablecloths. We ordered a bottle of wine and appetizers. I selected escargot with polenta in creamed spinach and Linda chose lobster fettuccine in a light wine sauce. For the entrée the waiter recommended the steak. It was perfect. For dessert, we shared tiramisu.

During the evening, an older man sitting at the bar seemed to be holding court. Linda said, "I bet he's the owner. He looks interesting. Let's join him."

We joined him at the bar and ordered a glass of Grand Marnier. He volunteered his story. He emigrated from Italy to New York City in 1976. He married an American/German student and has five children. One of them had been our handsome chef. The owner appeared to be quite prosperous and was charmed by our attention. He bought us another Grand Marnier. I later remarked, "At least we can still hustle a drink. We must not be over the hill yet."

We walked down the street to an Irish pub and had a drink. Business was slow. We hailed a taxi piloted by a Sri Lankan and returned to the Waldorf, closing down a bar across the street.

There wasn't much traffic as an African taxi driver took us to La Guardia. Since we were early, we ate a large hamburger for $8 at the airport. It kept us satisfied all the way to Dallas and San Antonio, where with great luck we found the car where we left it. At the toll booth we owed $74. Linda had mistakenly parked in hourly parking. We paid and swore each other to secrecy.

In spite of my Texas mentality, I enjoyed New York City. About the only thing we didn't experience was a Broadway or theater performance. We agreed that would be on the agenda for our next visit.

Upon reflection, I realize that visiting New York City is similar to international travel. The city is truly a melting pot and I was not surprised to later learn that more languages are spoken in New York City than any other city in the world. It certainly isn't Texas, but this time I understood why everyone loves New York City.

49

Grandmama day care shuts down

When Molly and Theiss moved from the ranch, my role as provider of Grandmama Day Care ended. The day after they moved, I visited the local bank.

"Sonja, your eyes are swollen. Do you suffer from allergies?"

"No, I've been crying. My daughter and grandson moved to Alpine so she could finish her master's degree."

"Oh, I'm so sorry."

She was embarrassed by my answer. Heads had turned in the small bank, all ears attuned to the conversation. The canyon telegraph would soon broadcast the news. None of that mattered to me, I simply told the truth. I was sad.

As the days passed, I assumed a new role. I was back in charge of the ranch, having previously relinquished control to my daughter and her partner as ranch managers. And that was when I realized that I had been a sort of hostage on my own ranch. My home was up on a hill overlooking the creek bottom, barn and two houses. I maintained my home and grounds, wrote and kept my grandson.

I traveled too. My life slowed.

I encouraged my daughter to finish her degree and nudged her out of the nest. She was too young to do nothing with a degree and passion for environmental science. The fall from the nest was not without pain and suffering, but suffering is optional.

I became energized by the change and went to work with a vigor that I had abandoned for a few years. I cleaned, hauled off trash and lost a quick five pounds. I hired a friend to help and after a few weeks of hard work was pleased with the results. In short, I took my ranch back, realizing that I had almost lost my dreams.

The ranch soon had my stamp of approval. Then a hard rain revealed a leak in the roof of the lodge. A new roof had to be built. I included the rock patio under the new roof, added some rock sidewalks and began to furnish the lodge, decorating it with bright colors and new paint. The results were fun. I retrieved furniture stored in the loft, repaired some pieces and painted others. Some I gave away. I ordered globes for broken lamps, a new mattress for an old futon and cleaned out my kitchen cabinets, moving excess dishes down to the lodge.

Each morning I drove down to the creek bottom, surveying the changes, feeding the sheep and chickens, harvesting the garden and smiling. Purpose had returned. I still had some years left to run the ranch and by God, I would run it my way.

Daughter and grandson settled into the academic life. The university provided his day care. Daughter had an internship and would teach as an assistant while completing her second degree.

The two years had not been lost; they had been productive. I loved being with that little boy for the first two years of his life, but he was not my child. I was his grandmama and would always remain so.

Once I found someone to stay at the ranch when I was gone, I booked some trips. A month in China traveling by boat, train, plane and coach was my first choice. India, Indonesia and the Maldives was second.

Grandmama Day Care may have shut down, but was not out of business. There were years of opportunity for that. In the meantime, I was fit and living with dreams and passion. It was far too early to become sedentary and old.

50

Viva Big Bend

My friend Linda the singer/songwriter and I were so anxious to leave the summer heat of Uvalde, Texas that we skipped lunch. By the time we arrived in Marathon for an evening meal at the Gage Hotel, we were starving. Entering the bar through the courtyard, the dark cool was welcoming. Two women sat in the corner playing gin and sipping on glasses of red wine.

We ordered two dirty vodka martinis and some snacks. The brochure on the bar advertising the Viva Big Bend Music Festival stated that Drew Kennedy would be playing in the courtyard at 7 P.M. We adjourned to the courtyard and split the buffalo rib eye. The cool evening air and great food were complimented by Drew's original music. We visited with fellow diners from Galveston and Lubbock as well as with Drew's wife Holly.

Before the evening ended we had exchanged books, CD's and cell phone numbers, planning to reunite in Alpine. The trip was proving to be a good one.

After checking into the hotel in Alpine, we went to the desk to call a taxi. The man behind the desk gave us a card. Josh at Tipsy Taxi was available to drive us for $5 each to the music venues. He was there in five minutes, an enterprising student at Sul Ross State University.

Josh delivered us to the Granada Theater, where we listened to The Josh Abbott Band and then walked down the street to Railroad Blues to hear more music. The Tipsy Taxi delivered us safely to our hotel. It was 2 A.M. And the $20 taxi fares were much cheaper than a drunk-driving citation.

Friday was the reason for being at the festival. A book signing had been in the works for a year. A friend on the Alpine Library Board had offered to host it. The construction of their new library had been delayed, and a year had passed since my book was published. My friend Linda had agreed to play her guitar and sing some of her songs. Her talent and beauty would compliment my talk on travel and my recent trip to Cuba.

The room was full. Wine, fruit, cheese and crackers were served. My speech was well received. Linda's performance was entertaining, and we sold some books and CDs. Two of our fellow diners from the evening before attended. We were flattered.

The previous late night had taken its toll. We dined on Italian food and went to bed. No Tipsy Taxi that evening but Saturday we were primed and ready, shopping in the morning for a new blouse to wear that evening. We spent the afternoon at the Holland Hotel listening to performers and drinking Bloody Marys.

In the course of our wandering around the historic Holland Hotel we met the manager, an aggressive, well-spoken lady with many years of hotel service. She gave us a short tour, and when I pointed up to the roof and asked, "Is that the penthouse suite?" she answered with a chuckle.

"One of the previous owners had spent quite some time in jail, and when he bought the hotel he built a suite of rooms on the roof that resembled his jail cell. He was quite strange."

We learned that the new owners are doing extensive remodeling, restoring the kitchen and upgrading the facilities. Linda and I vowed to stay there next year. The convenience would be worth it in saving Tipsy Taxi fare.

After freshening up, we engaged the Tipsy Taxi and returned to the Reata to hear Drew Kennedy again and have dinner with our friends from Galveston. From the Reata, we walked to the Granada to hear the Texas Tornados. The music was fun and danceable. We danced until we were dripping wet, went outside to cool off and returned to dance some more.

We left Alpine early the next morning, agreeing to attend next year when my second book is published and Linda had produced a new CD. I say Viva Big Bend. We'll be back.

51

Pointless

Most of the things we do are pointless, especially texting, playing games on some latest technology and attending social events. Most of the words we speak are pointless too.

I have attended parties where the conversation tended toward the insane.

"Where do you get your pedicures?"

"Did you see the last episode of the new Dallas?"

"I couldn't find any cute decorator pillows at Walmart."

"Have you tried any of the new Texas vodkas?"

"I need to have my roots dyed."

Rather, I prefer the conversations with the older crowd's bridge club with whom I often play as a substitute.

"Have you read the book about India, *Freedom at Midnight?*"

"There's a book about China you should read."

"Would you like some peppers from my garden?"

"I don't think Iran is a threat to America. They have never aggressively attacked another country; whereas, we are the most warlike country in the world."

"Do you think the European Union is a failure?"

Those are thought provoking questions, indicative of analytical minds.

People are too involved in themselves, seeking instant pleasure and falling short in the development of social graces.

Script handwriting is no longer taught in our educational system. Does that mean that the younger generation will be incapable of reading a handwritten letter? I suppose so.

On a recent visit to Alpine, Texas, I was visiting with the bartender at the Holland Hotel. He referred to himself as an alternative student.

"What is an alternative student?"

"There are three of us in my English class. We are older."

"I think that's great."

Sonja Klein

"We had a recent essay assignment, and when I attended class, the professor said, "You alternative students are dismissed. What I have to say does not apply to you."

He continued, "I remained out of curiosity. We had all received good grades on our essays. She lectured to the class, telling them that text language was not acceptable on a written essay. Can you believe they thought those were words?"

Lack of imagination is rampant. When I was a child we were sent outside with orders, "Don't come home until dark." We found many things to do. When it rained, we dammed the gutters to see how much water would accumulate. We climbed trees, we played Hide and Seek, we caught butterflies, sucked the nectar from honeysuckle blooms and watched the clouds drift across the sky. We created homes with cardboard boxes.

Today preschoolers are using handheld computers, playing games. Sure, they are allegedly learning games, but there is so much more to learn outside, so many opportunities to expand and stimulate the mind.

I have read that fluoride in the water dulls the mind. Whether it's true or not, I don't know for sure, but I have witnessed the workings of a lot of dull minds in recent years. I have been on trips where lectures on history, geography, language and customs are available. No one attends. Instead, they go shopping, buying very little and dining a lot. They are only interested in pleasure.

I can't do that. I have to learn, to accomplish, to win, to succeed and to move forward or backward. At least I move. Where is the strength that developed America? Where is our courage and vigor? Our armed forces are instilled with patriotism. Our schools are failing.

People have become bovine. Perhaps it is pointless to ponder the issues but I don't think so.

52

Tattoo

The first tattoo I ever saw was when my father stopped to pick up a sailor hitchhiking on the streets of Houston, Texas. We were on our way home from church, driving down South Main Street. World War II was over. He had an anchor tattooed on his right arm.

I don't recall thinking it was good or bad. I assumed servicemen were tattooed. During the 1950's and 60's, motorcycle people often sported tattoos. During the 1970's, I owned a motorcycle dealership with my first husband. We mostly rode dirt bikes off the road but sold street bikes too. Tattoos were common on motorcycle riders, not admired by me but common.

My second husband had an X tattooed on his right hand in the niche between his thumb and first finger. On his right arm, halfway up between the shoulder and elbow, was the word "Killer." I tried to ignore his tattoos. They were crude, not professional. He kept them hidden as much as possible.

My fourth husband spent nearly five years in federal prison for conspiracy to sell marijuana. He had no tattoos. One day we visited one of his friends from the past. John had not seen him in years. His friend asked, "John, where are your prison tattoos?"

"I don't have any."

"I thought everyone who goes to prison comes out with tattoos."

"Not me. Why do you ask?"

"I'm kind of involved with this girl from California. She just got out of prison and has lots of tattoos. The tattoos turn me off."

"Leave her alone."

When my children were in high school in the 1990's, tattoos became popular. My daughter wanted one. I told both of my children, "If you ever get a tattoo, I will disinherit you and kick you out of the house."

One evening when I returned home from work, both of them were in the kitchen. My daughter sported a butterfly on her neck and my son had something on his arm. Before I went nuts, they laughed. The tattoos were stick-ons. I didn't find it funny.

Today I see young people with tattoos all over their bodies, displays that cannot be hidden by clothing. I question their judgment. Tattoos will jeopardize their future in the work force. Their careers will be limited. Can you imagine walking into a bank and meeting with a loan officer or a bank teller with tattoos? How about a doctor or an attorney or even a checker at Walmart? I know that times are changing but not that much.

And then permanent cosmetic makeup became vogue: translate tattoos. Women have their eyebrows, eyelids and lips applied with the revolutionary method of micro-insertions of natural pigments into the dermal layer of the skin. This state of the art technique is medically proven and specifically designed to be completely safe. Intradermal pigmentation is used for a variety of permanent cosmetic enhancements such as permanent eyebrows, eyeliner and lip liner/color. Other permanent cosmetic procedures include vitiligo, stretch mark and scar camouflage, areola restoration, hairline enhancement and more.

The procedure for lip color can appear to change the size and shape of the lips, as well as the color. The procedure helps prevent lipstick from bleeding into the surrounding skin. A soft pink, similar to a natural lip color, is popular for those wanting a natural look. A more dramatic color can be achieved if desired.

The procedure for eyebrows can mimic the appearance of hair on the brow line. Anyone who desires more fullness in the brows will save time by not applying makeup. Those who use pencil can go swimming, play tennis or wipe their forehead without the embarrassment of losing their eyebrows.

Implementing pigmentation in the lash line is popular with both males and females. Ophthalmologists recommend the procedure for those who are allergic to conventional makeup and for those wearing contact lenses.

This procedure is for those who want to look their best, busy people with no time to apply makeup, people with allergies, those who are physically incapable of applying makeup, burn survivors, people with flaws in their skin, those with oily skin who tend to shed makeup, and entertainers, actresses and models.

My sister-in-law was the first person I knew who had the procedure done. She looked good and was pleased with the results.

Soon I noticed that many of my friends of all ages were having their eyes lined.

I am a blonde and have very little hair. My eyebrows are nearly invisible. My entire life has been spent applying eyebrow pencil and applying eyeliner, which soon smears due to my oily skin and bad habit of rubbing my eyes.

My hair is long and straight. I do not visit beauty parlors except for pedicures and an occasional manicure. When the ends of my hair become stringy, my daughter trims them. In her absence I needed a haircut and called a beautician in the area, made an appointment for a haircut and, as a splurge, an eyelash and eyebrow dye, knowing that she was an expert in the permanent cosmetic procedure.

The lash and brow dye went so well and was so convenient that I made an appointment to have my eyebrows pigmented intradermally. Once I arrived at her salon, I decided to have the lower eyes lined but not the upper. Having had eye surgery four times on my left eye, I didn't want to risk injury to my bad eye. The lower lid seemed safe.

After I signed my life away and selected the brow color, she painted and measured my eyebrows. Once I approved she applied a topical anesthetic and cut into my skin with a small instrument that buzzed like a bee. It stung and it hurt, but the pain was bearable. Once the skin was opened, she applied more painkiller, and from there on it felt like she was only rubbing the skin. There was no pain. She carefully passed over my brow line about seven times, applying painkiller between applications.

The lower eyelash application took less time and was less painful. The first application did not sting as much as the brow.

The entire procedure lasted three and a half hours and cost $300. She sent me home with an antibiotic salve, applicators and a lubricant similar to Vaseline to keep the treated areas moist. I was admonished to not pick at the scabs and to apply the salve twice a day.

That evening my brows and eyelids were sore. The pain was bearable. The following morning the area below my eyes was swollen and darkened and still ached. I planned to stay home for a few days.

By the end of the week, my face returned to normal. I could go anywhere at a moment's notice without worrying about my eyebrows or eyeliner. I know that men don't care whether a woman has eyebrows or eyeliner. They're more concerned with the crotch.

Sonja Klein

I hope my children don't notice that I've been tattooed. I'll never tell.

53

China

I was never anxious to visit China, but when I realized I had recently visited two of the five remaining Communist countries in the world, my excuse seemed stupid. Since I had some credit vouchers with Lufthansa, I flew through Frankfurt on my way to Beijing. The food was adequate. If you have ever flown Emirates, you have been spoiled. I hear Qatar is even finer.

My seat neighbor was from Houston, an executive with a consulting firm in the oil business, a featured speaker at an industry seminar in Germany. We shared titles of books and an interest in genealogy. He admitted to having been in China 15 times and warned me that drinking any alcoholic native concoction would make me quite sick. I assured him that I have been similarly tempted with pisco sours in Peru, fermented mare's milk in Mongolia, slivovitz in Serbia and yak butter tea in Bhutan.

He commented, "They are quite fond of banquet sized dinners with a revolving server in the middle of the table. When they serve the watermelon, the meal is over."

The flight was short for intercontinental travel, a mere eight hours. I slept for a while and was awakened and offered breakfast, "Hot or cold?" What has happened to class or manners? Cold was sliced ham and cheese with some grapefruit and a roll. Hot was an omelette. The coffee was lukewarm. And I was flying business class.

October weather in Frankfurt was cold and rainy, and the morning produced a gray dreary day. The business lounge was quite busy, and since I had a five-hour layover, I extracted my new iPad and spent 30 minutes trying to type text and navigate without a mouse. The keypad was tiny and I continued to hit the wrong buttons until I allowed my coffee to wear off and settled down to typing more slowly than usual. The calmer mien worked and I discarded the impulse to throw the iPad in the garbage.

The five-hour layover was a rough one. I walked, I ate, I read and then I went to the bathroom. A nap was too risky. When at last the flight was called I was relieved to board the plane and relax. Although my seatmate was a German woman, men dominate business and first-class sections on airplanes. Those odds also apply to the business lounge. Two thoughts occurred to me: The business lounge is a good place to meet men and it's still a fucking man's world, even when most of the wealth in the world is controlled by women.

Air China definitely tries harder than Lufthansa. The food was a bit more innovative and the service much more elegant. I ate very little, having eaten at every opportunity. My pants were becoming tight much too early in the trip. The down comforter gently placed over my legs by a sweet smiling Chinese attendant was welcome.

Beijing

The 10-hour flight was just that, 10 hours of confinement. I read, slept and drank a lot of water. Dawn was still a thought when the plane circled the lights of Beijing and circled some more. The early expected arrival wasn't. A 40-minute taxied tour of the Beijing airport facilities followed our smooth landing. I didn't think we would ever find the gate, and when the plane finally stopped I descended the metal stairs and walked across the tarmac to a shuttle bus that finally delivered the passengers to an ultra modern terminal. Beijing time was 5:59 A.M. In two and one half hours I was expected to be in the lobby of some hotel I couldn't pronounce to join a tour of Tien'anmen Square.

What should have been an easy task was not. As usual I managed to stand in the slowest line to have my passport stamped. Carousel 39 never spit out my one suitcase. Fortunately I was not alone. A German man and I went to the lost baggage office and patiently waited while two skinny men from the United Kingdom attempted to convince a young Chinese lady that the dent in their shiny metal suitcase ruined it. Running out of patience I returned to the carousel and joined a small group who assured me that some pieces of luggage stowed in the front cargo part of the plane were expected any moment. My luggage arrived with the others.

I dragged that heavy thing past customs with a nod and summoned a taxi, showed the driver the piece of paper with the hotel's name and address and entered the back seat thinking I had ample time to arrive and meet the group. I was not surprised to be wrong.

Roundtrip from Texas

The morning rush hour traffic was awful. My driver couldn't speak a word of English and I soon realized that he most likely could not read or write. My suspicions were confirmed when he left me at a hotel that was not named exactly like the one in my letter. The man at the desk confirmed the mistake and summoned another taxi. Thirty minutes later I arrived at the correct hotel with 10 minutes to check in and return to the lobby. I succeeded and was welcomed by 12 other travelers and a charming Chinese lady.

The group was diverse: Canada, America and Sri Lanka.

The short ride to Tien'anmen Square was the third circuit of the area for me. The huge square was crowded with Chinese tourists. Our guide, whose name was Hui, pronounced "way," delivered a short lecture before she turned us loose to take pictures and wander through the square.

From our guide I learned that Beijing is the third largest city in China. The population is about 20 million and the district is composed of 6,490 square miles. The summers are hot but the fall weather is pleasant. She was correct. The day temperature was in the low 70's and delightful for walking.

I gravitated to the giant flower sculptures created for China's anniversary celebration. In the picture-taking process, I was approached by Chinese tourists who wanted to have their picture taken with me. I was the monkey in the zoo. We smiled a lot in the exchange.

From Tien'anmen Square, we traveled a short distance to the Temple of Heaven, a beautiful complex on a hill overlooking smoggy Beijing. The view was 360 degrees. The lovely buildings were in great condition and the area was full of tourists, mostly Chinese. The park and pavilions through which we walked were full of senior citizens sewing, playing cards, playing games with tiles, dancing and singing. They appeared busy and friendly. Retirement age for women is 50 or 55, depending on whether you work for the government or for the private sector. For men the age is either 60 or 65. With time on their hands, the retirees spend time together and take care of their grandchildren while the parents work to save money for the child's education. From our guide I learned that city workers can have only one child or must pay a large fine for a second child. Farmers can have two children and minorities can have more, depending on the status of their particular minority.

Chinese are limited in traveling from China. Fearing desertion, the government puts a high price on visas and requires that the traveler have approximately $10,000 in the bank, a secure job and a home, a reason for returning. Independent travel for a husband and wife together is not allowed. They must travel separately. Tourist group travel is allowed.

I learned that our guide does not approve of China's treatment of the Tibetans. She believes that other cultures should be preserved rather than be absorbed. She spoke quite freely with me but admitted that she would not do so in the company of other Chinese.

The traffic in Beijing was oppressive as we drove through the city. I noticed Kentucky Fried Chicken, Subway and McDonald's and learned there was previously a Starbucks in the Forbidden City but that the population protested so much, it was removed and replaced with a Chinese coffee shop.

The meals continued to be excellent. The large tables have a lazy Susan in the middle and the food is placed on the revolving circle. Dishes of pork, beef, chicken, cabbage, bok choy, soup, rice, noodles and often cucumbers are served, delicately seasoned. Tea is a staple, light and refreshing, never very dark. The arrival of a plate of watermelon indicates the end of the meal

That first afternoon Professor Lui Hao lectured to our small group in a conference room at the hotel. He explained some of the events of the Cultural Revolution. Educated people were humiliated and persecuted. For instance, a teacher had to wear a dunce hat and carry a heavy blackboard. Professor Hao's father, who was a teacher, was hit on the head with a brick and later died from the injury.

During the Cultural Revolution educated women were sent to the country to care for pigs and cows. The men were forced to work the fields. After several years, they were allowed to return to the city and work in a factory. Life was not easy.

Hui, our guide began the morning with a joke, "To the Chinese, hell is to eat British food, live in a Chinese apartment, be paid a Japanese salary and have an American wife. Chinese heaven is to eat Chinese food, live in a British house, be paid an American salary and have a Japanese wife."

Hui revealed her history. Her father and mother worked hard to send her to college. She now supports them. Her husband's family is wealthier and more influential. Through them she was able to obtain her current job. The choice is whether to work for the government or for foreign companies. She is not a Communist party member because she said the foreign companies prefer to hire non-Communists. She added that Communism is a joke and that no one believes it.

China is a good country to be old. Families take care of the aged and show them great respect. That treatment applies to elderly tourists too.

A Peking duck dinner was served that evening. The duck was delicately roasted, sliced and served with thin crepes. We were instructed to dip the sliced duck in plum sauce combined with cucumber and scallion slices and then roll it in the crepe, a Chinese taco.

Sleep was elusive, I awakened every few hours to check the time and was ready before daylight for the breakfast buffet and a visit to the Great Wall.

The smog and traffic were heavy. The journey to the Tianshou Mountains took about an hour and a half. I was not prepared for the rugged terrain through which the Great Wall of China winds. I learned that the wall was begun in the 5th century B.C., took 2,000 years to complete and is 5,500 miles long. Our guide stated that signal fires were lit to relay messages and that the smoke signals were ignited with wolf dung. How many wolves would you have to track to collect sufficient dung? That statement just doesn't fly. The average height of the wall is about 24 feet, the base being wider than the top, which is sufficiently wide to accommodate five horses and 10 soldiers. There is no way that wall could keep out invaders, any more than a wall between the U.S. and Mexico would restrain illegal immigrants from entering our country.

A bicycle race hampered our approach to the Great Wall. The guide hired two drivers to shuttle us closer to the entrance. Nevertheless, we still had a substantial climb to reach the ticket booth. The price of admission was about $7 and there were thousands of people on the wall in either direction. The top of the wall was steep and uneven. Heights are not my favorite. I took some pictures, had my picture taken and retreated for a cup of tea.

Following a buffet lunch at the base of the wall, we drove to the Ming Tombs, the resting place of 13 emperors from the Ming Dynasty. The park was peaceful and the pavilion leading to the center was flanked by large stone statues of guardians, people and animals. Mythical animals were also represented and I was told that dragons are only represented at imperial sites. I learned that man follows or respects heaven, heaven respects earth, earth follows the tao and the tao follows that which is natural.

Returning to Beijing, we passed by the famous Olympic venue that represented a bird's nest. It was phenomenal.

A typical Chinese meal followed at the hotel, and an opera began at 7:30 in the hotel theater. Actors portraying the emperor, his concubine and the enemy wore ornate costumes. The acting and singing were exaggerated and the subtitles displayed for the tourists were clear, but the audience was lethargic, not knowing when to clap. I dozed and finally left between acts, surrendering to sleep long before bedtime. As a result, I was awake hours before dawn, writing on my iPad; and when I went down for breakfast the dining room was inundated with German tourists who devoured the bread, cheese, coffee and eggs.

I returned to the lobby with my suitcase, which was to be checked the day prior to taking the train to Luoyang. From the lobby, our small group left to visit the *hutongs,* the ancient homes and alleys near Beihai Park.

Rickshaws were waiting to take us on a leisurely morning ride through the narrow lanes and alleys of an older part of Beijing. We stopped several times to admire the wooden doors and tiled roofs before eating a delightful lunch hosted by local families in a modest home. The food was freshly cooked and flavorful.

We spent the remainder of the day at the Forbidden City, home of the last emperor and his government and concubines. The Forbidden City is now called The Palace Museum. The ornate complex rests on about 200 acres.

Feudal society in China ended in 1911, and the last emperor left the Forbidden City in 1925. The day I was there, thousands of visitors crowded the city. Everywhere I looked were Chinese families. The grandparents were in charge of the children. Tour guides spoke loudly with handheld devices. We walked a good distance past the Temples of Harmony before we reached the inner city. Supposedly, 20,000 people lived within the walls, but after doing the math, that figured to one person every four square feet. Another tour guide statistic debunked. Then I realized that the Great Wall was erected to protect the Forbidden City. It didn't, and Mongol invaders entered the city. The emperor committed suicide.

After a long day of walking, my lack of sleep was taking its toll. The smog, traffic and 20 million Chinese encouraged me to move on. I was ready to leave the city. The train would take me to Luoyang.

The train station was huge. What I had not anticipated about China was the vast numbers of people, 1.3 billion, the most populated country in the world. Everywhere I went were thousands of people. The train station was no exception. The waiting rooms contained standing room only. When our train was announced, there was a mad rush of Chinese leaving the city for the weekend. It was Saturday.

Car 17 advertised a capacity of 108. There were at least 150 people. To get to my reserved seat, I had to step over luggage, people and packages. I fell into a small seat after a perilous walk. The train was electric, quite smooth and quiet, the passengers not so. They played cards, laughed and talked a lot, smiling all the time. Most of them were young. They work in the city factories while the parents live in the smaller cities and raise the grandchildren.

As the train left the station, I settled down to enjoy the scenery. I was prepared to see farmers in cone-shaped hats plowing behind water buffalo and small, quaint farming communities. Instead, the train rolled through the yellow air, thick as ocean fog, past coal plants, large cities with 30- to 40-story apartment buildings and massive construction sites. I did see a small herd of sheep grazing the banks of a poisonous colored ditch. Six hours later, at 80 miles per hour, the scenery had not changed.

Shortly before arriving at Zhengzhou, we crossed the Yellow River, which was actually yellow. The train ride had been cramped and confining, the aisles jammed with passengers. Tickets are sold, the first buyers being given assigned seats. After that, the tickets are the same price even though no seats are available.

Luoyang and beyond

After traveling through cities with names of Shijiazhuang, Baoding and Xinxiang, we arrived in the capital of the Henan Province. Zhengzhou boasts a population of 12 million and is located in central China, an area with the oldest and longest history.

Following a long walk through another huge train station, I emerged in the late afternoon to see my first clouds of the day. It is difficult to explain the yellow-colored air and crowded populace. At times I felt I was in a science fiction novel or in a post-nuclear disaster. I longed for stars, clouds, a rainbow, birds, butterflies and natural surroundings.

For anyone fearing invasion from China, let me reassure you that China has such immense problems that the United States is not the enemy. The Chinese government distorts economic indicators and reports just as well as any other country, and the citizens distrust their leaders, like any other populace.

A handsome young Chinese guide led us to a small coach and informed us that Henan is an agricultural province and that two crops a year are grown, primarily corn and wheat. A tractor factory, a scooter factory and a camera lens factory are among the industries that employ thousands of Chinese. A huge Walmart was busy in the early evening rush hour.

Night had fallen when we arrived in Luoyang several hours later. Luoyang is a small town of only 6.5 million, and I am not being facetious by using the word only. People were out in the streets, enjoying the weekend. Restaurants were illuminated, displaying Chinese diners. The traffic jam in front of the hotel was to be expected. I had yet to find a quiet nook or corner in China.

A dinner of pork, chicken, tofu, cabbage and eggplant completed the day.

Surprisingly, the hotel room was quiet and when I awoke in the morning and opened the curtains, the yellow fog was infused with a bit of pink. Below my 10th-floor room I observed Chinese citizens lined in rows doing tai chi. It was not yet 7 A.M. on a Sunday morning. I did not join them but instead enjoyed a full breakfast buffet, not unlike those in Beijing. Included in the buffet were small dates, grown in China.

China is toxic. The air and water are not safe. All tap water must be boiled; even the Chinese do not drink tap water. Electric tea pots are in hotel rooms as well as one or two complimentary bottles of water. All restaurant water is bottled. Coffee is dispensed from a machine.

The drive to the outskirts of the city revealed blocks of unfinished 20- to 30-story apartment buildings capable of housing thousands of Chinese workers. When we questioned our guide about the vacant buildings and those still under construction, he admitted that the housing bubble had collapsed.

Roundtrip from Texas

The Longmen grottoes along a dirty tributary of the Yellow River were flooded with Chinese tourists. The grottoes are carved niches in a limestone cliff. Most of the carvings inside the grottoes are Buddhist statues. Some are as tiny as one inch, others are stories high. Over 2,000 caves are in the area; most of the images were carved beginning in the 1400's.

The smog never lifted as the day progressed. Instead of walking back to the parking area, we took a boat ride down the river under a stone-arched bridge. Very little animal life existed along the river. A young Chinese girl who appeared to be about six began to sing. An even younger boy in the back of the boat sang a song about Mao. We took their pictures. They posed like movie stars.

Following a typical Chinese lunch, we visited a farming "village" that was not a village at all but a series of three-story concrete buildings separated by narrow alleyways wide enough for just one vehicle. There was a small plot of plowed earth in the area. People lingered in the alleyways, smiling. Babies were carried with the ass cut out of their clothing. The carrier held a sort of washrag over the buttocks area. Sometimes the bare butt was exposed. Small plots of herbs and flowers grew in front of the blocks of buildings.

We entered the home of one farm family. The rooms were minimal, concrete walls and floors, a small refrigerator, a propane burner or two, a wok and an electric rice cooker. A color TV was in the living room. There were no storage cabinets. The people own little. I felt very humble. They have a bathroom and running water, but it is not potable. Few families in rural areas own cars. Bicycles and scooters are common.

We visited yet another home owned by a widow. The home was older. She rented out rooms on the upper story. This "village" that was not what I considered a village housed several thousand people, most of them supported by their children who work in the city factories and come home on weekends, traveling on the same crowded train we rode.

The streets were busy as we returned to the city and visited the Horse and Chariots Museum. It houses artifacts from the eastern Zhou dynasty, which existed from 770 B.C. to the 250's A.D. Chariots and horses were discovered below the city, buried in ceremonial fashion. Luoyang was the King City and the emperors from the dynasty were buried here.

We walked through the city square, crowded with thousands of people singing, dancing, painting poetry on the pavement, playing games with cards and tiles and sewing. Strange as it may seem, we were the ones on display. People followed us, surrounded us when we stopped and stared not in an unfriendly manner but out of curiosity. Our local guide, Luh (rhymes with duh), said to keep moving so as not to be crowded to a standstill. Most of the people in the square were older and from the countryside and had never or rarely seen foreigners. I might add that I had yet to see countryside. Every square inch appeared occupied.

We returned to the hotel, and as I looked out my 10th-story window to the square below, I saw more tai chi and heard the crack of a whip that sounded like firecrackers. I had earlier learned that it was a form of exercise, a noisy one.

Visiting with the guide, I asked about social problems. He said, "China has many. We don't trust the government. They are corrupt. Suicide is a problem. Alcohol, not so much with the young. We would like more opportunity."

From our conversation I learned that the Chinese harbor much animosity against the Japanese, that English is required in the schools and that the guides are not allowed to take us to the really poor parts of China and everyone carries an ID card that identifies them as either city or country people. Country people are not free to move to the city and city people are not free to move to the country.

The Chinese government is quite arbitrary. When we left Beijing, we were instructed to remove all scissors and knives and bottles of liquids from our checked luggage and place it in our carryons in preparation for the train ride.

For the next train ride the instructions were reversed. No knives or scissors or bottles of liquids were allowed in our carryons. I hoped to get it right.

I cannot begin to describe the importance of family in the Chinese culture, at least that which I have been exposed to in north and central China. I have been told that the south is quite different, having experienced other cultures much earlier.

The parents work hard, sacrifice beyond measure and later raise the grandchildren. Chinese parents will do anything to provide opportunity for their child. In evidence as we checked in the hotel, a young girl of about 10 walked up and said hello and asked, "Where are you from?" in good English. We engaged her for a few minutes before the hotel staff signaled for her to leave us alone. Our guide explained that young students frequent tourist hotels to practice their English since few foreigners visit cities in the interior of China.

The following afternoon as we returned to the hotel, another young girl of the same age spoke with us. Her mother sat nearby. They had ridden their bicycle to the hotel so the young student could practice her English.

We dined at a nearby restaurant and conversed with yet another young lady, whose grandmother sat unobtrusively in the lobby. A walk around the square opposite the hotel revealed parents teaching their children to jump rope, Rollerblade, exercise and play games with other children. It is hard to imagine that this is the only open space. They live in 30-story high-rise apartment buildings. Their children are precious. China is a good country to be either very young or very old. In between, you work very hard.

The food became quite standard: chicken with some noodles or onions, always cabbage and carrots, pork, green beans with onions, bok choy and sweet-and-sour fried something. Eggplant was added, sometimes dumplings, but less beef than in Beijing. Hot peppers added spice to the meals. There were three or four of us that requested hot chili pepper oil. Occasionally, we were served butternut squash, which the Chinese label as pumpkin. Twice we were served zucchini. Desserts, if served at all, were watermelon, pears or apples.

Meat in China is served sparingly. When I mention pork, chicken or beef, the amount served is in small bony chunks and very little. A month after I returned from China, I noticed my fingernails were shredding and growing slowly. After some research I realized that it was due to a month of little protein. I might add that cheese and milk products are not common in China. The Chinese and the majority of the world's population is lactose intolerant. Only in several of the large hotels was cheese or yogurt available.

One morning I arose at 4:30, put some water on to boil, took a shower and sat down at my fully charged iPad. I love being able to write on it as I travel, much better than scribbling notes and waiting until I return home to transcribe the story. I find my observations much more insightful and the telling of the tale is passionate from being on the scene.

I walked down the quiet hotel corridor at 5 A.M. to return an iPad charger borrowed from a fellow traveler. He invited me into his room and we shared a cup of Nescafé while sharing impressions. We agreed that China's problems were no different than any other country and that the Chinese people were the same as people the world over. We differed in that he believed China was ascending in the world order and we were descending. I believe America continues to reign as number one. I returned to my room about 6 A.M. Daylight was threatening, and the sound of the bullwhip cracking on the square below sounded like firecrackers. Tai chi was scheduled for 7 A.M. I had yet to join the exercise. I found it hard to imagine a meditative regime among millions of people. My life was far too isolated to conquer those distractions without a great deal of practice. Instead, I mentally reserved the quiet of a riverboat for my first tai chi experience.

Current U.S. politics had only been summarily discussed among the Americans in the group. I was shocked to discover that they were quite liberal and that I was the only admitted conservative in the group. I wanted to shout, "Do you want the government to take your money and spend it recklessly? Obama has never held a job in the private sector. He's never even had so much as a lemonade stand." But I kept my mouth shut. Over two weeks of traveling together remained. I was determined not to make an ass of myself and become the scapegoat.

Most of them were academics, not business people. They were thinkers not doers. I doubt that any of them had ever picked cotton or dug a sweet potato or made pear preserves. Not so for the two Canadian ladies; they were real.

Below my window the groups of Chinese doing tai chi were organized like pieces on a checkerboard. There were two bullwhip crackers, and the city was coming to life.

Thoughts raced in my head. What was I doing in China? I travel for adventure. If a trip turns out as expected, it is not an adventure. China was definitely adventure. I was beginning to believe that Chinese supremacy is smoke and mirrors.

A mid-morning visit to a middle school proved quite interesting. Lower middle-class children attended the school, explained as a medium academic school. The noise, complemented by the trains passing a short block away, was deafening. The children wore red jackets, the school uniform. The teacher was a lady. She taught two English classes each day. The remainder of the day, she prepared tests and graded them. The students admitted to being 14 and 15. Some were shy and some were bold. They were typical adolescents, the boys being most uncomfortable.

We suffered through an entire class session which was taught from a PowerPoint presentation prepared by Microsoft. This lesson was about volunteering to help feed hungry children, clean up parks and assist the elderly. The vocabulary words being help out, clean up and volunteer. The teaching was done by repetition, with reinforcement in workbooks. Anyone who can read could have taught the class.

Following class, we were asked to spend 20 minutes speaking with the students so they could practice their English. I spoke with a group of boys. One had a cellphone. Most of them had one sibling. Two wanted to be doctors, one a soldier and the rest basketball players. I learned that only 30 percent of them pass the test to continue on to high school and only 50 percent of the high school graduates pass the test to continue on to college. At first thought, that translates into the Chinese education being no better than ours. I certainly did not see any evidence of a superior educational system. However, when you realize that there are 1.4 billion Chinese, the 30 percent and 50 percent figures take on a bit more meaning.

English is compulsory and taught every day. Funny, in the repetition exercises, the teacher said "uh" every few words. The students all spoke using the "uh" fillers.

Before departing on the bullet train, I ate my first bad meal. The pumpkin donuts were delicious but the fried chicken sticks could have come from the frozen food department of my local grocery store.

What a difference between first class and lower class. The commuter train that carried us to Zhengzhou was slow and crowded, the train station even more. This train station was huge, modern and not busy, one of the first public venues not teeming with thousands of Chinese, most likely due to the cost.

Xi'an

After a perfunctory security check, we sat in comfortable waiting-room chairs a short distance from the train loading dock. The bullet train arrived out of the smog like a giant worm. Time was short. The coach was clean and roomy, not crowded but full. In two minutes we were under way. The bullet train was quite expensive. A one-way ticket cost $30, the commuter train was $15. The train was quiet, smoother than an airplane and traveled 200 miles an hour. In an hour and a half, we were in Xi'an (pronounced see-ahn). Pronouncing and speaking the Chinese language was near impossible for me. I didn't even try and admit that I also did not use chopsticks; whereas, most of my fellow travelers were quite good with them.

A purple coach reeking of mildew met us in the thick smog. Our new, capable guide, who called himself James Bond, recited facts as we rode toward the art school. Corn, wheat and cotton are grown in the Shaanxi Province of China. The culture dates back over 5,000 years. Eight million people live in Xi'an, and 42 universities in the city educate Chinese students. According to James Bond, 30% of the residents are employed in the tourist industry. Six million tourists visit the city, five million of them being Chinese. One million are foreigners, mainly European. Our guide was quite humorous, stating that the popular colors of China have changed from red to pink to green and now to gold, signifying the change from red Communist to pink not so Communist to green beginning capitalism and now gold, meaning great wealth.

At the art school we took a tour of contemporary art, the folk art of farmers and the stylized higher art forms. The question posed was whether free style or stylized art was the higher art form. The answer was free style.

The lady in charge directed our attention to some of the Cultural Revolution art depicting the workers and slogans. She remarked that she found the slogans ridiculous. Her scorn for the Communist party was obvious.

Seated around a table, we were furnished a horse hair brush, a bowl of black liquid and a sheet of thin rice paper. We were introduced to the eight strokes used to create 50,000 Chinese characters. The strokes were not difficult, but putting them together into a Chinese symbol was, for me, nearly impossible. We contributed to tuition costs for the students by purchasing some of their artwork. I found two pictures I liked and lightly bargained, purchasing both of them for a modest sum.

We then stopped at a famous dumpling house for a world renowned dumpling feast, featuring 18 types of dumplings. We ate duck dumplings fashioned in the shape of a duck, vegetable dumplings that resembled lotus flowers, dark brown walnut dumplings that tasted like pecan pie, and all sorts meat and vegetable dumplings. I was overjoyed when they brought out the sliced watermelon.

The day had been a long one before we checked into a five-star hotel. The luxury did not impress me. I only cared for some quiet and a clean bed.

Lying in bed the following morning, I asked myself, Self, you have another two and a half weeks in China. What the hell were you thinking? You're a long way from Texas, dummy.

Thankfully, a cup of coffee dispelled those thoughts and I prepared for another day in China.

The breakfast buffet was quite elaborate, and the WiFi access in the lobby allowed me to check email. I had been reluctant in the past to carry portable communication devices with me, but had earlier succumbed to a Kindle rather than tote heavy books. The iPad was proving to be convenient and an improvement over note taking with pen and paper. With the iPad I could relate my impressions and experiences more thoroughly. Communicating with family and friends was optional.

Rain was falling lightly as we set out for the International Studies University. The temperature was in the 50's. James Bond began the morning with a story about Chairman Mao during the Cultural Revolution. Chairman Mao had gathered his generals to select one of them for a prestigious position. He posed the question, "Which is better, a black cat or a white cat?" One general answered, "The one that catches the rats." He received the appointment.

Construction of a second subway in Xi'an slowed our progress, and James explained that the first subway had been under construction for 15 years. The subway was about 30 miles long.

James also advised us not to visit the city wall or the Muslim quarter in the city because of recent events that made it unsafe for foreigners. Recent riots in protest to Japanese policy had targeted all tourists, not just Japanese.

The university was nestled among trees. The buildings were only two or three stories and the narrow streets void of cars, containing only students laughing and talking. This was more like the China I had envisioned.

Sonja Klein

The lecture room on the second floor was like any college classroom. The front two rows were empty, reserved for the dozen old foreigners. About 25 students quietly sat in the remaining rows, mostly girls, only four boys.

Our lecturer was Professor Yang, a diminutive middle-aged woman. She began her lecture with a statement that will always resonate:"There are two ways to enrich your life, read 10,000 books or travel 10,000 miles. You have done one of them."

She then lectured on Chinese culture and history. She spoke with passion for three hours, with a short break midway. From the historic age and Chinese creation stories, she led us through the early philosophers, Lao-zi and Taoism, Confucius and Confucianism and Xun-zi and Legalism. At one point she digressed to comment on Chinese superstition, how the Chinese consult fortune tellers and numerologists. As an example, she said the fortune teller might advise them to send some money to their parents or say,"This is an auspicious week to start a war with Japan." I later learned that riots against the Japanese are occurring throughout China, with Japanese cars being destroyed and Japanese tourists being assaulted. Professor Yang inserted her dislike of the Japanese into the lecture.

Beginning with the Qin Dynasty in 221 B.C. and continuing on to the Qing Dynasty that ended in 1911, Professor Yang kept our attention. The modern era from 1911 to the present was just as interesting. She spoke freely, ashamed of Chairman Mao and the 10 years that the universities were closed and the educated were sent to work the fields.

Following the lecture, she implored us to walk the campus with the students and ask them any questions. I had spoken with two of the boys during the break. All of the students attending our lecture were master's candidates in English interpretation, translation and reporting under Professor Yang. They were in their second year of a three-year degree. Their ages were 22 and 23. One of them wanted to work for the government and join the Communist party. The other wanted to work for a foreign or private business and was not interested in joining the party.

The two girls with whom I walked the campus were similar. One believed in the party and the security of a government job. The other had higher aspirations. All of the students expressed their fear of not finding a job when they completed their degrees.

Roundtrip from Texas

Following a typical Chinese meal at the university, we continued to the Shaanxi Museum of History. Museums in China are free. The government encourages the citizens to be proud of their history. It must be working because the museum was crowded with hundreds of Chinese tourists. The museum was well done, with beautiful grounds and artfully arranged exhibits. I was quite impressed and wished that museums in America were equally as busy.

We spent several hours in the museum before walking several blocks to the Hai Chao Yin Teahouse, where we attended a lecture on tea and a tea tasting. Samples of five varieties were furnished. I learned to drink the small cup of tea in three sips, one for happiness, one for good luck and one for good health. There are over 1,600 varieties of tea. None of the Chinese teas I had drunk so far were brown or dark or full of caffeine and none were brewed with tea bags. The teas we sampled were brewed in small balls or chipped off bricks or simply loose leaves. For the first time, I was enjoying warm tea. The teas were very light in color, almost like water. We were given a sheet of paper listing nine teas and their medicinal effects. I purchased some jasmine sphere tea and a green tea that moistens the skin and lungs. Applying the dregs on the face and skin for 20 minutes erases wrinkles. I also purchased some dragon well tea, supposedly the top Chinese tea. This tea is purported to make your energy come back, diminish inflammation and help assimilation. Four small containers of these teas were quite expensive.

A short ride back to the hotel left little time before walking down the street for more Chinese food. The eggplant, the noodles and the white sweet potato with apricot sauce were the best courses of the meal.

The day for a visit to the eighth wonder of the world dawned clearer than expected. The site of the Qin Dynasty Terra Cotta Warriors is about 30 miles from Xi'an.

The emperor Ying Zheng ruled from 259 B.C. to 210 B.C. He defeated the other warring states and consolidated China under his rule. The emperor began construction on his tomb at the age of 13 and continued until his death at the age of 49. He built his tomb in the feng shui tradition, paying close attention to the wind and water and the zen of the site, which was 300 acres, the largest tomb in the world.

Sonja Klein

His tomb replicated his life on earth, except it was built underground to compliment his life after death. The site was discovered in 1974 by farmers digging a well. From bamboo scrolls discovered in southern China, archaeologists learned that over 700,000 workers built the tomb and that over 8,000 terra cotta statues were created hollow, so that his soldiers' souls could inhabit them. The soldiers were divided into infantry, cavalry, archers and officers. Most of the statues were broken when discovered. Looters invaded the site during a peasant revolt.

The restoration is a monumental task being done exclusively by the Chinese, who also developed a software program to fit the broken pieces together from photos.

Pit number one includes restored warriors' bodies, no two alike. According to records, the army went to the site and their faces were drawn as models for the terra cotta figures, all of them being about six feet tall.

Standing on the edge of the pit in the presence of these solemn, silent figures over 2,000 years old, I felt immortal.

Two more pits are in the process of restoration, and seeing the crumbled clay parts of soldiers and horses lying as they have for thousands of years is an awesome experience. A fourth building houses artifacts, including two bronze chariots and horses built half scale.

The emperor's tomb has not been opened, due to a mercury vapor that poisons the air of the tomb. I didn't quite understand how that was possible. The explanation had something to do with two rivers being created within the tomb to replicate China's Yangtze and Yellow Rivers. The water comes from natural hot springs, which have something to do with the mercury vapor.

I spent most of the day at the tomb, but as we returned to the city we stopped at a massage parlor, and for $25 I had a one-hour foot and body massage. The only clothing removed was shoes and socks. It was the perfect end to a perfect day.

The evening meal at a nearby hotel did not offer one remarkable course. I was craving some real meat with bones and flavor.

I questioned the guide regarding facial hair. Nearly all of the terra cotta warriors were depicted with a mustache or a beard or both; whereas I had yet to see a modern day Chinese man with a fuzzy face or a tattoo. He replied that facial hair and tattoos are not popular, and if you want a job, it is best to be clean shaven and clear skinned.

The morning dawned cold, damp and gray, one of those bone-chilling days best spent at home simmering soup and feeding logs into a fireplace. Not so for the intrepid travelers. We spent the morning hours at a lecture informing us of the political events from 1950 to the present. None of the news was good. If the Chinese people were not being killed for being smart, they were starving to death or being informed upon by their neighbors or friends and then tortured to death or sent for re-education. Their recent history was not a pretty picture, but the lecturer asserted that the Chinese people are now not afraid to resist or speak out. Government corruption is the current topic and the citizens are critical of their leaders. I think it is a good sign.

In spite of the dreary weather, we managed to eat more Chinese food, again, not a remarkable dish but only the usual predictable sweet-and-sour chicken, pork, steamed vegetables, soup, rice and cauliflower.

We then traveled a short distance to the Wild Goose Pagoda, the largest water fountain show in Asia and the Small Wild Goose Pagoda. We heard two folk stories about the naming and building of the pagodas. You can easily guess that the stories involved a wild goose chase or quest.

A fellow traveler and I spent the remainder of the afternoon shopping the main boulevard. I purchased a charger for my iPad for $30, and we each bought a sweater for under $30. We walked briskly back to the hotel in the damp mist. The warmth of the hotel was welcoming.

Dinner was Chinese, surprise, surprise, and unremarkable. Bedtime arrived early since we had been promised a 5 A.M. wakeup call. I was lying in bed waiting when the call came.

Cruising the Yangtze

We left the hotel before daylight. The airport was not busy and the flight though full was smooth, a short one hour on a domestic Chinese airline to the city of Chonqing. The municipality of Chonqing hosts a population of 32 million, the city a mere ten million. It was the first mountainous town in China I visited. The Japanese bombed the city for six years during World War II. Most of it today is quite new.

Our first stop was the zoo. We were in panda country. Eight of them live in the zoo, and a breeding farm is located in the area. Since pandas are solitary and don't get along, they were in separate pens, lying on their backs eating bamboo. They were hilarious. Their bellies were littered with bamboo leaves. The pile of stalks was beside them and they would select a stalk, eat it and discard the leaves. A panda will eat about 40 pounds of bamboo a day.

Lunch was served on a rooftop garden in a quiet setting. The butternut squash and roasted green beans in garlic were tasty, the green tea quite refreshing. A chicken dish was served, and we were cautioned that it was spicy. It wasn't really spicy, but something ignited my palate like a strong mouthwash. No one could identify it. We were told it was a special small brown pepper that grows only in the Sichuan area called a tongue-numbing pepper. It was.

Following lunch we drove to an 18th century palace, the only remaining palace in Chonqing after World War II. Restoration was not complete, having begun in 2004.

Our next stop was the Three Gorges Museum, located in the center of town. The four-storied museum featured displays on the building of the dam, the history of the area and the relocation of the one million people displaced by the dam. One section revealed the history of the Han people and another the history of the city of Chonqing. From the square we walked to a hot pot restaurant. We were ushered into a private dining room and seated around a table with a burner in the middle. A pot within a pot stood simmering with a clear broth and some seasoning vegetables. Our local guide said the inner pot was spicy and the outside pot was mild. Then they started bringing food to boil in the pots: noodles, lamb, beef, sausage, tofu, mushrooms, pumpkin, chicken, pork balls, crab and carp (I don't eat carp). We were instructed to drop the food into the simmering juices and let it cook, then fish it out and dip it in our bowl of mixed soy sauce, garlic and sesame oil.

I can't say I was impressed. The end result was two bowls of slop. We fished stuff out and ate it, but everything was mixed together. At least ample meat served.

The day had been long as the coach pulled to the pier on the Yangtze River. An aging four-decker was waiting. A band played Yankee Doodle. We received a cup of warm tea rather than champagne as we entered the musty ship. Only two life boats were in evidence. I asked the guide where the lifeboats were. She replied that there were only two but that there were life preservers in each room and that each room had an outdoor balcony. Not very reassuring. The rooms were tiny but had a TV, telephone, bathroom and balcony.

The mandatory lecture and introduction to the ship was on the schedule. I had expected a safety drill and exit strategy. Instead the social director, a senior citizen from Phoenix, Arizona, introduced everyone from the chambermaids to the bartender. At one point I looked to my left and right. My fellow companions were nodding off and when I turned around, the people behind were asleep. I stood, returned to my room and went to bed.

The ship docked before daylight. I rushed to the upper deck for coffee and discovered tai chi. While I observed the tai chi participants, I visited with some ladies from the United Kingdom. They had just returned from Tibet and said they all became sick from the altitude and were disappointed in their tour, which was supposed to be small but instead had over 40 travelers.

I did not take part in the tai chi and while watching was relieved that I had not missed a defining moment. I don't believe tai chi is a regimen learned in a few morning sessions but rather a life discipline. None of the participants were Chinese other than the instructor.

While observing the tai chi students, I saw an elderly Chinese man walk out on the forward deck of the ship and in minutes execute some of the most beautiful fluid movements I have ever seen, a stark contrast to the jerky, unbalanced gyrations on the dance floor inside the salon. He then returned to the salon, sat down and drank from his cup of tea.

The buffet breakfast was as expected, except that it included scrambled eggs and there was no bacon or watermelon. We spent the morning on shore, visiting the home of a farmer who had been relocated because of the Three Gorges Dam. He was quite prosperous, owned a three-story home and currently farmed less than an acre. His five children all worked in the city in good jobs, and his wife took the bus every morning to care and cook for some of the grandchildren before returning home. At 70 years old, he still farmed and said how much better off he was than before the dam. I later learned that we were only allowed to visit Chinese homes where the inhabitants were prosperous and happy with the government and their lives.

Sonja Klein

The banks of the Yangtze were populated with factories. Barges traveled the river. I saw ceramic factories and sacks of rice being unloaded one at a time on the backs of shirtless Chinese men. Small plots of vegetables and fruit trees were cultivated on the steep terraced hillsides.

We explored the market in Hong Yan, crowded with families on a Saturday morning. Every imaginable meat, fruit and vegetable was on display, including pig snouts. Good thing I wasn't hungry.

After returning to the boat, lunch was a welcome change. There were lettuce wraps and good green beans and eggplant with a bit more of a global twist, perhaps to accommodate the Germans, Brits, Australians and Americans, even though over half of the passengers for the three-night cruise were Chinese.

A lecture on acupuncture from a Chinese doctor who also instructed tai chi was disappointing. She couldn't speak English and instead read a lecture delivered by an interpreter. The procedure lacked passion, even though she managed to stick needles in a German she persuaded to remove his shirt. I did learn that the purpose of acupuncture and acupressure is to stimulate the blood to circulate in the channels of the body. A lecture about the river, the dam and the gorges followed.

Later I visited with two young attractive ladies, one from Canberra, Australia, and one from Breckenridge, Colorado, near my mother's home in Silverthorne, Colorado. I love that part of travel, sitting at a bar on a riverboat on the Yangtze River in China, visiting with a young woman from a town in Colorado where my children and I spent many happy days enjoying winter and summer sports.

I declined to attend the native costumed dancing and music that evening. Instead I retired to read. Before daylight we docked with much banging and shouting outside my balcony. I observed the tai chi students. There were fewer than on the morning before. As I sipped my first cup of coffee, a man who spoke with a German accent joined me. He was American and lived in Minnesota. He was old enough to receive Social Security, dyed his thinning hair a light carrot red and spoke only of his son and business. He was traveling in China for the first time, paying for a trip for his German accountant and the accountant's wife. He was clearly lonely. When I asked him what he thought of China, he digressed into a lengthy discourse about how China is the only nation that was once great and is now making a comeback. I told him, "I'm not so sure I agree with you. I'll have to think about it."

I learned to play Mahjong before we entered the Qutang Gorge, a scenic five-mile stretch of the Yangtze. The game of tiles is similar to the card game of gin, only with dominoes picturing Chinese symbols. Once I learned the symbols, I managed to win at my table of four players.

The sun and some clouds were visible for a short time as I enjoyed the drink of the day, a Shanghai Sunrise, composed of vodka, cherry brandy and lime juice served straight up, that is with no ice, as all ice in China is very risky.

Passing through the Wu Gorge promised to be the feature of the afternoon. Our passage was punctuated with thunder and rain, quite dramatic. Upon arriving in Badong we boarded a large ferry boat and sailed up Shennong River, a tributary of the Yangtze until it became too narrow for the ferry. In the rain, we left the dry warmth of the larger boat and clambored onto small wooden sampans, with blue tarps for shelter. The wooden sampans were a conglomeration of boards and slats, not very reassuring and much like the flimsy life vests we strapped onto our torsos.

And then came that precious moment that memory stamps, sitting in a sampan, quietly rowed by three bare-chested ethnic minority Chinese, over the green waters of a narrow gorge, towering cliffs on either side, thunder echoing from the cliffs and a strong but gentle rain pelting the scraggly tarp above. Our guide, also an ethnic minority citizen, began singing a folk song in a clear young voice. I trailed my hand in the water. At last I was close to the essence of China. I later learned that her father, brother and uncle were trackers, men who, in the past before the dam, nakedly pulled boats through the shallow waters hauling freight along the Yangtze and its many tributaries. The building of the dam destroyed their jobs.

The return trip on the ferry was maddening. The Chinese are not quiet people; they are very noisy.

The sick among us had not improved. One man had developed a rash early in the trip. It had not cleared. He was on his third type of ointment and the Chinese doctor on the ship and other experts along the way had advised him to bathe three times a day, to drink no alcohol or tea and eat no fish. He had faithfully followed the orders. Another traveler had a similar rash but was not being treated. One of the ladies was suffering from dizzy spells, another from colitis. Two in the group had stupidly brushed their teeth with tap water and spent two days being very sick until the antibiotics took effect. The Chinese were all adamant about not drinking tea within 30 minutes of taking any medication because they treat tea as a medication.

That evening we dined at the captain's farewell dinner. Just the night before, we dined at the captain's welcome dinner. It was a bit silly, but the champagne was free both nights. The drinks in between were not. A beer was about $4, a glass of wine $7.50, a martini $6. The meal was elaborate and the Chinese tourists louder than normal. The tourists from the United Kingdom were a close second. Two Chinese men celebrated birthdays. The lights went out and small birthday cakes were delivered in the dark to each table. Toasts were raised, the Happy Birthday song was sung and I retreated to the quiet of my room. The adventure had reached the halfway point.

Before leaving the Yangtze River and the riverboat and continuing south, our guide had warned us to rest up, saying, "On the second half of the trip you will be continuing your march across China."

The morning we exited the boat, we visited the scenic Three Gorges Dam site. In the lightly falling rain, we first passed through a security check and then were escorted to the viewing area, featured with four levels of outdoor German-made escalators that comfortably carried us to the top of the mountain overlooking the 10 locks, the dam, and the ship elevator being constructed. For the first time, the skies had cleared so that I rediscovered the blue sky and clouds. The air breathed cleaner.

I learned that the dam generated electric power for much of south China and that by doing so prevented the burning of 57 million tons of coal. No wonder all of north China is under a surreal haze. I also learned the tallest dam in the world is in Tajikistan and the longest is in Brazil. The dam that creates the largest reservoir in water volume is the Aswan Dam in Egypt. A sign on the overlook railing read, NO TOOSSING.

Upon returning to the ship for lunch, I ventured into the tourist shop at the dock. There it was, the same blue silk jacket I had admired in two previous cities. In the first city the price was 280 yuan, in the second it was 560, in Yichang it was 120 but poorly made. I planned to wait for Shanghai.

Wuhan

Due to mudslides, we left the ship at a port earlier than scheduled and rode a bus to Wuhan. At last I began to see China through the eyes of a countryside traveler. Through the mountains and gorges we journeyed on wide smooth roads. Vacation homes, free standing for a change, dotted the hillsides. A chair lift rode up a sheer cliff. The poor live in the cities, stacked in 30- to 40-story buildings. The wealthy own vacation homes, travel and frequent the resort areas.

From Yichang, with a population of 4 million, we moved into the flat plains through fields of rice, corn, wheat, fish farms and lotus plants growing in ponds of water with water chestnuts. Cotton was picked by hand. Carp were raised in ponds. We had been served carp on several occasions. I had not tasted the fish as I prefer to not eat bottom-feeding fish and consider carp a trash fish.

As we neared Wuhan, with a population of 10 million, the traffic became congested, and the countryside lost its rural atmosphere. The province that contains the city of Wuhan also hosts 6.5 million Chinese. Wuhan lies on the river and is a great commercial trade center. Citroen, Honda and Nissan manufacture vehicles there. The city is also a center for textiles and shipbuilding and boasts a huge manufacturing center. I had mistakenly believed that we had left the Yangtze.

We enjoyed a delightful meal of the usual eggplant, green beans, bok choy, cabbage, cauliflower, onions, celery, soup, pork, beef and chicken before driving across the city in the evening traffic to check into a five-star hotel where Chairman Mao often stayed. The lobby was stunning, but what I was looking forward to was a hot shower and some WiFi access to check on pressing business.

The guide had raved about the hotel. When I asked her, "What makes this hotel so great?" she answered, "You'll see when you go to breakfast." She was correct. The dining room was huge, with Venetian murals on the walls and a glass roof, creating the illusion of being outside. Attractive young Chinese dressed in red hovered, anxious to serve. There were many islands of food types, even a waffle station and a noodle station.

After leaving the luxurious hotel, we joined a new guide who offered his name as Jeffrey Summer. He was passionate about his job. At first I surmised he was a Communist party member, but my usual probing questions revealed that he was not. He was anti-party. He said, "Only one out of 15 Chinese are members of the party, and no one believes the dogma of Lenin and Marx. They only join the party to obtain favors and better jobs."

For the third time I heard the story about Bill Clinton. The Chinese love Bill Clinton because in 1997 he visited China with his family and stood down in the pit with the terra cotta warriors. The leader of China practiced English phrases to use with Bill Clinton, but when the time came to speak he was so nervous he said, "Who are you?" instead of "How are you?"

Bill Clinton paused momentarily and replied, "The husband of Hillary and the father of Chelsea."

The premier, not realizing he made a mistake, thought the exchange had gone, "How are you? I'm fine." He replied, "Me too."

We soon arrived at the Hubei Provincial Museum. Like all the museums I visited in China, the grounds were well kept and colorful with seasonal flower plantings. Our guide led us through the displays in rooms related to the life of the Marquis Yi of Zeng. He lived in 400 B.C. and was an avid lover of music. His tomb was discovered and excavated in 1978. It contained many artifacts, including musical instruments and the bodies of his musicians so that in death he would be serenaded. Instruments from the tomb included bronze bells, marble chimes, drums, flutes, pan pipes and zithers. Bronze artifacts were intricately cast—large wine coolers, bowls and carved animals. Weapons, chariots and harnesses were also found in the large tomb, as well as gold bowls and jade jewelry. The display was amazing.

Following the tour of the museum, we entered a small auditorium and were treated to a musical performance using replicated instruments of the Marquis Yi of Zeng. Three tiers of bells from large to small, two zithers, chimes, drums, flutes and a pan pipe played Chinese music. The final song was Beethoven's "Ode to Joy." The moment defined an exceptional day in China.

Following a typical Chinese lunch, we drove to the train station and boarded a sleeper train for our third train ride. Car 16 was crowded with businessmen. A small compartment with three layers of bunks accessed by a narrow metal ladder was assigned to every six passengers. In the aisle were fold-up padded seats next to the windows. Mercifully, I was assigned a lower bunk. A Chinese girl sat inches across from me, and above me were two men. Above her were two more men. The aisle seats were full. Every so often a Chinese lady or man would push a cart down the aisle, selling drinks, fresh fruit wrapped in cellophane or giant cups of soup similar to Ramen noodle cups. The noise was deafening. The train lurched at unexpected intervals, and the bathroom at the end of the car was quite rank.

After an hour, a camaraderie among the passengers developed. We didn't speak the same language but instead spoke with gestures and smiles, my favorite communication.

This is how you understand a country. Do what they do, wait in the train station, ride trains with them, go to the market and visit their parks and museums. In China everyone goes to the parks and museums because there is so little free space.

Changsa

We arrived in Changsa, capital of Hunan province, four hours after leaving Wuhan. By then we were close friends. A late dinner at the hotel hosted by a new guide, Mr. Tan, provided some new dishes, edamame beans and frog. I was expecting bullfrog as I have eaten in Texas or Louisiana. Instead I ate tiny chunks of meat with many bones. I'd rather not think about what I was eating.

The guide sat next to me. He admitted to being 48, divorced and a Romney supporter. I was elated to be in the company of a conservative. His opinion of the Communist party was not good. He expressed hope in the United States as the world leader and was quite versed in economic affairs. More than once he said,

"America is the greatest nation in the world. I wish I could go there."

Three Chinese girls shared the elevator as we returned to our rooms. Dinner had been unusually late, due to the train ride. They were dressed quite provocatively and stopped at the 5th floor. Loud music drifted down the halls. Later we learned that a nightclub/disco for businessmen was on that floor and that women tourists were not welcome. You can guess why. Most of the better hotels in which we stayed had a special floor. In one hotel the elevator did not stop there.

Sonja Klein

Even though my room was on the 22nd floor, the street noise was bothersome until I closed the curtains and the city settled for the night, a city I later learned produced 300,000 Volkswagens per year.

My first breakfast in the Hunan province was disappointing. The coffee was bitter and the food appeared to be warmed-over Chinese dishes from the previous evening. There was no fruit, only boiled eggs and toast with no jam or jelly, but the taro rolls with sesame seeds were unusually good.

The morning began with a lecture by Professor Zhang, a professor of Maoism at the Central South University in Changsa. Tea was served. Large glasses similar to our ice tea glasses stood on the table in front of each chair. Large loose tea leaves covered the bottom of the glass. A young lady poured hot water to the top of the glass. The tea leaves rose to the top of the glass. We were instructed to wait until the tea leaves sunk to the bottom; the tea would then be ready to drink. Our guide, Mr. Tan, commented that a very expensive tea existed that rose and fell three times in the glass before it was sufficiently brewed for drinking. I immediately thought of Dom Perignon champagne and the spirit of the bubbles. From there, I thought of the husband who introduced me to expensive champagne. I looked around the room. I was in China.

Professor Zhang was a soft-spoken man in his early 50's who had suffered during some of China's tumultuous years. The lecture covered the many facets of Mao Zedong: the basic Mao, the neutralized Mao, the devil Mao, the heroic Mao, the personified Mao and the deified Mao.

More interesting was the professor's story. His father received a formal education and fought in the army with Chiang Kai-shek. His unit defected to Mao. He later retired from the army and taught school. Under Mao, for whom he fought, he was labeled a right winger and imprisoned for three years. In 1979 he was released from prison and restored to his post as a teacher. He was 88 when he died.

There was no education when the professor was young. He worked construction as a brickmaker and a bricklayer and educated himself. He later passed a test and attended college. He is a Buddhist. He was asked his impressions on the 1989 uprising on Tien'anmen Square. He said that no students were killed and that he believed soldiers, homeless people and dissidents provoked the protest. He added that many of his students went to Beijing at that time; and when they returned the university appointed him to the board to examine the students and determine who would be jailed. He tailored his questions to protect his students. He added that the protests delayed the development and progression of China to democracy by 12 years.

When asked his feelings on the treatment of Buddhists and the Tibetan people, he first expounded on the fact that the Dalai Lama is not the reincarnated Buddha, that he should not be secular and is in fact only a good politician. He added that the Tibetan people want to change their culture and be modern and that the Chinese government is only helping them. His comments were measured.

As we later walked to a nearby market, discussing the lecture, a member of our group spoke out, saying she did not agree with his comments. She had friends who recently returned from Tibet and said the Chinese soldiers throughout Tibet were oppressing the monks and Tibetan people.

Later at lunch, sitting with Mr. Tan, we asked him the same questions. He said he was a student under Professor Zhang and did not agree with his views on Tien'anmen Square and Tibet, as well as other issues that he did not mention. On the subject of the Japanese, he was in agreement with most Chinese who dislike them with prejudice.

After another unexciting lunch, we attended a lecture by Professor Peng, vice-president of the Hunan Province University of Agriculture. This man is world-famous and has traveled extensively, being involved in agricultural research in California, Canada and Ethiopia. He is an authority on rice. After naming the agricultural products of China, he focused on the development of rice to increase the quality as well as the quantity of production. He explained the recent reforms in rice—hybridization, shorter plants and higher yields.

We then accompanied him to the agricultural research station to witness the varieties and harvesting. I asked him about his recent visit to Ethiopia. He spent 10 weeks with other agricultural specialists, training 300 Ethiopians in improved farming methods. I asked him if he was optimistic about the future of some of the African countries. He replied that much of Africa has fertile soil, plenty of rain or water, 13 months of sunshine but no strong leadership; and that is the problem. Another of our group inquired about the use of human waste as fertilizer. The professor stated that a small percentage, perhaps one third, of fertilizers used is derived from human waste; but there is no effective means of collecting and treating it.

Later that afternoon, I asked Hui, our guide, about Tien'anmen Square and the Tibetan situation. She agreed with Mr. Tan. Tien'anmen Square was about the students. She was there. She also travels to Tibet several times a year and has seen the mistreatment of the Tibetans and the Buddhist monks. She said Professor Zhang is a good man and is only trying to work within the system until he retires next year.

A quick stroll through the market on the way back to the hotel netted some fresh Chinese apples, some roasted peanuts and a couple of bananas. I was becoming accustomed to the noise and crowds on the streets.

"Noisy" in China is not the noisy I know. I'm referring to firecracker blasts that resemble a firing range. Weddings are big celebrations. As a wedding party was leaving the hotel, strategic firecracker and rocket pads surrounded the hotel grounds. When the groom carried the bride, resplendent in her red wedding dress, through the lobby to the flower-decorated car, the explosives were ignited. The smoggy air was now blue with gunpowder. Everyone was smiling and laughing. The Chinese love noise.

Restaurants are just as noisy. Most of the better restaurants have a common dining room and many private dining rooms. Most of our meals were in private dining rooms, where we sat around a table for 12 with a lazy Susan in the middle. Eight to 12 dishes were then brought to the table. We spun the middle of the table and served ourselves, most of the time not very neatly. Think about noodles with chopsticks.

Breakfast was usually eggless; instead, I ate fried bananas, fried taro and a fried donut thing. The coffee was watery and the watery noodle soup that everyone ate never appealed to me. Time to move on.

We traveled to Hunan University, located at the foot of the Yellow Mountain. From there we walked through the tree-lined campus to the Ancient Academy, a school of philosophy built in the tenth century and a historical site. The Chinese style buildings and gardens were vastly different from the bustling cities. Here again, I glimpsed the China I expected. A sign in the gardens caught my eye, DO NOT ROMP IN THE GARDENS.

Following lunch, we visited Walmart. The escalators to the store that began on the second floor were moving ramps with no steps that allowed the shopper to take his basket. We had each been assigned to shop for a particular item written in Chinese and meet at checkout counter 20. I was so overwhelmed by the people and the store that I almost lost my composure. Instead, I wanted to flee far away; I experienced a moment of panic.

On the third floor I located the paper cups and returned to the meeting place, giving my assignment to the guide and rushing outside. For an eternity I did not realize that we had entered from the street and risen a story. Another panicky moment before I found the street and a Starbucks. Alas, I had trouble communicating that I wanted a frappuccino and then remembered about not drinking the ice. Fortunately, the manager spoke some English. The ice was made with purified water. I must admit, it was the best drink I had tasted in China. I savored the whipped cream and chilled frothy mocha drink.

Following a meal of snails and lamb almost too spicy for anyone but me, we adjourned to a conference room for a lecture on economics. I learned that the Chinese are taxed as much or more than Americans. They pay taxes for most every purchase, plus the value-added tax. Their income tax is taken directly from their salaries and no income tax is paid until the citizen makes 3,500 yuan a month, which is between $500 and $600. Our guide, in a position of great responsibility, makes 2,500 yuan, about $425 per month. Her husband, who works for a bank, is paid 7,500 yuan per month, about $1,200. Both of them have a college degree and have connections, very important to obtaining a job in China.

Taxes are paid on food and real estate purchases, ranging from construction taxes to education taxes to consumer taxes to luxury taxes. And they don't like it any more than we do.

The per capita income in 2011 was about $175 per month. Farmers make $75 per month and over 200 million Chinese make below $75 per month.

In Beijing, a city of 22 million, 3.8 million home units stand empty. Tall empty buildings characterized most all of the cities I visited.

The phone rang at 5 A.M. I had been awake writing for an hour. The luggage had been sent the previous day. It would take two days for my suitcase to find me. In the meantime I had a backpack with all my "weapons": a Swiss army knife, a pair of tiny scissors, two cigarette lighters purchased for gifts and a few small bottles of cosmetics. The reason for the delay in receiving my luggage was something about a train station being remodeled and not accepting a luggage car.

Sonja Klein

The train left at 7 A.M., another sleeper train. My bunk was a lower one, and again, I shared prison-sized space with five Chinese. Most of them were sleeping, one snoring lightly. The cubicle was littered with bags of food, shoes and canvas bags. The redeeming virtue of the sleeper trains and all hotels in China was the down comforter. I kicked my bag under the bunk, took off my shoes and laid down on the pillow, pulling the comforter over my torso and pretending that everything was clean. The books on my Kindle entertained me until I became sleepy.

When I awoke to the music of "Sounds of Silence," played hauntingly and looked toward my feet and the aisle, I saw two Chinese men, perched on the fold-down stools. One man with thinning hair, one hand on his knee and the other hand propping his head, was captivated by the countryside. The next man on the aisle was in a similar pensive position. The music had momentarily brought silence into the crowded train car. Tears rolled down my cheeks. I wondered what these men had seen as I saw the smog and empty shells of abandoned new construction, a coal yard, clothes drying on porches, and piles of rubble. And as I silently sat on my narrow bed with a wet face, I was sad for the Chinese people, their history of oppression, the low salaries, the poisoned land and corrupt leaders and I wanted to be them. I was angry at my fate of being born American, for my comfortable life, my freedom and my wealth. In that moment China had stolen me away from myself. It was a singular experience.

The Chinese are curious people. Being among the few foreigners on the train, they always looked for an opportunity to practice English. I met a man in his 40's who had been to Denver, Dallas, New York City and Orlando. He worked for a factory that manufactured tempered glass.

Ka'li

We left the train in Ka'li, a small village of 480,000 in a mountainous province dominated by minorities. The evening meal at the hotel was one of the best: a hot sour beef soup, lotus roots, pea pods with bacon, sweet sour pork and sticky rice with peanut and sesame paste. Sticky rice used in desserts is a totally different type of rice, snow white and rounded. I had always believed that sticky rice was sticky because of the method of preparation.

After an unremarkable breakfast we attended a lecture by Professor Wang, a Miao or Hmong minority citizen of the Guizhou province, also an autonomous prefecture. Anything labeled autonomous in China means that the majority of the population is composed of ethic minorities; they choose their own leaders and supposedly have more freedom.

Professor Wang grew up in a small village of Miao people and spoke mostly about the Hmong/Miao minority people, who compose 42 percent of the population. The Dong people comprise 38 percent. The Hmong/Miao people are also found in Laos, Burma, Thailand and Vietnam and were the neighbors of Clint Eastwood in the movie "Gran Torino."

From the professor, who admitted to being an avid singer and ballroom dancer, we learned the history of the Miao/Hmong people, their migration to the mountains from the Yangtze River area, their ethnic tasty pork and sour soup dishes and their rice wine.

He spoke of the many festivals, their silver jewelry, Dong batik designs and patterns, their covered bridges and stilt homes, as well as their rooster fighting, hunting, horse racing and boat racing.

We learned that the sour soup was made with fermented rice water and were instructed how to make the soup and ferment the rice water in a jar for a week or two. I think if I try to duplicate the soup, I'll simply use rice vinegar.

A short ride through the dense smog/fog led us to the 200-bed provincial hospital with an A ranking. The head of the hospital, a woman physician, met us in the lobby and escorted us to the second floor, the acupuncture, cupping and blood-letting department, some of the treatment methods of Chinese traditional medicine. The hospital specializes in both Western and Chinese traditional treatment.

The smell was not pleasant as we walked by rooms with people lying exposed with needles protruding from various body areas. I patiently stood and tried not to breathe, think or observe too closely.

We followed the doctor to the traditional pharmacy. There were old-fashioned wooden drawers, white-robed pharmacy people filling prescriptions issued from a man behind a computer and Chinese citizens lined up outside the glass window, patiently waiting in line. The room smelled like tea leaves or dried herbs. I opened drawers to find cinnamon bark, peach seeds, dried mushrooms and orange rind and was even shown a drawer with dried scorpions used to treat arthritis. Most of the treatments prescribed require a combination of many ingredients that are boiled into a soup or tonic and then ingested.

Across the lobby, the western pharmacy had no customers waiting for the boxes and bottles of pills and capsules. I believe in both methods of treatment, the holistic approach.

The lunch in this minority province was equally as tasty as the previous evening's meal: lots of pork, peppers and vegetables. The afternoon visit to two minority villages promised to be interesting. The bus ride wasn't. Leaving the mountainous city from our hotel, aptly named The Heaven Sent Dragon Hotel, on a bus titled Dragon in Flight on a six-lane highway, I observed the change in architecture. Whether it was the style of the minorities or a style dictated by building materials, I'm not sure. I suspect it was a combination of both. There was a definite similarity to the wooden homes in Bhutan and Tibet.

The small coach turned off the main highway onto a wide swath of destruction through a mountain valley. A new highway and bullet train track was being constructed. Heavy equipment, concrete trucks and workmen moved everywhere. Progress was slow. No detours were marked.

The mountains were lush, terraced to the higher elevations with rice, wheat, corn and vegetable plots. Lotus ponds grew in the lower areas. The sight was beautiful: mountains and terraces, crops lined in precision, marred only by the smog or haze.

Leaving the construction area behind we climbed on a two-lane mountain road, complete with hairpin turns, viewing gorges with water far below. Our bus driver was a bit reckless. He did honk his horn at every severe turn, a mountain-driving custom for trucks and busses.

After a scenic hour, we stopped in a small village of the Miao people. The villagers were waiting, some dressed in native costume, and the rest watching. As we walked up a stony path, we were stopped at three intervals and given a drink of rice wine from a buffalo horn. We could not touch the horn and were told that if we touched the horn we had to drink it all. The wine was smooth and strong, a nice buzz for the afternoon.

Stools had been provided. We were seated around the town circle, a paved area, and the music and dancing began. The music sounded Cajun and the dancers moved smoothly to the harmonious music. I told Bob, sitting beside me, "You'll know it's the last dance when they come and grab us by the arm and we dance with them."

We joined the circle, everyone smiling, laughing and taking pictures. Tables were set on the periphery of the open area. Bright and pretty batik crafts and silver jewelry were for sale. We purchased some of their crafts.

The coach continued into the mountains. The terraces consumed every inch of tillable land. Construction sites continued to rim the valleys. The government is promoting tourism, tourism for the Chinese people. With over one billion citizens becoming prosperous, the government is encouraging them to travel. Every city, museum, archaeological site, monument, park or hotel we visited was filled with Chinese tourists. Evidently, in the past, the Chinese people did not or could not move freely within their country.

While we continued through the mountains, our local guide told the creation story of the Miao people, how Mother Butterfly fell in love with a bubble and together with the bubble created man, the animals and the earth. I later commented, "I don't think I could have much faith in Mother Butterfly if she chose a bubble for a mate. She sounds like she doesn't make very good choices in men, kind of like me. I've fallen for some bubbles myself."

Wisely, Carolyn observed that Mother Butterfly probably fell in love with a reflection of herself as seen in the bubble. And someone else added, "Like Narcissus." It made sense. My opinion of Mother Butterfly changed.

Again we stopped at a small village of the Miao, this time to learn the old way of making paper. The Chinese contributed paper, printing, the compass and gun powder to civilization. An old man was squatted on the ground. Before him lay a small pile of pale soft strips of bark that had been soaked in a lime mixture.

The paper is made from the bark of the mulberry tree, which grows in the mountains. The bark is soaked and shredded, the dark parts removed by hand and then soaked several times in the lime mixture. Then the bark and lime liquid is put on a screen and later the wet sheets are laid against a charcoal-heated wall to become sheets of paper. Everything is done by hand. The family has done this for four generations and has a contract with the government to supply the paper for restoration projects. The process can produce 500 three-foot square sheets per day.

We walked down the narrow cobbled street of the village. Rice still in the hulls was drying on tarps, dried corn cobs hung from the wooden eaves of homes and clusters of peanuts tied with strings hung from porches. Old men played cards and smoked. Children played card games too.

Younger men were butchering a hog, boiling the hunks of fat in a large black pot. In another pot clumps of brains were boiling. A large yellow spotted hog lay dead and gutted but not yet skinned, the head intact. Around the corner another pig's throat was being cut. We could hear the animal squealing until all was silent. The village was preparing a feast to celebrate the completion of the framework of a large building on the outskirts of the village.

The afternoon was passing. Our driver wanted out of the mountains before dark. The return trip was shorter, most of it downhill. A Chinese dinner of mostly vegetables with a bit of pork ended another good day.

On our way out of Ka'li the next morning, we stopped at the Sunday market. Though it was early, the streets and alleyways of the market were busy. As we walked among the Chinese, I saw clothes being sewn with pedal sewing machines, stool legs being fashioned with a hatchet, fish being cleaned, pork carcasses being hacked and rice wine in barrels slowly aging.

The three-hour bus ride through the mountains on a four-lane expressway was scenic. The terraced fields and villages in the distance appeared well ordered. Trucks loaded with shiny new cars, mostly white, carried 18 vehicles. The highway was well policed. The radar detector on the coach went off about eight or nine times.

Guiyang

We arrived in Guiyang, the capital of the Guizhou province, in time for lunch. The city was another big one with a population of near two million. The city is a Chinese summer vacation destination due to its subtropical climate and 3,500-foot elevation. We dined on a delightful vegetarian lunch and then visited a school titled The Children's Palace. It is a nonprofit school teaching dance, gymnastics, Ping Pong and calligraphy to students in the after-school hours. Fees are charged, but the facilities are free to anyone. The preschool girls danced for us. We tried our hand at calligraphy with the long brushes and saucers of black ink. My Chinese characters were nothing to boast about, and one woman painted a mustache on her husband. We had all reverted to childhood fantasies. The young boys demonstrated handstands and breakdancing, and then we played Ping Pong outdoors with each other and the children. I was not as good a player as I remember and lost my game 11 to 6.

At the Provincial Museum we saw batik being made and silver ornaments being fashioned by a young artist. The museum displayed the history of the Guizhou Province in a pleasing manner. I purchased a small batik cloth and a wall hanging.

After checking into a nice hotel in the center of the city, some of us met in the bar for a before dinner cocktail. We were the only ones in the bar and the two young men could not produce any of the drinks on the menu that we indicated. After 20 minutes I finally received a glass with two shots of vodka, and Robert had a pink concoction with a can of club soda. Dawn ordered a beer and Margorie was drinking a dark mixture, supposedly Long Island Tea. The cost of each drink was about $6 and the beer was between $2 and $3. None of us dared to use ice.

The buffet dinner in the restaurant was supposed to be a western one. I selected mussels in garlic, lamb on a skewer, sole in a white sauce and some chicken Caesar salad. There were many other dishes on display, but the dessert table seduced us all. There was a walnut torte, tiramisu, mango mousse and chocolate pastry, as well as several flavors of ice cream and strawberry cake.

Returning to my room, I could not avoid thinking of the ways in which the Chinese conserve even though the country is so polluted. Everywhere, whether in public or private places, the garbage receptacles are in pairs, one for recycle and one for not recycle. The roadways are clean, not littered with plastic bags or bottles or cans. In many of the hotels the lights around the elevators and in the hallways are motion activated. The lights in the hotel rooms work only if the room card is inserted in the slot by the door. Option cards in the rooms encourage sheets and towels to be used more than once.

Carrying that issue one step further, the Chinese do not borrow money from banks. Rather, they pay for their purchases and obtain the money from their families. Children buy homes for their parents and grandparents. They save their money in banks owned by the government. They hope as we do that the banks don't fail and that their money is safe.

The rain fell lightly as we drove to the village of Jichang, founded in the 1300's by military soldiers following a conquest by the Han Chinese. The 6,000 inhabitants attempt to live in the old ways, which makes the village an excellent tourist attraction.

In order to reach the small open theater in an inner courtyard we walked by stalls selling silver jewelry, handmade slippers, wall hangings, carved wooden pieces and carved stones. The temptation was hard to resist. For less than a dollar I purchased a carved seed purported to keep away mosquitoes and insects. The smell was exotic. A comb carved from water buffalo horn was about $4.

A short operetta was performed by three masked soldiers in elaborate costumes dancing and singing to the rhythm of a drum. Their movements simulated the battle between the Han soldiers and the native population. The natives lost the battle and were conquered by the Han soldiers.

Our guide led us back through the alleyway, pointing out some older women whose foreheads were plucked free of hair. They consider it beautiful, but the younger generation does not follow the old custom. I think it would hurt.

We returned to the outskirts of Guiyang for lunch at a botanical garden and fish restaurant. Following a typical Chinese lunch in our private dining room where the chrysanthemum blossom tea was left too long to steep and turned bitter, we took time to stroll the large entertainment facility. There were tanks with fish, snails, razor clams, varieties of crabs, lobster and an aquarium with live scorpions, all available to be selected and cooked. I was glad I visited the aquariums after eating. They were smelly even though I am an adventurous eater.

I later heard a Chinese saying that the people from north China eat anything with four legs except tables and that the people from south China eat anything from the sea except a submarine. I believe it.

We then visited Stone Town, on the outskirts of Guiyang, another tourist destination with shopping opportunities. The main feature of the old town was a lovely home five or six hundred years old. Vendors along the walkway sold rose candy that tasted like roses smell, as well as a large assortment of Chinese crafts.

A private dinner at the hotel, hosted by a tour agency delighted to have foreign tourists, was tasty and well seasoned. I enjoyed the spicy food for which the region is well known.

Shanghai

The traffic was light as we left the hotel in the early morning darkness to fly on South China Airways to our final destination, Shanghai. Rain was falling lightly as the plane flew through the soupy clouds to the first true blue sky I had seen in almost four weeks. The blue color was uplifting, but temporary before we landed in Shanghai where we were back in the pea soup and lightly falling rain. The temperature was chilly.

As we drove from the airport on a freeway with four-layer interchanges, I saw the McMansions of the suburbs, single-family dwellings. A fellow traveler commented that her son had spent time in Shanghai and described the city as New York on steroids.

The Shanghai inner city was different from the China I had been visiting for the past weeks. Here and there I could see a part of the colonial past, balconies with scroll work and ornate architecture. There was a hint of old world charm and atmosphere. I thought of the colonial days, the British sitting under fans, drinking gin, household servants standing by, linen suits and arrogance.

The tour guide's voice interrupted my reveries. Shanghai was a small fishing village until the 1830's, when the first British vessel docked. Over the years the British introduced opium and conquered the city.

The hotel was luxurious, the lobby busy with Chinese businessmen; and after checking into our rooms, we took a bus ride to the banks of the Pu River to see the unique skyscrapers across the water. The tall buildings were architecturally diverse and beautiful to see, if you find beauty in structures.

During the course of the rainy afternoon, I discovered that Shanghai is one of the four municipal districts directly controlled by the central government. The population is about 23 million. Shanghai is the financial, trading and economic center of China. One third of the population is migrant, that is to say they are temporary and do not carry an ID card identifying them as city residents. This means that medical care is not free and that their children can attend school only until the eighth grade. They are not eligible for high school in the city. That doesn't have a ring of the truth, but that's what the guide said.

The climate of Shanghai is subtropical monsoon, and navigating my first afternoon in the rain, I could believe the guide on that statement.

Some of us who wanted to buy knock-off designer goods were told that the Chinese government had recently forbidden market sales of such products since the authentic designers were opening stores in Shanghai.

However, enterprising shoppers are not thwarted. We found a third-story walk-up deemed safe and were escorted to a room with Prada, Coach, Louis Vuitton and other purses and wallets. Ladies and men's Rolex watches were also available. The prices were high; bargaining made them more reasonable but not by much. We made purchases and snuck out of the building like criminals.

The rain had stopped but the weather remained cool. We dined not far from the hotel. The fresh fish and beef were a welcome change. We were on the edge of the Pacific Ocean, the confluence of the mighty Yangtze and Pu Rivers. It seemed as if the Yangtze River had been keeping us company because every time we moved around inland China and thought we had left the river behind, we found ourselves once again on her banks.

From my 11th-story hotel room, the sky was trying to be blue. The elaborate breakfast buffet of Chinese food, but including eggs and a platter of white cheese for a change, was welcome. The Chinese do not cook much with dairy products. More varieties of fruit were offered, and there was a coffee machine that with the press of a button offered latte, espresso and cappuccino. I selected latte and watched the milk overflow and heard the machine belch suspicious noises. The end result was satisfying.

We left the hotel marveling at the faint blue sky, and I walked along the banks of the Pu River gathering my coat close. The wind was blowing. Following the brisk exercise, I spent the remainder of the morning at the Shanghai Museum with a telephone guide close to my ear. I visited the floor displaying native costumes of the many ethnic minorities, the jade carvings, the bronze artifacts and different types of coins. I learned that jade is white and that mineral impurities cause the greens, purples and reds, and that the dark green jade is the most highly prized.

Many of the items date from 3200 B.C., over 5,000 years old. There were tiny intricately carved jade figures and complicated bronze pieces.

A vegetarian lunch was served near a pagoda frequented by Buddhist monks who eat no meat. Tofu was served every which way. I had been eating tofu three meals a day in China and was not excited to try some more disguised as meat. The deep-fried and sweet-and-sour tofu were my favorites.

We spent the afternoon at the largest silk factory in China. We began with the moth and finished with a cocoon, seeing the moth eggs, baby moths and finally the single and double cocoons being stripped of a kilometer or more of silk thread. We saw the silk thread being spun on a spindle directly from the pile of cocoons. The process was fascinating. The prices of the finished products were exorbitant. We were told that silk is healthy for asthma and allergy sufferers. Pillows, comforters, sheets, pillowcases, table runners and clothes of every description were displayed for sale in the showroom. A set of sheets sold for over $200, blouses and jackets from $60 to $400. Men's silk boxer shorts were about $40. I purchased a table runner for about $25. It was a gift.

We walked to the evening meal at a Japanese restaurant near the hotel. Seated in front of a grill, I watched an attractive lady chef cook my meal, a rice mixture and some of the most tender beef I have eaten. The change was ever so welcome.

The bus drove us to a theater where the famous Chinese acrobats perform. I am not clear as to what I saw. The theater was darkened, and we were seated midway on the first floor. The stage became illuminated and for an hour and a half I thought I had suffered a stroke. My vision was double. The faces and movements of the acrobats doing amazing balancing and gymnastic feats were blurred almost to bizarre. I took off my glasses, cleaned them and tried to see the show without them. It didn't matter what I tried; everything was distorted.

Several times between acts, when the lighting was changed, I glimpsed what I thought was normal. I suspected the lighting was contrived to distort or disguise. I looked around the theater. I seemed to be the only one having vision problems.

The final act included a large ball that consumed most of the stage. One man rode a motorcycle onto the stage and entered the ball riding round and round within it, even upside down going in circles that included the roof. One by one, six more Chinese men on motorcycles entered the ball and joined the others, until there were seven motorcycles humming, flashing lights and honking horns, crisscrossing at breakneck speeds. It was impossible. The stage and the ball were not large enough to contain the seven motorcycles. The audience loved the show and gave a standing ovation.

The normal theater lights came on, and my vision was restored. I was relieved. As I suspected, the show was partly, or perhaps mostly, illusion. The amazing thing was that no one in the group suspected illusion or experienced impaired vision. No wonder the world is in a mess, if the populace can be so duped by manipulation that what they see and hear is designed to misrepresent truth. But then, what is truth? I then remembered what a Russian guide said to me in Vladivostock, Russia, "You can't trust the Chinese. They are sneaky." The Chinese are not unique in being sneaky.

At breakfast I attempted to engage someone in questioning the feats of the Chinese acrobats. There were no takers. One of them even said, "That's not a new trick. I saw it done by Cirque du Soleil, and they had nine motorcycles in the circle instead of seven."

I replied, "It's still an illusion. There's not room for all of them at that speed in the ball."

Someone else joined, "I saw them go in the door to the ball."

I added, "They went through a trap door."

Now I had them thinking. Bob spoke again, "If you noticed, some of them stayed in the lower part of the circle."

They lost interest and continued with their coffee. Not one of them even hesitated to doubt what they had seen, except for twirling and balancing of the plates on a stick and the glasses balanced on the forehead. Most of them agreed that the glasses were probably attached with velcro and that the plates were fastened to the sticks. They seemed to like the illusion. Silently I wondered how much of our lives is an illusion.

The blue sky lost the battle. It turned grayish yellow as we left to visit the Yu Garden built in 1559 by a wealthy merchant. The garden possessed the four requisites for a Chinese garden: plants, water, rocks and pavilion. The grounds were crowded with Chinese tourists, but today there was a tour group of Russians, mostly men, who were feeding the large koi in the ponds and then trying to snatch them out of the water with their bare hands. I caught them in some funny poses with my camera.

Free time in the old town bazaar provided pleasant shopping and bargaining. I bought some silk pajamas and a few last-minute gifts before we traveled to an upscale part of town that rang with a distinct European flavor. Restaurants from every nation ringed the walkways. High-scale shops dotted the area. Margorie noticed an attractive wool cape in a store window. The price was 5,400 yuan, about $900.

We walked past French, German, Thai and Chinese restaurants offering dining inside or outside. Menus and prices were openly displayed on outdoor easels. I saw Reuben, my favorite sandwich. Three of us ordered Reubens, the fourth a healthy salad with mango slices. The sandwich was 48 yuan, the water 15 yuan, total cost about $10. I might add that it was delicious.

I returned to the hotel to pack for my return home trip. Only the farewell dinner, awkward goodbyes and reflective analysis remained. I was ready for the journey to end.

We walked in the chill of the evening to a fourth-floor restaurant. The public dining room was full of noisy businessmen. Our dining room was down a hall. We passed private dining rooms full of Chinese people drinking and laughing, bottles of beer and liquor displayed on the table with bowls of food.

Our meal began with some pickled vegetables and four large bottles of ice-cold beer. In the hinterlands of China, the beer was not always chilled. The meal was good. A new addition graced the table, a dish of fried eel with sesame seeds, seasoned with hot red peppers. I ate more than my share. Boiled shrimp, shrimp croquets, tender beef and vegetables, pork, chicken and tofu were prepared in delicate sauces, dishes to which we were accustomed. Sticky rice balls with sesame filling swimming in a sweet sauce completed the meal, along with a platter of watermelon.

And then the part I always dreaded, the goodbyes, the how much fun we had, the what a great guide you are, the what a great group we are, and the how this was the best trip ever and the what was my favorite part of the trip. I quietly sat through that necessary segment, hurriedly walked back to the hotel in the evening chill, took a shower and crawled in bed. The long flight home would begin in the morning.

Sonja Klein

For some unknown reason, I was squirmy on the flight to San Francisco. Instead of sleeping I tossed and turned, trying to quiet my thoughts. None of the usual techniques were successful. I merely suffered. Customs and Immigration in San Francisco went smoothly. I didn't have to change terminals, and my sweet daughter-in-law met me at the baggage claim area in Houston.

She drove directly to a Mexican restaurant, where I savored the beef enchiladas covered in onions and jalapeño peppers. I promised myself to eat Mexican food for a month.

I find it interesting that Chinese food in China is the same as Chinese food in America. Some of the spices in the dishes are more subtle and delicate, but the food is essentially the same, except for less meat.

The long drive to Ambush Hill Ranch allowed time for reflection. The trip had been more comprehensive than I had imagined, which classed it as a good adventure. I was returning to Texas with excellent knowledge of ancient and current Chinese history, even familiar with the ancient dynasties and current politics.

China is dealing with a wealth of problems: a vast population, pollution, low employment, poor education and massive government overspending and corruption.

The people are friendly and kind. Families are revered. They take care of each other.

A strange thing occurred when I returned home and kissed the earth. No days were wasted gathering myself back from China. I had left little of myself behind, just a part on that train ride and a part up the gorge being rowed in a sampan. Texas is my home, and that is where my heart resides.

54

Food as medicine

When I realized that food was the most important medicine I could ingest, I admitted that at last I had developed that extra sense, wisdom. No longer was I the mother/wife/sister/daughter or bitch.

Since I don't take vitamins, supplements or anything except Premarin, I am obviously anti-chemicals/drugs/prescriptions or supplements. The Premarin story, I am reluctant to tell.

With endometriosis, they treated me with fertility drugs that caused cysts on my ovaries. By the time I was 40 and had adopted two children, I had a complete hysterectomy. The doctor prescribed hormones. I said no, but before the year was out, I was taking Premarin.

The night sweats and hot flashes were overwhelming. At the time, I had two children under the age of six. I still justify it by convincing myself that it is just mare's urine. Not very realistic.

When I was in my 50's my mother asked, "Are you still taking Premarin?"

"Yes, Mother, but it's a low dose."

"You need to quit taking it. Just quit."

Being a good daughter, I just quit like my mother said. Big mistake. I wasn't prepared for a return of the hot flashes and cold sweats.

All I could say was, "Oh, shit."

I lasted nearly a year before I restarted taking the Premarin, which I still take.

Every week I eat fresh beets, Brussels sprouts, greens, fruit of all colors and ranch-killed meat. I do not eat chicken, except when as a guest I cannot refuse. I do not eat farm-raised seafood of any kind and eat sardines every week.

Years ago, I gained weight eating the leftovers from my children's plates. Somehow, I came across a book advocating a diet according to my blood type. The book informed me that being German from southeastern Europe, my blood type was one of the oldest, that I was nomadic and adaptable. Food from the new world was not assimilated well. Those food included peanuts, tomatoes, avocados and corn. I knew I had stumbled on some sort of truth because I could never digest corn and didn't eat it by choice.

I convinced myself that if I ate those forbidden fruits I would gain weight. Once on the right path, my weight has stayed constant for over 30 years. I became a believer in eating for my blood type.

Elderly friends regularly visit the doctors. One of them was given cholesterol medication at the age of 77. I asked her, "Did the doctor mention anything about your diet?"

"No, he just said my cholesterol was high and gave me a prescription."

I told her, "You know you can lower your cholesterol by changing your food habits."

She answered, "It's easier to just take a pill. I'm too old to change."

I persisted, "What if you had to pay for the prescription? I think the pills are pretty expensive."

She was stubborn, "I have Medicare and two supplemental insurance policies. I never pay more than a dollar or two for any of my medicines."

I much prefer food to pills. I put a dash of dark unsweetened cocoa and a dash of cayenne pepper in my coffee each morning. I eat oatmeal and fruit. I don't use sugar substitutes or butter replacements. I avoid high fructose corn syrup. I use no black pepper. I try to eat pure and unprocessed foods. I like to think that my body is a Mercedes engine and I shouldn't fill it with kerosene. It runs best on premium unprocessed food.

Most of the time my system works. I feel good and have no aches and pains. But recently my stress level went off the charts and my body responded appropriately. My blood pressure became elevated. There were reasons. I had an infected finger; I needed a tetanus shot and my daughter's partner's teenage daughter and son from a previous marriage were living on the ranch. Reluctantly I visited a family doctor in Rocksprings. My blood pressure was alarmingly high, but my urine was clean and I didn't have diabetes. I could have told him that. He prescribed a low dose of blood pressure medicine and within three days, my blood pressure was normal.

After a week of taking the medicine, I suffered leg cramps and realized that the diuretic in the medicine was flushing out all the good minerals I was ingesting. I bought a blood pressure monitor at the nearest

Walmart and began to meditate and breathe deeply as well as cut out the kosher salt that covered every bite. In the meantime the teenagers left to live with their mother.

My blood pressure returned to normal. I didn't pay a return visit to the doctor, quit taking the blood pressure medicine and continue to fuel my Mercedes engine with natural foods.

55

Families

The simple family consists of a mother, father, sister and brother. Not so anymore. This is the era of extended, complicated, fractured families.

Man marries woman, and they have children. They divorce. Woman marries man with children and has children with second husband. Divorced man marries woman with children and has more children with new wife. Custody battles ensue. Siblings are separated. Divorce occurs again and the pyramid's base becomes wider.

For the grandparents, the family becomes even more complicated. There are step-grandchildren and a vast array of in-laws that aren't really in-laws.

The custom in Texas has been, "What do you do? Where are you from? What is your family name and history?" Everyone seeks a connection, even a remote one. Lineage was important. No longer true. Now, if you ask someone, "Who is your family?" they look as if you have asked them the amount in their bank account.

And then there are the adoptees with birth mothers, adopted mothers and siblings that aren't really siblings. The adopted children seek their roots, which once again complicates the situation for the bewildered grandparents. How does one deal with birthdays and Christmas and Thanksgiving and Mother's Day and Father's Day and even Grandparent's Day? I'm sure Hallmark has a nice expensive card for every situation and occasion.

When I noticed the price of cards, I quit buying them, writing a silly message or poem instead, probably saving myself at least $50 per year, maybe even more.

The family that exists today is not what I call blood relatives. The family is a loose unit of involved people. Friends are called aunts and uncles. The godparent is not an important figure in a child's life, if the child even has godparents. Most children aren't baptized with ceremony or are even baptized.

Family loyalty seems to have flown the coop. I remember my family on both sides always helping out when needed. Now families go years without visiting or speaking, "I have a sister, but we're not close."

I think, *For God's sake, you grew up together. What happened?* Are people too busy with their ego-infested lives that they can't keep in touch?

Even funerals are becoming outdated. People live too far apart to attend. The deceased desires to be cremated for financial reasons. Funerals are damned expensive. Some are prepaid. Memorial services are productions that can be ordered by mail—programs and mementos sent in a box to be handed out at the service. The orchestration of the ceremony precludes meaningful spontaneity. Preachers and funeral directors speak over the body of someone they never knew. Ponderous songs are sung that increase the burden of grief.

And then there is the yearly family reunion. Only the very young and the very old attend. The middle-agers think they will never die or grow old. The old enjoy social stimulation. The very young go because they have no choice.

Family is family. The past is the past. The present is where I want to be and the family is my choice. I can't imagine a day that I don't speak with family members.

56

I think I've changed my mind

Back in the 1960's, I believed in UFOs. I was young and free and full of rock and roll. Then came the years when it didn't matter. I became a wife and a mother. I tried the best I could to be a good mother and raise my children in the Christian life style and beliefs that my parents imbued.

I always believed in a supreme being and in loving my neighbor as myself. And who was my neighbor? The obvious answer—everyone with whom I came in contact.

I read many books. I studied religions and embraced the Buddhist belief in reincarnation and non-action. When my fourth husband died, I once again attended church, mostly for social reasons but also for spiritual energizing.

Then I began watching the History Channel and the International History Channel. The only conclusion from all the shows concerning aliens was that, yes, we have been visited for thousands of years by aliens, that they are more intelligent than us and that they were responsible for many of the monuments and structures that we can't explain

Sumerian tablets reveal that we were created as a slave race to mine precious metals and minerals necessary for alien technology. From time to time, they castigated us for our devious ways, which explains the flood, the tower of Babel, famines in Egypt and wandering in the Sinai.

The next question becomes what of life after death, the tunnel of light, heaven and hell, the other side, another dimension and reunion with loved ones upon death.

The tunnel of light so common to those who have experienced death and rejuvenation becomes one of the body's response in shutting down. Heaven and hell go to hell. God becomes an alien. Perhaps the soul is not dissipated but becomes energy elsewhere.

The government becomes the bad guy for not admitting there is someone smarter and that there are greater beings than us, all in the name of protecting us from mass panic. The predictions of the world ending in 2012 may or may not be real. Maybe the Jews have the right idea. When you die, you die. You are dead. You live only in the memories of those you leave behind.

Maybe we are all controlled by the alien beings that created us and appear to be monitoring us. There is seemingly too much evidence to prove the contrary. We are not alone and we are not supreme. I always knew that. But I don't know exactly how to integrate that into my belief system. I was indoctrinated from my earliest memories into the Christian faith, namely Missouri Synod Lutheran. I find it hard to stray from that belief, but it is becoming easier as the years go by.

The Bible becomes a children's story to explain God in parables. That I can understand. Angels become aliens sent to help us out in times of distress. Jesus was an alien. Enoch was an alien.

Ancient civilizations looked to the stars and the gods for guidance. They had a lot of help from above. Where does it end? The masters of the universe become the warriors of good and evil. They war over controlling us. Who will win the battle of the universe? I suppose time will tell.

In the meantime, I will continue watching the History Channels and living from day to day, being kind to my neighbors and admitting that I am not God but that I definitely have some of him in my genetic configuration.

57
Brother John

Early December each year, my three brothers and I meet to administer the charitable trust foundation that my parents established years ago. In the past we met at my brother Allan's home in the heart of the Klein Community.

Since my brother John began hosting a gala holiday party in December, we moved the meeting to coincide with the weekend of his party. The change has been successful and we exchange books and stories as well as take care of the business.

For me the drive begins the day before. Four hundred miles lie between my ranch and John's. A pattern has been set. I arrive late in the afternoon, unload my modest suitcase in the lodge and walk over to the main house for a glass of wine and dinner with John and Maria. This year the weather was unusually warm for early December. We sat out on his back deck overlooking the Trinity River bottom and fields of coastal Bermuda grass that nourish his cattle. We shared a bowl of roasted pumpkin seeds liberally salted and sprinkled with olive oil. My fingers were greasy.

A squirrel scampered in the large oaks in front of us. John noticed, "Maria get my gun." In less than a minute she handed him a shotgun. It must have been inside the door. He stood, took aim, fired and the squirrel fell from the tree. And then he said, "Let's eat. I'm hungry."

Dinner was light. We parted early and I returned to the lodge to read, after being instructed, "Coffee at 7 A.M. Sleep well."

Following some strong coffee and a hearty breakfast John stood and ordered the same as he had in the past few years, "Come on Sis. Ride with me."

"Do I have to open any gates?"

"Maybe one or two."

"How many?"

"What difference does it make?"

"I curled my hair and it's damp outside and I've got on a new $90 pair of shoes."

"Get serious. Come on."

"You do this to me every year. I'll never forget the year I was recovering from gall bladder surgery, wasn't supposed to even drive. It was freezing cold. I had to climb out of the truck and open gates. It's a wonder I didn't die."

"Let's go."

"Okay."

There weren't any gates for the first miles. His ranch is large. We did stop and John picked up some metal fence posts lying beside a cattle guard. He threw them in the back of the pickup, "These cost over $2 a piece."

John then spent the next minutes driving around barns and storage sheds looking for a pile of fence posts on which to add the four in the bed of the truck. He succeeded and we continued the journey. John drove through pastures of cattle, grazing on the lush grass. Calves played alongside their mothers. Soon the Trinity River was beside us. The trees and vines were thicker. I spotted a clump of mistletoe high in a tree before us, "John, stop, I see some mistletoe."

The previous year there had been a last moment effort to find a clump of mistletoe. We had failed. John stopped the truck and grabbed an automatic rifle wedged between us. He stepped outside and began to shoot at the clump of mistletoe. I dodged the brass shells hitting my chest. Even when a branch was separated, the thick foliage prevented the cluster of leaves from reaching the ground.

We did manage to leave the scene with a small scraggly bunch of mistletoe attached to a thin stem.

As John approached one of duck sloughs, he stopped the truck and retrieved another gun from the back seat, "Watch this." He then fired a few rounds and birds from everywhere took flight. Ducks, geese, cormorants, herons, eagles and crows arose in a cacophony of sound that became a bird symphony. I was standing in bird paradise.

Like our father John backed the truck until he tapped something and then he looked back, redirected and we continued through the river bottom until I spotted a clump of mistletoe almost within reach. With a limb I found, John loosened a pristine clump of the poison Christmas kissing leaves.

"Where's that shot up bunch mistletoe?"

"Right here between us."

"Throw it out the window."

Sonja Klein

As we returned to the house, Maria and the decorator were adding the finishing touches to the mantle. John proudly announced, "We found some mistletoe."

Under the archway leading to the formal dining room he paused, indicated a ladder in the corner and instructed, "Sis, grab that ladder and hang this mistletoe from that hook up there on that arch."

"I don't see any hook."

"You will when you get up there."

"John, I'm 70 years old. I don't need to be climbing ladders. I'm leaving for India in a few days."

"Just climb up the ladder."

He held the ladder. I climbed, found the hook and carefully stepped down.

"You hung it the wrong way. Go back up and reverse it."

"Are you kidding?"

"You can do it."

I admit it did look better. John walked around the corner, "Come see Maria. We have the mistletoe hung."

Maria gave the mistletoe a quick glance, "John, no one's going to notice it. It needs a red bow."

John looked at me. I shook my head, "I can't tie bows. I'm going over to the lodge and rest. I'll see you in a few hours."

58

India

Every trip begins and ends with people. I spent the hours waiting at the airport, watching travelers and reading a book written by a woman who fell in love with the country of Bhutan and married a Bhutanese man. Having visited Bhutan, I agreed with many of her insights and opinions.

Once settled on the plane, I turned to my seatmate, a young man in Bermuda shorts with a shaved head. I learned that he was from Michigan, was a geologist, worked for an American oil company and was on his way to Perth, Australia, where he would be working and living for at least a year.

The 14-hour flight passed more swiftly than some, mainly because I slept well. When I awoke, breakfast was served and the plane landed shortly thereafter in Dubai. Putting on shoes after a long flight is like stuffing marshmallows into a toothpick holder, a discomfort that soon goes away with the long walk to customs and baggage claim.

While waiting for my baggage, I struck up a conversation with a young man from Houston who had also been on my flight. He worked for a drilling company and had been in the service of his company for a few years. He liked his job but didn't like being away from his family for long periods.

I was met by a young man from Sri Lanka holding one of those cards with my name on it, who then led me to the driver of a new Audi, a man from Bangladesh. He spoke well, and when I asked him if he was from Dubai, I received the usual answer, "Dubai people are boss, not drive tourists." In the course of the conversation, I learned that he has been in Dubai for 22 years.

The young bellhop who delivered my bags to the hotel room at the Intercontinental was from Kenya and had been in Dubai a mere 11 months. He politely explained the details of the room and showed me the master switch, shower and bathtub enclosure, safe, minibar and climate control. I found it interesting that he took me out in the hall and pointed to the emergency exit, a good thing to know since I was on the 20th floor.

Sonja Klein

It was too early to retire, so I found my way with help to the five-story mall near the hotel. My quest was to find a Harley tee shirt for a friend. Unfortunately the mall was far too upscale to have a mere tee shirt shop, and I carefully found my way back to the hotel for a shower and some emails and writing since I had the luxury of WiFi in my room.

I knew I had retired too early when I awoke at 3 A.M. After trying my go-back-to-sleep tricks and failing, I read for a while, dozed a short time and finally gave up at 5. I sent some emails, wrote a bit and dressed for breakfast. The dining room was quiet and the buffet was elegant and complete with every imaginable food on any continent. As I looked around I noticed the obvious, couples and singles like myself suffering from travel disorientation. A man from Seattle sat next to me. A couple, obviously American, were nearby. Certainly I would see them on the ship.

Still trying to kill time, I picked up a copy of the *International Herald Tribune* and the *Gulf News*, reading them from cover to cover and lamenting the fact that international news is incomplete in America. I read about protests in Egypt, riots in Ireland, elections in India, Israeli expansion on the West Bank and Jordan hosting hundreds of thousands of Syrian refugees.

The concierge directed me to the Dubai Mall, where I could find a Dubai Harley Davidson tee shirt. The mall had many levels and included an ice rink. After some good exercise, I found the shop. The morning was passing rapidly. I wanted only to board the ship and take a nap. I had been on the move for six days, time to stop and settle down.

I boarded the ship with ease and was escorted to the lounge, where I was photographed, given an ID card and my room key, as well as a glass of champagne and some fancy snacks. I sat in a comfortable armchair and visited with a lady from Montana and a couple from Australia. We were all waiting to be escorted to our rooms. As the room filled, I noticed that many of the passengers were American, in fact about half. The other half were mostly from the United Kingdom and Australia. There were a few Germans and some Latin Americans.

That first evening I dined with a table of Australians and enjoyed escargots and a rare steak with caramelized onions. I excused myself before dessert and went to bed early, awakening before dawn as we cruised the Strait of Hormuz, which connects the Arabian Sea with the Gulf of Oman. Security measures were in place since we were sailing waters that border Pakistan and Iran on the north, Oman on the south and the United Arab Emirates on the west.

I attended a lecture on India before lunch, played a game of Trivial Pursuit, some duplicate bridge and listened to another lecture in the afternoon.

The morning lecture, given by Dr. Paula Smith, was enhanced with photographs and a map, as well as a PowerPoint presentation. She spoke with passion and humor. I learned that the 2010 population of India was 900 million, and that India's climate and geography is diverse, ranging from desert to the Himalayas. Dr. Smith cautioned us to not apply western values to what we would see in India.

I learned that 18 languages are printed on Indian currency and 1,652 languages are spoken in India, not including the various dialects.

The predominant religion is Hindu, but there are also Christians, Buddhists, Muslims, Sikhs and followers of Jainism.

Dr. Smith touched lightly on the caste system and explained that there are four classes of castes but also many subclasses. The system is complicated, but the boundaries are gradually dissolving.

Northwestern India in the area of the Indus Valley was a thriving civilization at the time of the pyramids, with large cities, predating Europe by 4,000 years. Rule was based on religion and not upon military leadership.

About 2,000 B.C., fair-skinned people invaded, coming through the Khyber Pass into northwest India. In 326 B.C., Alexander the Great invaded the Indus Valley.

Dr. Smith spoke of Ashoka the Great, an early leader, and of Siddhartha Buddha—the Enlightened One, born in 566 B.C.

Vasco da Gama discovered India in 1498, and when Columbus discovered America, it was the riches of India he was seeking not the country itself. Cloth, lumber and spices were among India's riches. By the mid-1700's, the English had subdued the various Indian tribes, but in 1857 an Indian uprising threatened British control. Independence and the partition of India into India and Pakistan was completed in 1947.

The British contributed to the unification of the country, as well as establishing and building railroads, ports and roads. Corruption was common in the past as well as today. Dr. Smith ended the lecture with a quote. I don't remember who said it but I found it interesting, "The world won't become free until the last king is strangled with the entrails of the last priest."

Following the lecture, I moved to the upper deck for a game of Trivial Pursuit. Of the seven Trivial Pursuit teams, ours won first, and of the 10 members on our team, I was the only American. The remainder were Canadians, Australians, New Zealanders and British, all of whom were quite smart. I earned my place on the team by providing the meaning of the word ecclesiaphobia. The consensus was that it meant a fear of religion, but I insisted that you could not fear something that was intangible and the definition had to be fear of churches, real buildings. I prevailed, and our team was the only one that answered correctly. The rest of the teams said ecclesiaphobia meant fear of religion. Thank heavens they didn't listen to me on the number of attendees at the Last Supper. The team agreed on 13, but I thought one of the disciples had been missing. I was wrong.

I enjoyed a hamburger on the pool deck and returned to my room for some reading and a nap. The days and nights were still a bit confused. I was recovering from my usual "What am I doing here?" routine and surrendering to the adventure of the journey and the company of my fellow travelers.

Ambassador Krishna Rajan lectured on India, one nation, many worlds. He was a pleasant middle-aged man and an excellent speaker. His wife was on my trivia team and was quite interesting. The two of them had served their country of India, living all over the world. I learned that India is the second largest country in the world population-wise, the largest democracy and the largest English-speaking country, with a current population of 1.2 billion citizens.

The ambassador said that 400 million Indians are middle class and that 300 million live on $1.25 per day.

The ambassador also said the Indians gave us the number 0 and the value of pi. Continuing, he stated that the first university in the world was in India in 700 B.C. and that Sanskrit is the mother of the European languages. He explained that India is a functioning anarchy and that there is dignity in poverty because this life is but a small journey on the path to nirvana or heaven. He referred to epics like "Ramayana," mentioned that India has the fourth largest economy in the world and that today India has a Muslim president, a Sikh prime minister and even a Catholic leader.

The ambassador's lecture and the computer Internet signup finished the afternoon before a cocktail party and captain's welcome dinner. The captain is from Denmark, and the crew is truly international, representing 30 countries. A total of 168 passengers from 13 countries were on the ship. The number of crew members almost matched the number of passengers.

After the cocktail party I was invited to dine with the ship's doctor from the Philippines. Some Aussies, Brits and "Kiwis," as New Zealanders are known, joined us. The company was very entertaining.

The meal began with salmon and caviar. Lobster and lamb were the choices for the main course, and I enjoyed the lobster with a lamb chop on the side and some fresh greens. Goat cheese and walnuts finished the meal.

I skipped the late-night entertainment and went to bed with the curtains open, awaiting the dawn as we cruised the Arabian Sea.

The morning skies were the palest pink and the waters deep blue. Warm oatmeal, fresh fruit and strong coffee, delivered at the earliest time possible, arrived late for me. I was waiting.

The early morning grew dramatic as I gazed out the window and imagined the early trading vessels from 3000 B.C. following the coastal sea routes, which usually began in the Far East sailing into the Gulf of Aden and then into the Levant or south into Alexandria via the Red Sea. Each of the major routes involved transshipping to pack-animal caravans, travel through desert country and the risk of bandits and extortionate tolls by local potentates. The potential profit was well worth the risk.

After the modest breakfast, I attended a lecture on what to expect upon setting foot in India. I learned that dollars are preferred and that small bills are better than large ones. I was told to be open-minded and that India has been described as organized chaos or orchestrated anarchy.

The main purpose of the lecture was advice. Dress modestly, cover the shoulders and legs and don't wear expensive jewelry. Don't eat raw food from the street vendors. Remove your shoes when entering temples. The pavement will be hot. Either wear socks or carry a pair with you. Expect beggars and crowds of people. Do not be offended by the poverty. Indians consider it noble (bullshit). When making purchases, bargain; it is expected. In closing, the lecturer quoted Mark Twain. I never knew Twain visited India, but the quote in effect said that nothing has been left undone by man or nature to make India the most extraordinary country in the world.

The ambassador delivered a lecture on Gandhi who the Indians regard as a saint. I learned that Gandhi studied and became a lawyer in England, and during a visit to South Africa he was removed from a seat on the train because of his color. From that time on, he championed the rights of others using nonviolent civil disobedience as a political tool to accomplish independence from the British. He often fasted to the point of death to prevent his people from misbehaving.

Other leaders and prophets influenced Gandhi, namely Mahavira, Buddha, Asoha and Christ. Gandhi believed that if one took an eye for an eye, it would result in a world that was blind.

I earned my place on the trivia team by answering whether the statement that in ancient China the Chinese committed suicide by eating a pound of salt was true. The team voted false, but I insisted otherwise, "I've just returned from a month in China, and while there attended a lecture at which this fact was stated. It is true." We were the only team that answered correctly. By the end of the session, we were still in first place.

I enjoyed a light lunch with some of my team members from Australia and barely had time to freshen up before an afternoon of bridge with a delightful partner from Australia. We scored highest among the four tables playing.

A time comes on each trip when you know you are totally there. That moment came on my second day. Three people invited me for dinner. People waved with acknowledgement. We were on a journey together.

I returned to my room to watch the afternoon lecture I had missed while playing bridge. Dr. Paula Smith spoke of Rudyard Kipling, a very interesting man, a prolific writer and apparently a decent human being. He was a loyal husband without any of the addictions or vices common to many famous writers.

I had been invited to join another lady traveling alone for dinner on the upper deck. We shared life stories over a few drinks and a steak. She was interesting, separated from her husband of many years. He found a younger woman. She had been a nurse in Vietnam and is the mother of three sons, two of whom are firefighters.

I returned to my suite, set the clock forward an hour and went to sleep, lulled by the light rocking of the ship, another day at sea. India was in the near future.

An early morning session of writing, eating oatmeal and fruit and taking a quick shower began the day.

Mumbai (originally called Bombay) was the subject of Dr. Smith's morning lecture. She explained that the city is multicultural and that the 16 million people who live there are short on space. The Portuguese named the city Bombay, which means good place, and the British developed the area into a trade center. Cotton became the major export during the late 1800's. The British government leased the port of Bombay to the East India Company for a pittance and the rest became history.

Dr. Smith emphasized, as have most of the speakers, that India is a land of extreme contrast, extreme poverty and extreme riches. She then presented a slide show featuring the prominent landmarks and sites of Mumbai and a brief history and description of each. The name of the city was changed to Mumbai in 1996, being named after an Indian goddess.

Among the featured sites were the gateway to India arch, Bombay University, The Prince of Wales Museum, The Taj Hotel, the gothic Victoria Train Station, various temples, Gandhi's modest home and the famous open-air laundry.

Following the lecture, I adjourned to the lounge for the third day of Trivial Pursuit. Again we won, and I feasted on a Greek salad and grilled lamb chops out on the deck while visiting with a couple from Vancouver. They were lamenting the loss of the hour due to the time change. The lost 60 minutes cancelled their exercise time. Somehow that didn't seem right. They must have been smarter than that.

The afternoon's agenda included bridge and an introduction to wearing the sari, a demonstration to be given by the ambassador's wife. My Australian partner and I played well, finishing in time to learn about saris. A sari is a dress made from a piece of cloth 45 inches wide and from four to nine feet long. The fabric—silk, cotton or synthetic—is wrapped, pleated and tucked into a flattering flowing garment. The sari is not the dress for me. I'd trip or strangle myself in the fabric, or it would fall off.

Sonja Klein

I dined in the main dining room as the social director's guest. The dialogue was interesting and the company enjoyable. I ate lightly on roasted beets, asparagus and lamb loin.

I was anxious to enter India after being prepped by the lectures. I had discovered in the course of the day that only 10 of us were going inland for five days, and unbelievably, five of us were Texans. There would be one other single woman and four couples.

We lost another half hour in the night. I awoke thinking of the French couple from Vancouver and how they were losing their exercise time.

The harbor was foggy as we slowly approached the dock in Mumbai. Only a few men in white shirts were present, but gradually the scene became a bit more hectic.

Indian customs insisted on a face-to-face, which means that every passenger on the ship was required to meet the Indian customs officers and have their face compared to their documents before having them stamped. Fortunately, there were not many people on the ship. I cannot imagine what it would be like for a large cruise ship with thousands, but then I suppose that is why we suffered the face-to-face, because it was logistically possible.

A scenic trip through Mughal taught me more about the most populous city in India. Mumbai is the richest city, as well as the commercial and entertainment capital of the country and accounts for the majority of India's maritime trade.

Delhi

A flight to Delhi, the capital of India, consumed most of the day. The vegetable curry served on the plane was spicy and satisfying, and the hotel that was to be our home for the night was elegant.

Security in India was evident everywhere. The hotel was enclosed as a gated community. There were guards with guns at the gates, a bomb-sniffing dog and a mirror on a pole to search the coach's undercarriage for explosives.

Before I was allowed to enter the lobby, I went through a scanner, and had my large purse inspected. After that, it was all elegance,—a fresh flower lei of carnations, a glass of mango juice and smiling faces.

Roundtrip from Texas

The lunch buffet in a beautiful setting overlooking lush gardens and two blue swimming pools was beyond description. One serving area offered fresh oysters and seafood of every description. There were curries, roasted meats and some of the best okra, roasted beets and cauliflower I have tasted. The flavors were delicate, similar to Vietnam and Cambodia but spicier.

The elevator only worked with a room key. My room featured teak walls, a marble bathroom and heavily carved furniture. Every amenity was included.

Outside the hotel grounds, the guide led us with competence. I learned that Delhi was built over 450 years ago by a succession of empires, first the Hindu and Muslim dynasties, then the Mughal dynasty, which ruled until the British prevailed.

The Mughal were from Uzbekistan and Central Asia and invaded India coming through the Khyber Pass.

Delhi, which blends Indian and British styles, was designed in the 1920's by British architects as the imperial capital. Its shaded streets and gardens were quite a contrast to the desert of Dubai. The Indian guide informed us that Delhi is one of the greenest cities in the world, even though it is the second largest city in India.

We visited the tomb of Emperor Humayun, the second Mughul emperor and the father of Akbar the Great. The tomb is rated as a World Heritage Site. The red sandstone monument was built by his first wife, who supervised the unique construction that was the basis for the design of the Taj Mahal nearly 100 years later. Two domes dominate the tomb, and after climbing the steep steps, the view of Delhi lies before you. The weather was in the low 70's, a nice afternoon in December.

When I commented to our guide that there was little pollution for such a large city, he answered that all public transportation including taxis is fueled by compressed natural gas.

On the drive to the site, I noticed billboards that read, PLANT A TREE THIS MONSOON. Delhi is indeed a green city.

Winter evenings come early in India, and I welcomed an hour of rest before we traveled to a middle-class neighborhood for a dinner party. Driving through Delhi, we saw cars decorated with flowers, men wearing colorful costumes riding well-groomed horses and festive red tents splendid with lights. Weddings were being celebrated, the time being auspicious.

Sonja Klein

Our guide said weddings are lavish and last for days and admitted that after 14 years of marriage, he is still paying his wedding debt. As we approached the home through a guarded gate, fireworks were ignited as a welcome gesture. Then we were gifted with a bracelet of fresh flowers. As the hostess fastened the flowers on my wrist, I felt petals on my head and shoulders. The owner of the home was tossing red rose petals from the balcony above.

We were escorted with great hospitality to the second-floor living area, given wine and invited to sit. A fire was burning in the fireplace and the balcony doors were open. Young men of the family served vegetarian snacks of corn, potatoes and lentils. Family friends also attended, and we visited before the buffet dinner was served.

The family members were very handsome. Wedding pictures decorated the mantel; and the owner, a handsome middle-aged man, put his arm around me and showed me pictures of his grandfather and father who owned the construction company that built Delhi. A certificate of appreciation signed by the viceroy in 1931 was framed on the wall. In front of the whitewashed palace where he was born stood a large handsome family. He explained that his cousins were fighting over ownership of the palace and that it would probably end up in state hands. There was also a photograph of his father with Lord Mountbatten, who oversaw the partition of India and completion of independence. And this family was represented as middle class. I was impressed, not by their wealth and influence but by their genuine kindness and affection. I have never felt so welcome.

The buffet was everything you would expect in an Indian meal—spicy curry, roasted chicken, a cottage cheese vegetable dish with peppers and wonderful warm breads. For dessert there was a berry cheesecake and a dish that resembled ground carrot slaw. I learned that it is a special holiday dessert made from carrots, almonds, pistachios and a bit of sugar. I had three helpings. It was light, healthy and very satisfying.

It was late when we left amid hugs and kisses and affectionate goodbyes. I don't think I have ever met a more gracious family.

Wedding celebrations were in full swing as we drove through the city to the hotel. Again, we were security screened as we entered the lobby. The soft bed brought a sigh of pleasure.

Still on weird time, I awoke very early and tried to return to sleep. I failed. I arose, looked for a coffee pot and found the pot but no coffee.

After writing for an hour, I ventured into the lobby and discovered coffee and several other travelers unadapted to the time. One was a tourist and the other a businessman. We shared conversation until the restaurant opened. My breakfast was light, fruit and eggs.

Five newspapers were at my door and I read them all before checking out in the morning chill and beginning the trip to Agra and the Taj Mahal. The exit from Delhi was frantic in the morning traffic. At last we entered the new tollway from Deli to Agra. A nap was impossible because the tollway was rough. Instead, I gazed out the window and saw fields of rice, wheat and, surprisingly, mustard—one of the main crops grown in the region.

Agra

We arrived in Agra and entered one of the most beautiful hotels I have seen, The Oberoi. The grounds and architecture were stunning and the service impeccable. The lunch was Indian and continental; I dined on lamb curry.

The hotel room was stunning, every detail perfect; and my room had its own terrace. In the distance was the Taj Mahal, white and much larger than I had imagined.

On the way to visit the Agra Fort, I learned that Agra was the capital of the great Mughal Empire in the 16th to 17th centuries and is the repository of many famous monuments and places of interest, some of which date back to the Afghans, who predated the Mughals.

Emperor Akbar built the Red Fort as his citadel over the years 1565 to 1573. The magnificent fort with its imposing gates, walls of red sandstone and moat, dominates the center of the city. It was here that Emperor Shah Jehan died as a captive of his third son, Aurangzeb, passing his last days gazing at the Taj Mahal, built as a monument to his wife. Shah Jehan was captive because his third son disputed his older brother's claim to be emperor. The son also questioned the exorbitant expense of building the monument, which more or less bankrupted the empire.

I learned that 75,000 to 100,000 people per day visit the monument. I think they were all there as I walked the grounds with a fellow traveler. The visitors were mostly Indian, with a sprinkling of obviously foreign tourists, myself included. We sat on a stone bench on the grounds,

Sonja Klein

pondering the sunset and the monument. I remarked, "I don't think anyone ever loved me enough to build such a monument to me."

The fellow traveler answered, "I bet they told you they did."

"Probably so; I don't remember."

A group of young men approached, appearing to be of high school age. There were maybe a dozen of them. They asked if they could take our picture. The lady beside me had bright purple hair, and I'm blonde. We were the monkeys in the zoo. Before long, they were all having their picture taken with us, with their arms around us or on our shoulders. The session lasted forever; and when they finally signaled their departure, each of them formally shook our hand, bowed and said, "Thank you."

As the two of us sat enjoying the grounds as much as possible with thousands of visitors, an elderly man using a cane approached us, "Come, come. I will show you the best place to take a picture as the sun is going down. Hurry, there is only a few minutes. I am the head gardener and have worked here for 35 years. Follow me."

He stopped at a spot thirty feet from where we were sitting and tapped a spot on the concrete with his cane. We dutifully snapped photos. For the next twenty minutes we followed him like sheep all over the gardens, taking pictures, tiring of the procedure after a while, and then agreeing between the two of us to give him $5. When I tendered the bill to him at the end of the session, he turned it over in his hands as though it was poison and said, "Only $5 for two. I need $10." We turned, walked away and left him standing there. I had noticed that there were times when he did not use the cane. We later learned that a couple in our group gave him $10.

We returned to the hotel after dark, and I enjoyed a vegetable curry dinner and fell in the soft bed like a rock.

The sun had not quite risen as we rode a golf cart to the main entrance of the Taj and waited until 7 A.M., the opening time for the monument. I had eaten some seasoning on my eggs for breakfast that didn't taste right. Fortunately, it was only a small spoonful; otherwise I might have died. The misery didn't arrive until the bus left, but my body was communicating that something was wrong.

Following our guide, Novene, we walked directly to the Taj, put on shoe covers and followed him up the steps to the tomb. In the early morning, the tomb was not crowded and we could see in clear detail the inlaid marble flowers in the walls—some blossoms two inches across and containing 100 pieces of malachite, jasper, lapis and carnelian.

I learned that 20,000 workers laboring for 22 years completed the tomb. No wonder Emperor Akbar's son imprisoned him. It was a bit extravagant, even for an emperor.

On our way out of Agra we stopped at a factory where white marble inlaid with the semiprecious stones is crafted, mostly by hand. We saw a man who polished and cut tiny leaves of malachite and flower buds of lapis. The man next to him was chiseling a design in the marble, carving the place to inlay the flowers and petals. The guide said it takes two weeks to craft a plate.

There were four showrooms featuring everything from 12-foot tables to tiny boxes, plates, vases and lazy Susans. The prices were extravagant, thousands of dollars but free shipping to anywhere in the world. For $75 I purchased a small saucer. I guess I'll put olives on it.

Jaipur

I fought nausea all the way to Jaipur, the Pink City. The road was rough and sleep was impossible. When we arrived at the Rambagh Palace, I went straight to my room, skipping lunch, determined to continue, which I did.

The Rambagh Palace Hotel was even more magnificent than the last hotel. It was a real palace, built in 1856, complete with a polo field, gardens and lancers riding white horses on the grounds. We were showered with rose petals, given a drink and presented with a garland of sweet-smelling flowers. I regretted that I was too ill to appreciate the splendor.

Following the short rest, we drove to the Amber Fort. On the climb to the mountaintop, I learned that Jaipur is a town of 4.5 million inhabitants and is a worldwide center for textiles and gemstone cutting. Most of the world's gemstones are polished and refined in Jaipur, and the industry employs over 200,000 people in the trade. The textile industry provides work for over 400,000 Indians.

We drove to the base of the Amber Fort and then rode by jeep to the fort, sitting on the crest of a rugged hilltop overlooking Lake Moata. The fort was built in the 8th century, and the palace was added in the 1500's. From the outside, the fort is an imposing defensive structure.

The ornate and lavish interior was influenced by both Hindu and Muslim styles of ornamentation. The courtyards and palace rooms seemed to go on forever. The fort was the city itself until the city of Jaipur was built in the valley below.

On the return to the hotel, we stopped at a jewelry-manufacturing center and were shown how the stones are polished and refined for setting. The showroom had magnificent jewelry, all for a price. One of our group admired a topaz ring. The price was $7,000. No purchases were made.

My queasy stomach had returned. I skipped dinner, took a shower and went to bed. The following morning I was up before dawn to see the sunrise from my palace room's private balcony. As advertised, it was pink. I put on a pair of pink slacks and felt pretty pink myself. I had recovered.

I was reluctant to leave one of the most beautiful hotels I have ever visited. The lancers on horseback were patrolling the driveway. No rose petals were thrown as we left. Our guide shared an anecdote with us about the owner of the palace. Sons are very important and when, after many years, the owner's wife presented him with a healthy son, he filled the large swimming pool with champagne. The boy grew up with the nickname Bubbles. I later learned that two of the hotels at which we stayed were on the list of the 1,001 best hotels to visit. I believe it.

We spent the morning exploring the City Palace, a complex that continues to evoke the splendor of a bygone era. The palace is a showplace of Hindu and Mughal architecture. Next to the City Palace is Jantar Mantar, literally translated as calculation instrument. This oversized observatory is in a courtyard within the City Palace complex. As I entered the courtyard and saw the modern angles and circles of the concrete structures, I thought I was in the wrong place. The observatory was built between 1728 and 1734 and is one of five built by Jai Singh, whom the Indians regard as a very smart man. Two sundials stand in the courtyard, one accurate to within 20 seconds, the other to within 2 seconds. I agree that he was a smart man.

After walking through courtyards, we finally reached the inner gate to the palace. The family of the Maharaja lives there. He died several years ago, and his wife, daughter, son-in-law and their three children now reside there. Only a son, a direct heir, can inherit the title, so before the

Maharaja died, he adopted his daughter's son, who is now 13. He will be the next Maharaja of Rajasthan.

The royal spokesman met us at the gate and led us into the inner courtyard, where a pavilion dominated the space. He explained that the courtyard and facilities are rented for events and weddings. The parties are lavish. The palace can arrange for elephants, camels and chariots. Guest are brought into the courtyard in or on any of those conveyances. Music and dancing girls entertain the guests. The facility can accommodate up to 500 guests.

We entered the palace and visited the roof terrace and a formal reception room. The floor was thick with lush carpets and cushions. I posed for a picture lying in splendor among the soft surroundings.

Prince Charles with Diana and later with Camilla, Jackie Kennedy, Bill Clinton, Oprah Winfrey and other celebrities have been guests at the palace. The main palace dining table seats 24 and is made of Lalique, French crystal. The dining room is available for private dinners for a minimum of 15 people. For $300 per person you enter on camel, elephant, and chariot; are showered with rose petals and garlanded with fresh flowers; given champagne and cocktails; entertained by music and dancing girls and served a fabulous dinner. One of our group said he spent that much on a dinner in New York.

In a quick moment, I imagined inviting my brothers to a dinner party in Jaipur, staying at the Rambagh Palace Hotel and having a private dinner party at the City Palace.

We were besieged by vendors as we emerged from the palace complex of over 700 rooms, 400 of them currently not in use. The vendors were selling everything from puppets to spangly bracelets, fountain pens, postcards, bejeweled boxes and wall hangings, everything for $2. With much laughter, we all joined in a buying spree.

But the laughter soon died when our guide told us our flight was delayed by two hours. He suggested a fabric establishment where we would learn the Indian technique of block printing on fabric. The demonstration was fascinating, and we entered the showrooms prepared to purchase fabrics. I purchased a silk blouse and a cotton dress to be worn over tight slacks, total cost about $60.

During the course of our visit to Jaipur, I learned that the city was founded in 1727, the first planned city in that part of the world. When

Prince Albert visited, it was painted pink in his honor. Today, the pink is more of a terra cotta but still very attractive.

The time for lunch arrived. Still trying to kill time, we drove to the Ramada Hotel for the buffet. The hotel was busy and definitely not the Rambagh Palace. The flight delay was extended another two hours until we were in danger of missing the connecting flight from Mumbai to Cochin. With luck, the second flight was also delayed, and we made the connection with ample time for our luggage to join us.

By the time we arrived at the Vivanta Malabar Cochin, it was late. Fortunately, the bar was open. It was a pleasant way to unwind after a day of flying in India.

Cochin

When I arose at daylight I discovered that my room overlooked the Indian Ocean and that the harbor was lined with colonial mansions. I walked the grounds, took some photos and witnessed our luxury yacht steaming into the harbor. For a moment, I imagined myself a colonial wishing to escape the heat and poverty of India. I was being rescued. It was a gallant feeling.

Being an intrepid traveler and an energetic lady, I was ready to leave India. The country had taken a lot out of me.

The few minutes before leaving the lobby were spent filling out forms for customs required for exiting the country.

We spent the morning visiting the city of Cochin, a major trade center and one of India's largest ports. The thriving palm-fringed city has one of the world's finest natural harbors, located in the state of Kerala on southern India's Malabar coast. Built in the 1920's, Cochin has a population of about 800,000. The city consists of a series of islands connected by bridges. It is the business capital of the state of Kerala, which also hosts the largest Christian population in India.

Agriculture is the dominant industry, dotting the landscape with rubber, spice and tea plantations. As we drove into town, we passed yards of piled teak logs awaiting export for use in furniture manufacture.

Cochin was first settled by the Portuguese in the early 1500's. Rivalry for the spice trade began between the Portuguese and the Dutch. The Dutch East India Trade Company forced the Portuguese out in the 1600's, and later the British edged out the Dutch.

I learned that black pepper was known as black gold, being more valuable than gold for its ability to disguise the smell of rotten meat.

King Solomon is said to have stopped at Cochin in the 10th century B.C. on his quest for timber to build his famous temple. Many Jews fled to this area of India when King Nebuchadnezzar occupied Jerusalem in the 6th century B.C.; and according to ancient documents, St. Thomas, one of the 12 apostles, introduced Christianity to the region.

We drove through Fort Cochin and watched the Chinese fishing nets counterbalanced with stones in cantilevered structures suspended over the sea being raised and lowered. We walked to the Church of St. Francis, constructed in the early 1500's, the burial site of Vasco da Gama. His remains were later moved to Lisbon, Portugal. We then visited the Dutch Palace constructed by the Portuguese, enhanced by the Dutch and later occupied by the Indian Rajahs. Our last stop on the hot morning was a synagogue built in the 1500's in the Jewish quarter of the city.

The old part of the town is likened to a bazaar, with stalls lining the narrow streets. Shopping time was welcome and air-conditioned shops the most popular. I visited a spice co-op run by Indian women and purchased a variety of spices at reasonable prices. Across the street, I found some silk blouses and an unusual shawl.

After going through customs, I boarded the ship and returned to the comfort of my suite. It was good to be "home" with a hamburger on the deck to finish my day. I returned to the room, unpacked, took a shower and a nap and planned to hole up and reflect on India as we sailed at sunset.

The lectures on India had warned me that India was a land of contrasts. It was. The wealth of the Maharajahs paid for palaces gilded in gold. The Indian royalty today is rich and thriving. The poverty I witnessed came not with the despair I had seen in Africa. The children in the slums were smiling and happy. Poverty is regarded with dignity and not to be judged. Hindus believe in reincarnation, thousands of incarnations. Thus this current life is short and is to be endured. Better lives will be experienced on the road to nirvana.

I found the caste system still to be in place. No one marries out of their caste, and there is prejudice against the lowest caste, the untouchables. They receive benefits and preferences not available to members of higher castes due to affirmative action.

Sonja Klein

Cows, pigs, dogs and water buffalo roam the streets rummaging in piles of garbage but everyone feeds them fresh grass and food; for it is good karma. Supposedly the animals belong to someone.

Any medicines can be purchased without a prescription except sleeping pills because they can lead to suicide. When I asked about pain medication, I learned it was available without prescription, whatever you want.

The Indian culture is one of horoscopes and religion. Religion is their way of life and permeates every action, whether it be feeding a cow or consulting an astrologer.

In a modern country of cellphones and computers, 95 percent of all marriages are still arranged. Many of the grooms never meet the bride until the veil is lifted after the marriage ceremony. Families choose the spouses, with the option of rejection open to all parties. Families meet, interviews take place and weddings last for days and cost thousands of dollars. The divorce rate is less than 2 percent. Obviously, they are doing something right.

I found the people affectionate. There is no reluctance to touch, hug or kiss. Children are treasured. Old people are respected. I loved India, and in spite of myself, I think I came to understand it—the largest democracy in the world and yet so vastly different than my own democratic country, America.

As for the future, I learned that Indians are more concerned about their relations with Pakistan than with events in the rest of the world. They accuse their leaders of corruption and graft, and hope for better jobs, opportunity and a stable economy.

As I sailed out the port of Cochin, I recalled the smell of India. I will remember the incense and lingering fragrance of woodsmoke mingling with the odor of garbage and animals. The colors of pink sunrises, pink sunsets and gray dust covering the landscape are etched into memory.

Awakening in the comfort of my suite, sipping coffee and looking out the large picture window to see the roiling blue oceans, I thought about China too. I realized that in the past two months, I had visited the largest Communist country in the world and the largest democracy in the world. I had not planned it so, but in reflection, I suspect it was an unconscious effort to fully understand the world in which I live.

I must admit that I don't understand it at all. In essence, there is no difference between China and India. Certainly, their cultures are different; but as to the people and the manner in which they live, there is little difference. Their leaders, past and present, have abused wealth and power to extremes. The people are kind and work hard, hoping for a better life for their children. They find their freedoms within their systems as best they can. They are suspicious of what they read and what they are told. They are distrustful of neighboring countries. They honor the past and work for the future. Most of all, they pray for peace and harmony. What is so different about that?

59

Thailand, Malaysia, Indonesia and Singapore

The seas were rough as we left the safety of the Indian coastline, cruising towards Thailand. I spent the morning writing and relaxing before attending a lecture by the ambassador titled "The Tigers and the Tiger Cubs." I could not imagine the subject of the lecture and was pleasantly surprised to discover it was about the major powers, China and India, and the ten countries that comprise the Association of Southeast Asia Nations, the alliance known as ASEAN.

The ten countries, or "tiger cubs," living in the shadow of the "tigers," China and India, are Myanmar (or Burma), Brunei, Cambodia, Singapore, Laos, Vietnam, Indonesia, Malaysia, the Philippines and Thailand. Though these countries are different in culture, size and religion, they share a strategic location with access to plentiful natural resources. Much of the world's commerce passes through this area, the Strait of Malacca. Providing political stability in this part of the world is important to the rapidly reshaping balance of power.

As these countries became independent, they looked to each other for stability. ASEAN has become one of the most successful regional organizations in the world, with a combined gross national production of 1.9 trillion, larger than India's. The economy of these countries is growing at five percent and 600 million people live in them. Leading nations are lined up to do business with them. I was looking forward to visiting some of them.

Our trivia team began the day in first place; but we answered poorly, having correct answers but abandoning them for wrong ones. We dropped to second place.

I was pleasantly surprised to find that the specialty of the day was Mexican food. Unfortunately, it was not Tex-Mex, but it was an adequate substitute to make me yearn for some enchiladas. The chili was not bad, but the beef fajitas were not well seasoned. I still enjoyed the meal, careful to not overeat before bridge.

Roundtrip from Texas

My Australian bridge partner and I played well (except for a few miscommunicated bids) and then adjourned for afternoon tea, where we shared insights over water and coffee. There wasn't much time left to dress formally for the captain's cocktail party and dinner, and I do so enjoy dressing up and feeling elegant.

The cocktail party was in honor of those who had previously traveled with the exclusive cruise line. The two Australian friends with whom I had journeyed to the Taj Mahal were honored for having cruised over 100 days. More honors were awarded for sailing over 250 days. Generous applause sounded for an elderly couple credited with over 800 days.

I joined the Australians for dinner and was surprised to discover that our waiter was the same one, Pedro from Spain, who had brought my breakfast that morning. Earlier in the day when I asked him how he was enjoying his job, he admitted, "I am the most truthful waiter on the ship. I don't like it and I am going home. I miss my wife and my young son."

"How old is your son?"

"He is two and a half years old."

"I don't blame you. I would go home too."

I was happy to see him and told my companions that Pedro was the most honest waiter on ship. We again shared his story; and he added, "I am trying to make arrangements to leave at the next port, Phuket, Thailand. I have a job at a new hotel in Madrid." We wished him luck.

I dined on lobster ravioli, beef tenderloin and green vegetables. As always, the staff was a miniature United Nations. One waiter was from Montenegro, another from Romania and another from Belgium. We lingered and laughed over a cherry dessert, and then I welcomed the soft bed and comforter.

The six-foot seas had calmed a bit when I arose at dawn for my oatmeal and coffee. On the TV in my room I watched a lecture I missed while playing bridge. The lecture was about a Chinese admiral eunuch during the 14th century who had sailed the Chinese fleet to the Middle East and Africa. I cannot pronounce his name, much less spell it, but he was over six feet tall and a Mongolian. He was captured and castrated as a young boy, and his family was killed. He became advisor to the emperor and an admiral in the Chinese navy, quite an interesting man and possibly the source of the fictional accounts of Sinbad the Sailor.

Sonja Klein

Our trivia team was crashing. We had dropped from first to third and continued on our downward spiral, again discarding two correct answers. We now were eight points away from first, with only three days left to compete. I joined friends for a light lunch. Chinese was the specialty of the day. I ate a Caesar salad instead, having sworn off Chinese food for at least a year after my recent trip to that country.

I dashed across the pool deck in the refreshing tropical rain and wind before going to my suite to dry off and prepare for an afternoon of bridge. I played well, but my defensive playing was imperfect. I was elated to discover that my Australian partner and I had placed first the previous day. It was a perfect day for bridge. The seas churned at three feet, the skies were gray and rain fell intermittently. We must have been in a sea lane because there were always tankers in the distance. We were cruising in the Bay of Bengal.

The time passed swiftly as I joined friends in the lounge for teatime and then rushed to dress for dinner and drinks in the bar, where the discussion was lively. An American businessman was engaged in a conversation about China. I joined and found a kindred spirit. He agreed with my assessment of China's possible power ascendancy: It's not going to happen. These seasoned travelers were well versed and opinionated on world affairs; and I was nearly late to join the social director, the Indian ambassador and his wife and some Australians for dinner.

Having had a few glasses of wine and being overstimulated in the bar, I was pretty chatty. The Indian ambassador had the misfortune to be sitting next to me, and I bent his ear on world affairs and threw in a few questions about the Indian royalty.

When the conversation turned to the shooting of the children in Connecticut, the Australians at the table voiced their opinions against guns. Of course we were in conflict, and the conversation became quite heated. I was the last to finish eating; and before I left the table I apologized for the intense discussion. They took it well. They all smiled and spoke with me the following morning, so I suppose I didn't offend anyone too badly. Humility usually works.

I slept late since we lost yet another hour. The morning lectures focused on our next ports of call and piqued my interest. Our trivia team moved up a place. I answered a four pointer, knowing that Rudolph the Red Nosed Reindeer's daddy was Donner. I don't know how I knew that answer, but I did. I joined an Australian couple for lunch in the main dining room, having a Greek spinach-and-cheese sandwich with a salad before joining my Australian partner for bridge. We played well, but our opponents played better; and following teatime, I adjourned to my suite to dress for dinner.

Over drinks at the bar, I discussed large schools versus small schools with an educator who establishes schools for at-risk children all over the world. We agreed that small schools as well as small ships were the most effective. I joined some Australians for a long dinner of conversation and good food. The evening was balmy and soft as we moved to the top deck to sit outside, listen to music and enjoy one last drink.

The following morning I attended a lecture on Phuket, Thailand, our next port of call. I learned that Phuket is the largest island in Thailand, lying just off the southwest coast in the warm waters of the Andaman Sea. Phuket is a world class destination for tourists drawn to the beaches, blue seas, exotic marine life and lushly forested hillsides. The island is home to over 350,000 Thais and has a rich history, due to its location on the major trade route between India and China. The wealth of Phuket derives from tin and rubber. Today, a bridge connects the island to the mainland, and the mainstays of the economy are rubber and tourism.

The ambassador delivered a lecture on the Dragon and the Tiger, better known as the countries of China and India. He titled the lecture "The New Jungle Book." The ambassador said there are so many possibilities for an Asian century. He focused first on India, remarking that India is at a crossroads between religion and rituals, progress and cynicism, austerity and materialism. He added that Indians need to bring fortune to the bottom of their society. Continuing, he said India has the largest film industry in the world, producing more films than Hollywood. He commented that young Asians are attracted to western culture, Scotch whiskey, western fashion and technology. He said Asians are converting to secularization, gender equality, capitalism and individuality.

I found it interesting that he remarked on Asia's lack of capacity for innovation and said Japan and South Korea as well as China improve on western technology, but only improve upon products and services. They do not invent. The ambassador admitted that the poor education in Asian countries sends many young people to Europe and America and conceded that there cannot be an Asian century when Asia's security depends upon a non-Asian organization for military stability, namely the United States. There will be no economic progress unless the nations make economic progress together. He stated that the United States is going to remain a presence in the Pacific for a long time and has inserted itself into many of the boundary issues between the Asian countries. In other words, the American eagle has landed in the jungle.

He spoke of the advances made in China and of the world's hope that China will reform its corrupt government and become more environmentally conscious with its water, which is becoming more precious than land. He compared figures of gross national production between China and the ten ASEAN countries. The ASEAN countries combined produce more than China. I found this very interesting in the light of the hype about China being the emerging world power. The ambassador commented on China's recent tough diplomatic stance, citing that it stems from insecurity because of its internal problems and efforts to inspire nationalism.

Australia becomes the "elephant" in the Asian Jungle Book, lumbering and progressing. The ambassador concluded that the United States will continue to be the superpower. The elephant, the tiger, the dragon and the eagle—who are dependent upon each other—must learn to trust. He said, "Let everyone relax and find the way."

The trivia team moved up another notch. We were now in second place and suspected a team near us was cheating. All of this for the prize of a bookmark or sun visor. After a light salad-ridden lunch, I played bridge. I played well. The game was enjoyable.

Teatime included a style show, after which I hurriedly dressed for a culinary feast and champagne in the reception area before attending a small cocktail party for one of the ladies who had journeyed with me to the Taj Mahal. She was in her 70's. We sang "Happy Birthday" and dined in the main dining room at a large, noisy table. A few of us late revelers then sat on the upper deck and watched the stars while listening to guitar music by Danielle. I stayed up far too late.

The harbor in Phuket was as pretty as the pictures I had seen of this popular tourist destination, and I left the ship early in the morning for a guided half-day tour. Our first stop was the Chalong Temple, the largest and most sacred temple on the island. The complex consists of several buildings and gardens. The buildings are elaborate and lavishly decorated with gold. There were many tourists on the grounds, and the guide told us they were from a 2,500-passenger ship that had docked that morning. He added that over six million tourists visited Phuket the previous year.

From the temple, we drove to an elephant camp and rubber plantation. At the rubber-tapping demonstration, I learned that 60 percent of the people on the island are involved in the rubber industry. The rubber tree begins to produce rubber after seven years and can be tapped for the white latex daily for 23 years. The tree is then cut and the lumber used for various products. The sticky white latex is strained for impurities; and then formic acid is added to the latex in a tray, where the latex becomes like jelly or tofu. Then it is emptied out and rolled flat several times with a rolling pin. After drying for four to seven days, it is then hung and ready for sale. One sheet of rubber weighing about one kilogram sells for $5 to $6.

The workers tap the trees once a day and work from midnight to daylight because of the heat. By the time we walked from the rubber lecture to the elephant mounting pad, I was dripping wet. This was winter in Phuket.

The elephant ride through the jungle was hot and rough. When the elephant stopped briefly, dipped her trunk into a stream, she sprayed herself and part of me too. The young man riding on the head of the elephant in front of me wove a star out of grass, and when he turned to present the star, he smiled. His teeth were rotten and his gums red from his betel-chewing habit.

A baby elephant show was next. Two young elephants aged six and 10 danced and performed a few tricks, and then the audience was invited to experience an elephant massage. One by one the tourists filed down to the arena, laid face down on a mat, had a dirty towel placed on their back and the elephant put her foot on their back. I remained on the bench. It was too hot for a massage.

The cashew nut factory was busy with tourists from China and Russia. I saw the fruit of the cashew, which resembles an apple. The cashew nut hangs from the bottom of the round fruit. The cashew nut tree originated in the rainforest; and in 1901, the former governor general of Phuket brought cashew seeds into the southern territory of the Siam Kingdom, now Thailand.

We watched young workers cracking nutshells to remove the nuts, which are then dried and transformed into mouth-watering snacks and sweets.

We were given every variety of cashew to taste, plus a small shot of cashew juice, not at all tasty. The flavored cashews were barbecue, wasabi, sour cream, chocolate, honey, sesame, butter, chili and some others I can't remember. I bought some chocolate and sesame cashews. By the time we returned to the ship, it was very hot. I ate a light lunch and left the ship to shop at some stalls along the dock, purchasing a few inexpensive gifts for friends and family.

Malaysia

Leaving Thailand, the ship sailed for Malaysia, a federal constitutional monarchy in southeast Asia consisting of 13 states and three federal territories. The South China Sea separates Malaysia into two similarly sized regions, Peninsular Malaysia and Malaysian Borneo. Land borders are shared with Thailand, Indonesia and Brunei, and maritime borders with Singapore, Vietnam and the Philippine Islands. The capital city of Malaysia is Kuala Lumpur. The population is over 28 million. Since independence in 1957, Malaysia has had one of the best economic records in Asia, with growth averaging over six percent for almost 50 years. The economy is fueled by natural resources.

Langkawi, our first stop, is an archipelago made up of some 100 islands lying about 20 miles off the northwest coast of the Malay Peninsula. Today, luxury resorts and hotels line the beaches, and a ferry connects the islands to the Malay mainland.

The history of the islands includes pepper production, Dutch and British influence, Siamese domination, Japanese conquest during World War II, independence in 1957 and formation of the Federation of Malaysia in 1965.

As we sailed into port, the air was clear and the water blue. The harbor is surrounded by lush tropical islands too small to be inhabited.

I took advantage of a free shuttle bus to a resort and beach area, a short ride from the pier. The shops had not yet opened, so one couple and I engaged a taxi to convey us to the Atma Alam Batik Art Village, where we visited a batik workshop. The fabrics and artwork were colorful and expensive. We continued on to Kuah, the island's main town. There, we walked and shopped the streets, and I purchased lovely cotton blouses and a dress before returning to the shuttle stop. I returned to the ship while my friends walked to the beach for a quick swim.

Something about the island exuded peace and progress and an unhurried atmosphere. Langkawi is a nice place.

A notice on the free brochure and map advertised in capital letters, TRAFFICKING IN ILLEGAL DRUGS CARRIES THE DEATH PENALTY.

I noticed that some of the drivers at the taxi stand were missing teeth, exhibiting the red gums and bloodshot eyes characteristic of betel chewers.

Penang was our next port of call. The island is known as the Pearl of the Orient, lying off the west Malaysian coast in the Strait of Malacca. Only fishermen and pirates inhabited the island until Captain Francis Light founded a British trading post now known as Georgetown. Penang is one of Malaysia's leading ports, handling tin, rubber and copra. The island is the site of the oldest British settlement in Malaysia.

In the early 1800's, European planters established spice plantations. Then later, sugar cane was introduced. In the 1850's, the opium trade flourished. During World War II, Japan conquered and occupied the island for over three years. In 1948, Penang became part of the Federation of Malaysia; and in the late 1980's was cited as the Silicon Valley of the east. In 2007, Georgetown was named the most livable city in Asia. Today the island hosts a population of 1.4 million, and a bridge connects the island to the mainland.

As I entered the coach for a day tour of the northern part of the island, I learned that I could travel across the bridge to the mainland and drive south all the way to Singapore or north to Thailand and beyond.

Leaving the bustling seaport, we traveled to the Thai Buddhist Temple, which houses the world's fourth largest reclining Buddha. Having arrived in 1956, he wasn't very old; but he was quite long, 108 feet. He was arrayed in bright gold, and his toenails and fingernails were mother of pearl.

Continuing on to the northern tip of the island, we passed coves, bays and sandy white beaches below forested hillsides. Expensive villas dotted the slopes.

The guide stated the necessary facts of any tour. The population of Penang, one of 13 Malaysian states, is 60 percent Chinese. A new leader is elected every five years, chosen from one of the nine sultans who rule the states.

We then visited the Butterfly Farm, a walk-in aviary providing sanctuary for over 1,000 butterflies, as well as tropical insects, anthropoids, jungle lizards and frogs. The butterflies of many varieties and colors were best viewed on trays set throughout the sanctuary. The trays contained either red hibiscus flowers or slices of pineapple. Butterflies covered the trays, feeding on the flowers or fruit. The contrasting colors were dramatic.

Our next visit was not quite so dramatic. We stopped at a batik fabric workshop. The patterns were colorful, but I was disappointed in the rayon fabric and the outrageous prices.

I dined that evening with friends. It was the captain's farewell dinner, and grilled fresh lobster was the preferred fare. I retired early, as the next day promised to be a long one.

Indonesia

Sumatra, Indonesia, is a green mysterious island of soaring mountains, active volcanoes, dense jungle and plunging waterfalls. The equator runs through the middle. The population contains a wide variety of ethnic groups. Most of Sumatra is Muslim, although there are about seven million Christians.

More than half the income of Indonesia is generated by the island of Sumatra, which extends 1,100 miles from one end to the other. The mineral wealth of the island includes tin, oil, coal and gold. Vast plantations also produce palm oil, rubber, tobacco, coffee and sisal.

We entered Indonesia through the main port of North Sumatra, Belawan, the gateway to the provincial capital of Medan, 16 miles away. The Dutch settled in the area in the early 1800's, and many old buildings exhibit a Dutch influence.

But it was not to Belawan or Medan where seven of us were destined. It was to Lake Toba and Samosir Island, home of the Batak people.

On route, we learned more about Indonesia as we drove through its plantations. Rice fields grew on the terraces as we approached the hills.

Indonesia is composed of over 17,500 islands and has 250 million inhabitants. Muslims dominate and account for about 60 percent of the population. Java and Bali, the famous island in the movie "South Pacific," are in Indonesia. New Guinea is also a part of Indonesia. Jakarta is Indonesia's capital.

We stopped in Pematang Siantar for a short break of coffee and fried bananas. Caramel sauce and melted sugar were served with the bananas. Having left the ship very early, it was a welcome break and snack. The drive to the lake had been advertised as shorter than the six hours it took.

The streets outside our coffee stop were lined with large signs about four by eight feet. The signs were gaudily decorated with plastic flowers, and the lettering also done with plastic flowers. All of them started with "Dauid," and a few lines below was the word "Irene." After reading them all, we assumed that David and Irene were the most popular people in all of Pematang Siantar and that the signs must be congratulating them on their marriage. Satisfied with our assumption, we took our photos and got on the bus. I asked the guide, "Who are David and Irene?"

"There's no David or Irene. Dauid means from and Irene means—." I forget the meaning of Irene, but it was something equally insignificant like the word "from." We enjoyed a good laugh.

Along the narrow road were small wooden stands and stalls with smoking clay pots, obviously containing food. One of the group asked the guide what the vendor was selling. The answer was, "Dog and pig meat."

I was sitting further back in the small coach and assumed he had said "duck." I was wrong.

On the way, our Sumatran guide told some jokes that were very off color. He read them from a book and had no idea how inappropriate they were. I must repeat this one:

A plane was flying over Indonesia when the pilot came on the speaker and announced that the plane was preparing to crash land and everyone should prepare. The beautiful blonde combed her hair and put on some lipstick. Other passengers asked her, "What are you doing? The plane is getting ready to crash."

She replied, "The rescue people will first go to the prettiest one, and that will be me."

Sonja Klein

The brown-skinned girl took off her blouse. When asked, "What are you doing? The plane is getting ready to crash," she replied, "The rescue people will go first to the sexiest one, and that will be me."

The black girl took off all of her clothes. When she was asked, "What are you doing? The plane is getting ready to crash," she replied, "The rescue people always look first for the black box."

That is the cleanest of the three jokes he told.

As always, some fellow travelers were not very informed. One of the men asked, "What are those plants with the big wide leaves?" The answer was banana trees. He was from Minnesota, and I suppose there are no banana trees there. When we passed by some corn fields, one lady asked, "Is that rice when it grows up?"

I learned that many of the plantations through which we passed are owned by foreign investment companies, the British company Bridgestone being one of them. Monkeys and motorcycles lined the road as we moved into higher elevations. Northern Sumatra is home to the rainforest as well as to an active volcano.

We finally arrived at Parapat, a small resort town on the shores of Lake Toba, a crater lake formed by a volcanic eruption thousands of years ago and the largest lake in Indonesia.

We boarded a small boat for a trip to the island of Samosir and a traditional Batak village. Three young boys serenaded us with Batak songs. Cruising the beautiful lake and listening to music with rain falling in the distance was a defining moment.

Arriving at the island, we enjoyed a light lunch while learning about the Batak tribe. The island of Samosir, with an area of 243 square miles, is larger than Singapore and is the cradle of the Batak culture. Their religion was animistic, but today most of them are Christian, having rejected the Muslim religion, which prevented them from eating dogs and pigs.

Following lunch, we visited the royal cemetery with stone tombs over 400 years old and also viewed some old Batak houses set high on poles. They are made of wood with no nails, only pegs and ropes.

The rainstorm caught up with us; and as we returned to the distant shore, I was struck by the beauty of the high, verdant hills cloaked in clouds. They matched a lime-green parka I was wearing.

The long return trip was sheer torture made even more so by arriving too late for the barbecue party on the ship's deck.

Singapore

Having survived the many hours of riding in a small coach, I awoke the following morning, my last day at sea, to cloudy skies and an ocean horizon dotted with tankers and container cargo ships. We were on our way to Singapore, an island nation roughly 26 by 14 miles and a dynamic republic between the Indian Ocean and the South China Sea, just one degree of latitude north of the equator.

Singapore City was my destination, a city with over 5 million people, a spick-and-span garden city and thriving financial center for all of southeast Asia.

In an earlier lecture, I had learned that Singapore is a "fine city," having fines for spitting, chewing gum and not flushing public commodes. Needless to say, its crime rates are among the lowest and its standards of hygiene the highest.

In 1820, Sir Stamford Raffles arrived in Singapore and chose it as a port for the British. He worked for the East India Company founded by Queen Victoria in the late 1700's. He was an administrator and a humanitarian, and the famous Raffles Hotel in Singapore, where the drink the Singapore Sling was invented, is named after him. A Sling and a visit to Raffles was on my list.

There was still that one last day of shipboard cruising. I attended a lecture on the history of scandals in the British royal families, beginning from the time of William the Conquerer in 1066. The lecture was not pertinent to anything but purely entertaining, with pictures of the British royalty that were not flattering.

The final day of trivia was disappointing. Beginning the contest, we were in second place, and at the end we risked betting all our points and losing them. We finished dead last, with a score of zero, but consoled ourselves over lunch that we possessed the courage to go for broke. Besides, none of us needed a bookmark, a sun visor or even a teddy bear.

The final bridge game for the championship dominated the afternoon. My Australian partner and I won, my prize being two decks of cards with pen and score pad in a nice leather case, better than a bookmark. Packing was simple, and I met with some Australian friends for a drink before dinner.

I dined the final evening with friends, savoring the steak and lamb, and then retired early.

In the clear morning air, I was off the ship and on a coach in Singapore for a day tour. Skyscrapers stood giant-like against the flat background. Colonial architecture was evident as we drove to our first stop, a Buddhist temple. A boat ride on the river through the center of town was pleasant. We then visited the palace of the royal native leader who sold Singapore to the East India Company.

Along the way, I learned that Singapore is a multicultural society and that the Chinese constitute the majority, with the Malays and Indians next. I noticed signs posted along the road: DON'T DRIVE TO DRINK AND YOU WILL NEVER DRINK AND DRIVE. It took a while to understand the wording.

Our guide was a young Chinese woman who spoke to us as though we were in kindergarten, asking stupid questions to engage us. At one point, she asked how many windows we thought were in a building to which she pointed. A voice in the back of the coach said, "I don't care." Fortunately, she did not hear him. She talked too much, and her voice was shrill. But she meant well. Only then did I realize how excellent was our Indian guide. He was truly professional.

One interesting fact is that Malay is the official language of Singapore. I would have guessed Chinese or English. I managed to purchase a tee shirt that advertised the fines of Singapore before we visited the famous Raffles Hotel. The Singapore Sling was thirst quenching as we ate peanuts, throwing the shells on the floor. My Australian friends had never been in a bar where you throw shells on the floor. They quite enjoyed it.

The cost of a basic room at The Raffles Hotel is $1,400 per day. The coach dropped me at the Four Seasons Hotel, where the rooms were a mere $600 per day. It was very elegant and colonial in style.

I checked into my room and then took a taxi to a shopping area, returning to the hotel for lunch. The lunch buffet was $108. I ordered a veggie sandwich for $30. Singapore is expensive.

A shower and relaxing afternoon watching the storm clouds and rain from the eighth floor consumed my afternoon. My wakeup call was set for 3 A.M.

I left Singapore in the dark and flew to Tokyo, where I connected for a direct flight to Houston. It was Christmas Eve.

The long flight home afforded ample time to reflect on the countries I had visited. Southeast Asia is thriving. I especially liked Malaysia for its scenery and burgeoning economy. I agree with the Indian ambassador's assessment of the future. America will remain the superpower for many years. Our presence in southeast Asia will continue for a long time. All the countries of the world have a symbiotic relationship; and we should relax and let things develop at their own pace rather than interfering and manipulating, good Buddhist thinking.

60

The rollercoaster

Life is full of ups and downs and the living journey has often been compared to a roller coaster ride, which is not a bad analogy. We all know about yin and yang, positive and negative, and yea and ugh.

Being in the last quarter of life (that sounds terminal), I reflect on the past, not dwelling on it overly but in fond retrospect. My life is easily condensed into highs and lows.

The high of graduating from the University of Texas with honors was offset by the low of having no job. The high of getting married by the low of discovering he was unfaithful.

The low of being divorced and short of funds was offset by the high of getting out of debt. The low of my father dying of cancer by the high of getting married again and having two children. The low of having a husband in prison with cancer by the high of his release and recovery. The highs and lows of divorce and remarriage (pretty common by now) are offset by the low of having children quit college and by the high of seeing them graduate.

The high of reuniting with my favorite love and moving to a ranch, was offset by the low of him dying of cancer three years later. The high of writing my first books, short stories and essays by the low of being alone. The high of winning awards and publishing my first book by the low of stagnant sales. The high of traveling all over the world by the low of still being alone. The high of my first grandchild by the low of my mother's death. The high of romance and dancing by the low of rejection. The high of giving speeches and marketing my book by the low that is just over the horizon.

With one, you receive the other. I'll ride this roller coaster until it quits, and if I have to, I'll find another one that's running and get on board.

61

I have learned

I have learned that travel is enriching, that people all over this earth are innately good. I have learned that evil exists and is the absence of love. I have learned to avoid evil and not let it into my life.

I have learned that all religions preach the same message, that all are trying to achieve a better place after death. I have learned to look in the mirror and like what I see. And I have learned to not believe everything I see, hear or read.

I have learned that good manners are most important and can carry the day in any situation. I have learned that adversity and change are good seasoning that enhances the flavor.

I have learned to say no in a diplomatic manner. I have learned my limits and sensed when to lose the battle but win the war.

I know what I like and what I dislike. I have learned to shun those who don't like me and to not be involved in their drama. I can't change anyone except myself. Bless them and send them on their way.

I have learned to carry no guilt or anger. I have learned to laugh every day, especially at myself. I have learned that I can do anything if I believe passionately and never, never, never give up, that persistence triumphs.

I have learned that telling the truth is much easier than telling a lie and I have learned to stand up for the truth.

I have learned often the hard way that the flavor of the month is not the love of a lifetime. I have known love and lost love. I have had respect and lost respect, never to be recovered.

I have learned that marriage is not forever and that humans were not created to be monogamous. Not everyone agrees with me. I know of very few marriages where both spouses have been faithful throughout the marriage.

I have learned that children are a blessing and are among the best teachers. I have learned that family is the root that anchors the branches. I have learned that it is easier to forgive than to forget.

Sonja Klein

I have learned that possessions can own you rather than you owning them. I have learned that money is only good to the extent that it gives you freedom. I have learned to live life with passion and that I want to draw the card in the deck that is the highest and the wildest so I don't ever want to draw again.

I have learned that death is not the end.

I have learned to savor the smells and taste the beauties of all of the senses. I have learned to take nothing for granted.

But most of all, I have learned that to live life fully, you must act with love and passion.

Order Form

Sonja's books are available both in print and as ebooks online or directly from Ambush Publishing:

Fax Orders: Send this completed form to 1-830-234-3155.

Telephone Orders: Call 1-830-234-3156.

Email Orders: Visit www.sonjaroseklein.com

Postal Orders: Send this completed form to:
Ambush Publishing, PO Box 192, Barksdale, Texas 78828

Name: _____

Address: _____

_____

City: _____ State: _____ Zip: _____

Phone: _____ Email: _____

ROUNDTRIP FROM TEXAS

Number of Copies: _____ @ $15.95/book Subtotal: $ _____

HONK IF YOU MARRIED SONJA

Number of Copies: _____ @ $15.00/book Subtotal: $ _____

Add $5.60 for priority shipping in United States.

Shipping: $_____ Total: $_____

Make check or money order payable to Ambush Publishing.
If you wish to pay by credit card go to www.sonjaroseklein.com

Made in the USA
Charleston, SC
13 December 2013

6